Alastair Sawday's

Special
places to stay

IRELAND

Edited by Stephen Tate

Typesetting, Conversion & Repro: ..... Avonset, Bath

Maps: .... Maps in Minutes, Cornwall

Printing: .... Stige, Italy

Design: ....Caroline King
& Springboard Design, Bristol

UK Distribution: ....Portfolio, Greenford, Middlesex

US Distribution: .... The Globe Pequot Press,
Guilford, Connecticut

Published in January 2001

Alastair Sawday Publishing Co. Ltd
The Home Farm, Barrow Gurney, Bristol BS48 3RW

The Globe Pequot Press
P. O. Box 480
Guilford, Connecticut 06437
USA

Third edition 2001

A catalogue record for this book is available from the British Library.

Alastair Sawday has asserted his right to be identified as the author of this work.

ISBN 1-901970-15-9 in the UK

ISBN 0-7627-0887-5 in the US

Printed in Italy

The publishers have made every effort to ensure the accuracy of the information in the
book at the time of going to press. However, they cannot accept any responsibility for any
loss, injury or inconvenience resulting from the use of information contained in this guide.

Alastair Sawday's

Special
places to stay

Ireland

"Ireland is HEAVEN, everyone is so dotty and delicious and none
dreams of taking anything seriously except, perhaps, the Horse Show."

Mariga Guinness

The
Globe
Pequot
Press

Guilford
Connecticut, USA

Alastair Sawday Publishing
Bristol, UK

Contents

Contents

Some places are too special even for us!

8

Acknowledgements

My Introduction suggests that finding Irish editors is easy. But I should add that once they are there they face a baffling array of hurdles: oceans of hospitality, rivers of booze, babbling conversation to arrest Samuel Johnson in his tracks, and a zest for life that is at odds with the climate.

Stephen has tackled these with consummate skill and diplomacy: never, to the noble purpose of gathering professional intelligence, refusing a drink; rarely turning down a good offer of a bed; never cravenly avoiding a good chat; always yielding to the charms of his hosts. From beautiful house to beautiful host he bravely weaved his way, ever alive to the need to get there before dinner and never to leave too early. For a book such as this cannot be written by a man or woman who has neglected the task of getting under the skin of Ireland.

So it is in a state of near-total envy that I write this Acknowledgement. I am now stuck behind the parapet, shuffling paper, while younger men enjoy the fruits; but I take comfort from the certain knowledge that no pleasure can last indefinitely - or can it?

However, Stephen has produced a wonderful book - with the brilliant help of Sally George in the office and Caroline King on design, with Julia Richardson in constant support. Thank you, all.

Alastair Sawday

Series Editor:.. Alastair Sawday

Editor:.. Stephen Tate

Production Manager:... Julia Richardson

Managing Editor:.. Jackie King

Administration:... Sally George, Kate Harris

Accounts:.. Bridget Bishop

Additional inspections:.. Victoria Brann
Cairlinn Carroll
Lorely Forrester
John Galloway
Kim Sankey
Mary Treacy

Special thanks to: Terry McCoy and Hamills Rent-A-Car (www.hamills.com) for saving a trip from the brink of disaster; Noel Comer; Mary and Declan Kelleher for help with the place name glossary. And extra special thanks to Kim, Grace, Folly and Meret.

Introduction

We never have any difficulty finding a good editor for our Irish book; they instinctively know they will have so much fun doing the job.

I'm not recruiting, only preparing you for your own bit of fun, for within these pages lie some of the most deliciously eccentric, ineffably friendly, unstoppably hospitable hosts you will ever encounter. So be prepared to be welcomed with rare warmth and to be pressed into accepting unusual quantities of kindness. The rewards will be great, especially if you are the sort who will turn no hairs at the entrance of the parrot into the drawing room to join you after dinner, or at being asked to bear a candle to the burial of your host's cat.

Yes, so many Irish seem to behave exactly as they are portrayed, using language with rare vitality and getting more fun out of life than most of us. (So it's not the sun we're missing; it's something else.) Where better to get the best out of them than in their own homes or hotels, where they can be themselves on a grand and often impressive scale.

Stand by, too, for some of the loveliest buildings anywhere in our books. You may find yourself having difficulty climbing into the elevated 4-poster, or in detecting the bath in the vast spaces of the bathroom. Yet on another night you could be tucked up in a tiny cottage after a modest supper with engaging people. Each place, as in all our books, is very much its own - there are no slaves to fashion here, no-one in pursuit of corporate trends. We encourage people to be themselves, to welcome you in their own way, and to abandon all the conventions of hospitality if that is their way of making you feel special. Some will be conventional, others will not - they will all be worth a detour, as Michelin says.

So enter Ireland, and the pages of this book, with an open mind and a sense of humour. We can promise you some memorable encounters.

Alastair Sawday

Introduction

Ireland is for dreamers, romantics and those bored of the run of the mill. Lounge in a castle, hobnob in a Georgian country house, heave ho in an inn, drift away in a thatched cottage, or even billet in a lighthouse.

This is not a book for those who expect to be waited on hand and foot. That's not to say you won't be well looked after. The owners we have chosen love to entertain, love to meet people and love to introduce travellers to the untold idiosyncracies of this richly textured country.

We don't subscribe to the philosophy of treating people as mere bed nights. Industrial B&B and bland hotel formulas belong elsewhere. This is an antidote to the mediocre and your stay will live long in the memory.

Ireland as a destination

You won't go far wrong travelling in Ireland if you remember the Irish saying: "When God made time, he made plenty of it." Plan the absolute minimum, leave the fat itinerary at home and take your time. You rush here at your peril.

There has never been a better time to visit Ireland. The exchange rates between Ireland and the UK and the US are extremely good value and thankfully, Northern Ireland increasingly appears to be settling its grievances in the debating chamber.

The republic is also undergoing enormous change with a booming economy driven by rapid growth in new technology and computer industries. Economists predict the so-called 'Celtic Tiger' to grow further as the present Irish government shows a fiscal prudence hitherto lacking in previous administrations and the US continues to pour money into a country for which it has always had a soft spot. The book has been divided gegraphically into the pre-Christian kingdoms of Ulster, Connacht, Leinster and Munster; Ulster for the north, Connacht for the west, Leinster for the east and Munster for the south. Dublin has its own section.

Ulster consists of the counties of Donegal, Monaghan and Cavan in the Republic of Ireland and Fermanagh, Londonderry, Tyrone, Down, Antrim and Armagh in Northern Ireland. **Connacht** consists of Galway, Mayo, Roscommon, Sligo and Leitrim. **Leinster** consists of Meath, Louth, Westmeath, Longford, Offaly, Laois, Kildare, Dublin, Wicklow, Carlow and Kilkenny. **Munster** consists of Limerick, Tipperary, Clare, Kerry, Cork and Waterford.

According to Irish tradition, Ulster represents battle, Connacht learning, Leinster prosperity and Munster music.

Introduction

Geography

Imagine that Ireland is shaped like a saucer, with mountains around the edge and flat land in the middle. Geologists believe that four thousand million years ago, Ireland was two separate halves; one attached to early America and the other attached to early Europe. When the two continents collided, Ireland was squashed together and raised above sea level. Ireland has many inland bogs because the mountains prevent surface water from running into the sea.

As for the climate, there is a lot of truth in the saying that you can see the four seasons in one day. The south-west can be extremely mild, thanks to the Gulf Stream.

Northern Ireland

"If you're not confused by the situation in Northern Ireland, then you don't understand it," explained one Belfast resident. Sure, the politics are complex but a brief history may help. It all began in the 17th century after the English divided up Ulster into plantations after the so-called 'flight of the earls'. The land was settled by Protestants, many from Scotland forces.

Northern Ireland came into existence with the Government of Ireland Act of 1920 which partitioned the six counties listed above that make up the province today. The other three counties of Ulster were not included because they were largely Catholic areas and considered harder to control by unionists who wanted to be ruled from Westminster. Further south, the act vindicated the Irish Republican Army's war of independence and led to the creation of the Republic of Ireland and self-government.

The current tensions in Northern Ireland erupted at an Apprentice Boys march in August 1969, which was celebrating the siege of Derry in 1689 when Protestants withstood the might of James II's Catholic army. The march provoked rioting, British troops were called in, the IRA re-emerged, direct rule was introduced and 30 years of troubles began.

Moves towards peace began in the mid-1980s under John Hume and a dialogue between the UK government and the IRA's political wing Sinn Fein (meaning 'ourselves' in Gaelic) began in 1993, culminating in the Good Friday Agreement signed in 1998.

On 29 November 1999, a coalition government was formed with unionist leader David Trimble as first minister. Sein Finn members have been appointed as ministers. The coalition has started shakily with decommissioning of IRA arms a sticking point. However, the future looks promising.

Introduction

When to go

The population of Ireland reportedly doubles in July and August as tourists flock to Kerry and Cork in the south-west and Connemara in the west. Tour buses thunder round the Ring of Kerry anti-clockwise from Killarney to Kenmare and you should do the same otherwise you will be dodging one after the other round every bend. Inishmor, the largest of the Aran Islands, is another tourist magnet. Ireland is best visited off-season.

Getting there

Unless you are planning to see Dublin and the surrounding area, try and avoid Dublin Airport because it can be difficult to get to and from, particularly at peak time. Try the smaller airports, such as Derry, Cork or Knock.

Roads

In Ireland you drive on the left and the upper speed limit on all roads is 60mph (100kph) and 30/40mph through villages and towns. Speed limits in the Republic are given in miles. Navigating is problematic as road signs giving distances are a law unto themselves. Sometimes they are given in miles, sometimes in kilometres. Generally, older looking signs are in miles and newer ones in kilometres. I would recommend taking the excellent Ordnance Survey holiday maps.

Petrol

In Northern Ireland, petrol costs the same as in the UK; it is much cheaper in the Republic, so if you are the near the border, hop over and fill up.

How we choose our Special Places

We search for the best of everything and write a book without fixed boundaries. If we discover a place where the art of hospitality is practiced with flair, good humour and commitment, we want to include it. We evaluate each place on its own merits, not by comparison. We visit every property; value for money and atmosphere are key considerations. We like people who do their own thing, though eccentricity is no excuse for poor standards. Good views are more important than a trouser press, good walks more important than a fitness centre.

What to expect

B&B

The range of B&Bs in Ireland is astonishing. Broadly speaking, the more expensive they are, the more luxurious they are. Prices have been creeping up in more popular destinations.

Introduction

Hotels

We have included those that pride themselves on creating a warm, homely atmosphere with all the added extras that a hotel can provide.

Inns and restaurants

Inns are busy places, often with live music and extended opening hours. That is part of their charm. Those wanting absolute peace and quiet should take this into account. Restaurants with rooms tend be less hectic and offer extremely good food.

Self-catering

We have introduced a smattering of self-catering places in this edition, covering most of the country. The aim was to spare you the hassle of sifting through huge catalogues trying to work out confusing grading systems which invariably tell you little about the place.

How to use this book

Maps

When you know where in Ireland you want to stay, look at the map at the front of the book, find your area and look for the houses nearest. Don't focus on counties, as this can be misleading.

Rooms

We state if rooms are double/twin/single, and if beds are king-size or four-poster. If a bathroom is en suite, you don't have to go through public areas to get to it and we say if there is a bath or shower. A private/shared bathroom means that it is not en suite and will have either a shower or a bath and a wc and a basin; the former you will have to yourself, the latter will be shared with other guests or family members.

If you'd like your child in the room with you, ask at the time of booking if you may have a foldaway bed and what the charge will be.

Prices

The Ulster section has places that quote prices in either Irish punts (IR£) or pounds sterling (£) depending on whether they are in the republic or Northern Ireland.

Ireland joins the European single currency in January 2002 after which the Irish punt will cease to exist. The currency conversion table on page 264 gives you an idea of what the punt is likely to be worth in euros.

Introduction

Telephone numbers

People from the UK calling Northern Ireland can dial the listed number direct. Calls from outside the UK to Northern Ireland should be prefixed with 00 44 and the first zero in the number dropped. All calls to the Republic should be prefixed with 00 353 and the first zero dropped.

Symbols

We have an explanation of our symbols at the back of the book, on page 263. Use the symbols as a guide, not an unequivocal statement of fact.

If an owner doesn't have a symbol that you are looking for, it is worth discussing your needs - one that doesn't have a Child Welcome symbol, for example, may be happy to have your children to stay if you are booking all of the bedrooms.

Quick reference indices

At the back of the book we have given at-a-glance information to help direct you to houses perfect for your needs.

Practical matters

What to take

Warm clothing, stout footwear and a first aid kit that includes pills in the event of a hangover will serve you well in Ireland. Walkers would also do well to take a compass and the Ordnance Survey Discovery series.

Meals

Breakfast - The Irish know how to do a good breakfast. There are often several courses with several main options. The staple fry up remains a firm favourite with black and white pudding included.

Dinner - Ireland's days as a gastronomic wasteland are long gone and the range of good cooking today is phenomenal. Many owners cook with passion and imagination, using the freshest ingredients; in houses where the host doesn't cook, ask for local restaurant recommendations.

Bookings and cancellations

Hosts will take bookings by post/fax/e-mail although most like to chat on the phone - that way you can get a feeling for each other. Some will ask for a deposit - often non-refundable if you cancel and they can not re-let.

Do let your host know roughly what time you will be arriving and call if you are severely delayed. Most will want to be there when you arrive and to spend some time with you. It's especially important to be prompt if you have booked an evening meal.

Introduction

Payment

All of our owners take cash and cheques with a cheque card. If they also take credit cards, we have given them the appropriate symbol - if yours is an obscure one, confirm on the phone that they can accept it.

Children

The Irish, generally, love them, but do discuss the age of yours and their needs when booking.

Even in those houses that do have the child symbol, we do ask you to be sensitive to other guests. If you have a child who often cries in the night you'll feel more comfortable in, say, a large farmhouse rather than in a small cottage where you'll be cheek-by-jowl with others.

Dogs

Many of you love to travel with your hound and many owners love dogs enough to make yours welcome. Some may have them in the house, a few accept them in the bedrooms, others may provide a kennel or ask that yours sleep in your car. Discuss house rules when making your booking.

Smoking

The No-Smoking symbol means no smoking anywhere in the house. The absence of the symbol obviously doesn't mean that you may light up anywhere, rather that you ask the owner where you may smoke. And don't forget that other guests may have strong feelings.

Tipping

Few owners expect you to tip them. If you have encountered extraordinary kindness, you may like to leave a little gift or send a thank you card. It is rewarding for owners if you write to tell us of your good fortune - we record all feedback from readers.

Environment

We seek to reduce our impact on the environment where possible by:

- Planting trees to compensate for our carbon emissions as calculated by the Edinburgh Centre for Carbon Management at Edinburgh University; we are officially a carbon-neutral publishing company.

- Re-using paper, recycling stationery, tins, bottles, etc.

- Encouraging staff use of bicycles (they're given free) and encouraging car-sharing.

- Celebrating the use of organic, home and locally produced food.

Introduction

- Publishing books that support, in however small a way, the rural economy and small-scale businesses.

Subscriptions

Owners pay to appear in this guide, their fee goes towards the high production costs of an all-colour book. We only include places and owners that we find special. It is not possible for anyone to buy their way in.

Special Places to Stay on the Internet

We have an online database with roughly a thousand entries. These are from the various titles in the Special Places to Stay series, so if you like the places in Ireland, why not browse some of those further afield?

We flatter ourselves that the 8000 visitors a month who come to the site have good reason to, and we think you should join them! Not only do they have access to open, honest and up-to-date information about hundreds of places to stay across Europe, but they also know that if they want to buy any of our books, their best option is to come directly to our window on the world wide web: www.sawdays.co.uk

Disclaimer

We make no claims to pure objectivity in judging our Special Places to Stay. They are here because we like them. Our opinions and tastes are ours alone and this book is a statement of them; we hope that you will share them.

We have done our utmost to get our facts right but apologise unreservedly for any mistakes that may have crept in. Sometimes, too, prices shift, usually upwards and 'things' change. We should be grateful to be told of any errors or changes, however small.

Finally

Let us know how you get on in these places. We value your feedback. And tell us about anywhere you find that you think should be in the book. We will send a free copy of the next edition if it goes in. Fill out the report form or e-mail us at ireland@sawdays.co.uk.

Work away.

Finally an Irish proverb for you:
Never bolt your door with a boiled carrot.

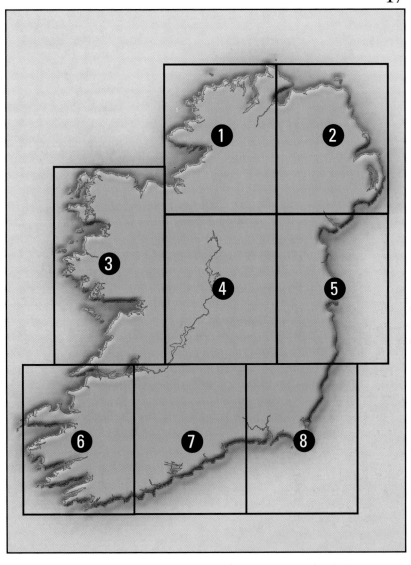

Guide to our map page numbers

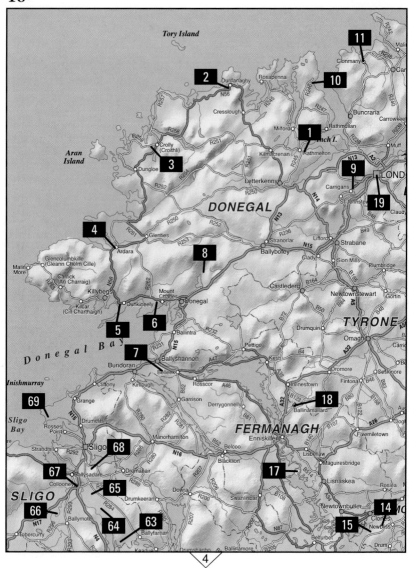

Map 1

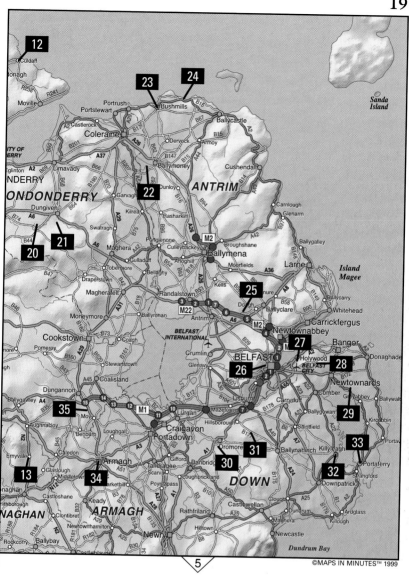

Map 2

©MAPS IN MINUTES™ 1999

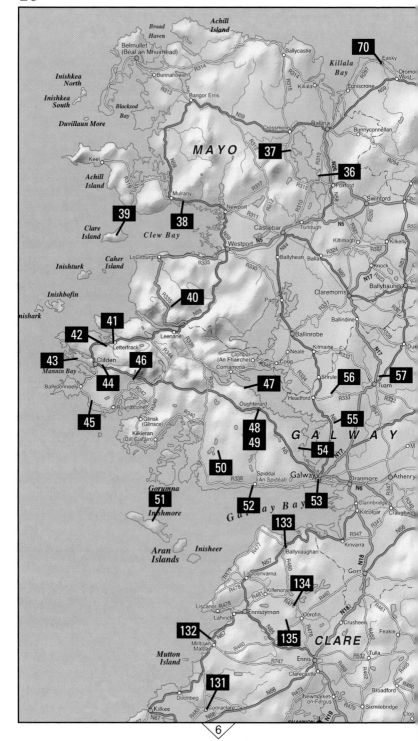

Map 3

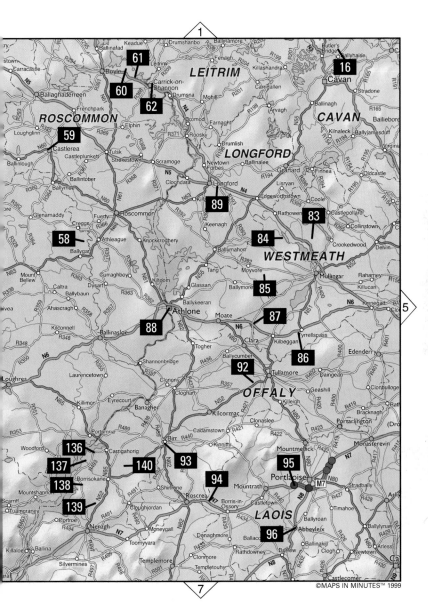

©MAPS IN MINUTES™ 1999

Map 4

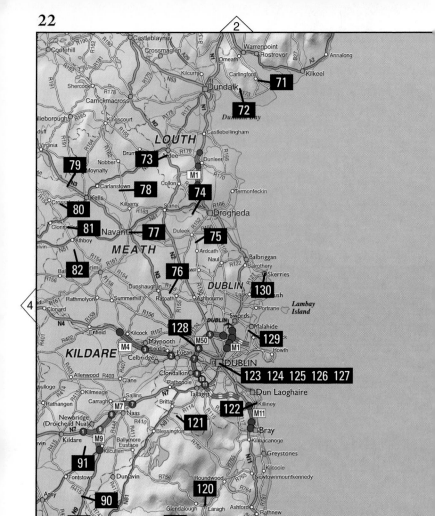

Map 5

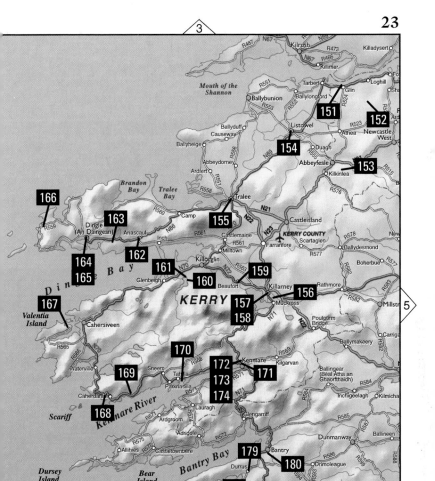

Map 6

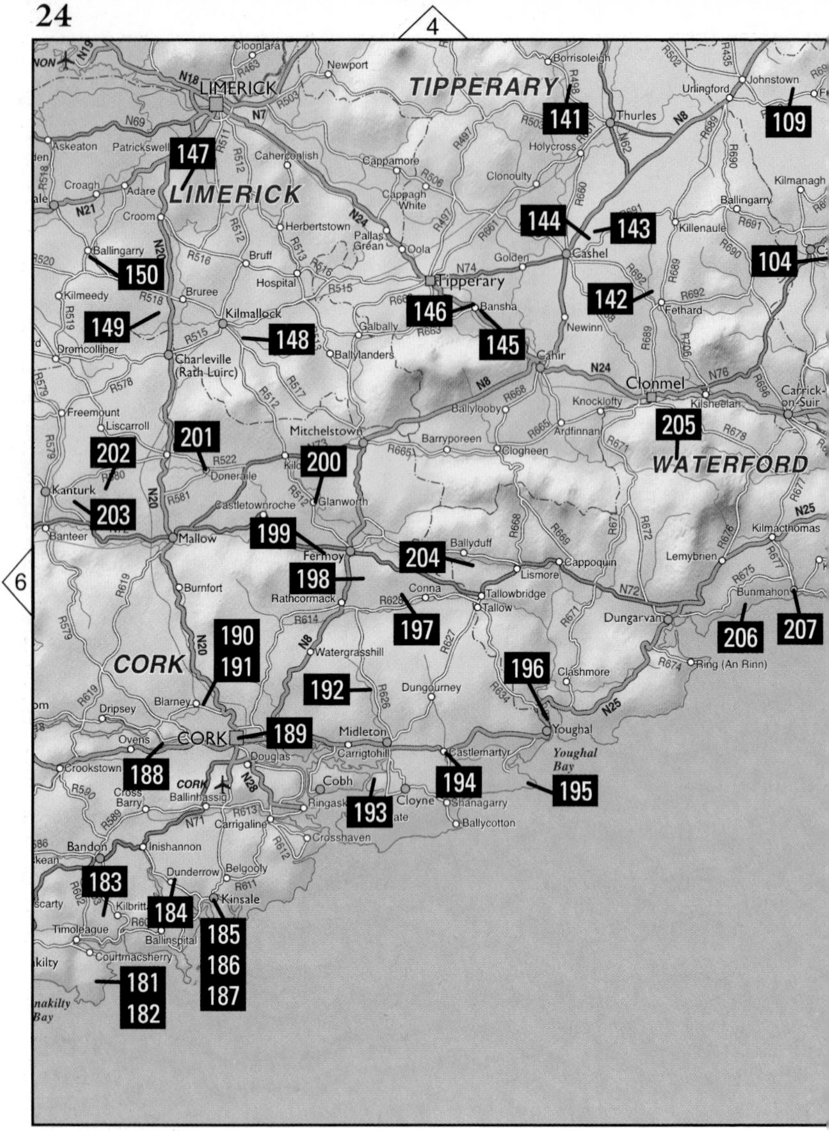
4
6
TIPPERARY
LIMERICK
CORK
WATERFORD
Limerick
Cloonlara
Newport
Borrisoleigh
Johnstown
Urlingford
Thurles
Holycross
Askeaton
Patrickswell
Caherconlish
Cappamore
Clonoulty
Kilmanagh
Croagh
Adare
Cappagh White
Ballingarry
Croom
Herbertstown
Pallas Grean
Oola
Killenaule
Cashel
Ballingarry
Bruff
Hospital
Golden
Tipperary
Fethard
Kilmeedy
Bruree
Kilmallock
Bansha
Newinn
Dromcolliher
Galbally
Ballylanders
Charleville (Rath Luirc)
Cahir
Clonmel
Kilsheelan
Carrick-on-Suir
Freemount
Ballylooby
Knocklofty
Liscarroll
Mitchelstown
Ardfinnan
Barryporeen
Clogheen
Doneraile
Kanturk
Glanworth
Castletownroche
Banteer
Mallow
Fermoy
Ballyduff
Kilmacthomas
Lemybrien
Cappoquin
Lismore
Burnfort
Rathcormack
Conna
Tallowbridge
Tallow
Bunmahon
Dungarvan
Watergrasshill
Clashmore
Ring (An Rinn)
Dripsey
Blarney
Dungourney
Youghal
Ovens
Cork
Midleton
Carrigtohill
Castlemartyr
Douglas
Youghal Bay
Crookstown
Cobh
Cross Barry
Ballinhassig
Ringaskiddy
Cloyne
Shanagarry
Carrigaline
Ballycotton
Crosshaven
Bandon
Inishannon
Dunderrow
Belgooly
Kinsale
Timoleague
Ballinspittal
Courtmacsherry
Clonakilty Bay
N7
N8
N18
N20
N21
N24
N25
N28
N62
N69
N71
N72
N73
N74
N76
141
109
147
144
143
104
150
142
149
146
148
145
205
201
202
200
203
199
204
198
197
206
207
190
191
196
192
189
188
194
195
193
183
184
185
186
187
181
182

Map 7

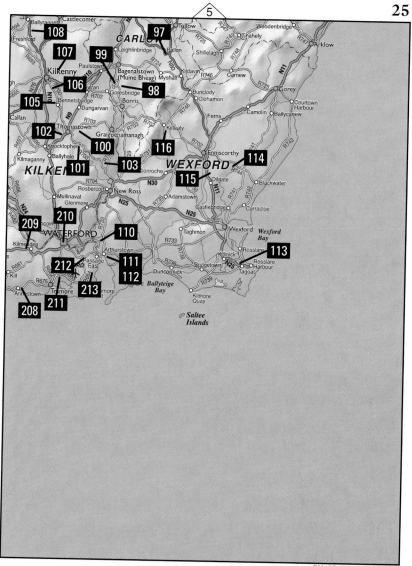

Map 8

Ulster

"It's a queer world, God knows,
but the best we have to be going on with."
Brendan Behan

Frewin

Ramelton
Co. Donegal

Tel: 074 51246
Fax: 074 51246
E-mail: flaxmill@indigo.ie
Web: www.accommodationdonegal.net

Thomas and Regina Coyle

Thomas and Regina have taken Irish hospitality to a new level in this lovely, relaxed house; elegant, uncluttered bedrooms have big, beautiful bathrooms and lush, woodland views. My highlight was a wonderful dinner with other guests under a chandelier of lighted candles. Regina's cooking is delicious. This Victorian house used to be a rectory, while the earlier fortified annex reliably dates to 1698 when landowners needed protection from the odd bloody uprising. Thomas, an avid antique collector and restorer of historic buildings, also discovered a family link; his great-aunt Susan had inscribed her name on the back of a cupboard in one of the bedrooms. He has set up a small museum in her honour. Ask him about the boxing gloves exhibit over a nightcap in the snug library covered with old Vanity Fair prints. Ramelton is a timeless place on the banks of the River Lennon famous for producing McDaids Football Special, a sweet pop drink loved by children across Ireland. In the village shop, a red-haired girl gave me directions to Frewin while Irish folk music played in the background. It was one of those magical moments when you realise you are in a foreign country. *Self catering cottage available. Sleeps 4.*

Rooms: 4: 1 family suite with en suite bathroom; 2 mini-suites, 1 with en suite bath, 1 with en suite shower; 1 double with private bathroom.
Price: IR£35—IR£45 p.p.
Breakfast: Included — full Irish/buffet.
Meals: Dinner, 3 courses, IR£20, by arrangement.
Closed: Never.

How to get there: From Letterkenny, R245 to Ramelton for 8 miles. Approaching Ramelton, take right fork after petrol station. House 300yds on right.

Map no: 1

Entry no: 1

The Mill Restaurant
Figart
Dunfanaghy
Co. Donegal

Tel: 074 36985/36983
Fax: 074 36985

Susan and Derek Alcorn

It is not hard to see why the north-west of Donegal has fostered a unique painting tradition. Exposed to the mercurial temperament of the Atlantic and enclosed by the Derryveagh Mountains and Mount Errigal, its hostile beauty is manna to the artist. Acclaimed watercolour artist Frank Egginton moved here in 1949, buying this 19th-century lodge on the shores of New Lake to work in until his death in 1990. Now his granddaughter Susan and husband Derek have breathed new life into The Mill, opening a B&B and an exceptional restaurant. Derek cut his teeth at the prestigious Gleneagles Hotel in Scotland but always wanted to return to his native Donegal to cook with the fabulous local ingredients. Donegal lamb, oysters, duck, salmon, mussels, everything he uses is fresh and in season. Susan is a charming host, ensuring guests and diners are well looked after. Pleasant bedrooms have sleigh beds, Egginton paintings on the walls, pretty tiled bathroom floors and lake views. A living room for guests also upstairs is full of Egginton's collection of antique oak furniture — ideal to relax in after dinner. By day, take a ferry to Tory Island where fishermen artists produce acclaimed work, or bring your own paintbox.

Rooms: 6: 3 doubles, 1 twin, all with en suite bathroom; 2 doubles, both with en suite shower.
Price: IR£25—IR£30 p.p. Sing. supp. IR£5.
Breakfast: Included — full menu.
Meals: Dinner from IR£21. Sunday lunch from IR£14.50.
Closed: Mondays.

How to get there: From Dunfanaghy, N56 Falcarragh Rd past gallery on right and down small hill. Entrance on right. House overlooks lake.

Entry no: 2

Map no: 1

Danny Minnies Restaurant

Teach Killindarragh   **Tel:** 075 48201
Annagry, Rosses   **Fax:** 075 48201
Co. Donegal

Terri O'Donnell

The west coast of Donegal: deep green sea, long white beaches, rugged hills, waterfalls and a music that finds its melodies in this poetic landscape. Some of Ireland's best folk acts started in the local pubs and bars of Donegal. Enya and Clannad still play at Leo's down the road. It is just a shame about the 'bungalow blight'. A house with character like Danny Minnies sticks out like a pretty shell on a pebble beach. Terri took an old pub, painted it olive green, added a baronial, wood-panelled entrance gallery, several fireplaces and an inglenook, exposed the dark old beams and made lots of extra space. Downstairs is now a celebrated restaurant, with sunken parquet floor, low lighting and award-winning atmosphere. It specialises in spanking fresh seafood; Annagry means 'place of the sand eels' and this local delicacy is harvested from a nearby beach in summer and served up. After your meal, sing along to live music well into the night. Teri is a hugely sociable woman with a passion for life. Her children are all creative as well, playing music or painting and everyone cooks. The rooms are quirky but comfortable; one is in tartan, another has an oriental feel. Beds are good and the breakfasts are taken at a leisurely pace.

Rooms: 5: 3 twins, 2 doubles, 2 with en suite bathroom, 3 sharing bathroom.
Price: IR£28 p.p. Sing. supp. IR£5.
Breakfast: Included — full Irish.
Meals: Dinner from IR£20.
Closed: Never. Book in advance.

How to get there: From Letterkenny, N56 through Kilmacrenan. 3 miles on, left signed Glenveagh for 13 miles, then left, rejoining N56 for 3 miles. Right on R259 to Annagry. House on right in village.

Map no: 1   **Entry no: 3**

The Green Gate

Ardvally   **Tel:** 075 41546
Ardara
Co. Donegal

Paul Chatenoud

Paul has been described as a cross between Jean Paul Sartre and Charles Aznavour. How this Parisian exile ever ended up living a hermit's life on a hillside overlooking Donegal's rugged western coastline is remarkable. He was born in Morocco, studied philosophy at the Sorbonne then set up the first shop in Paris to sell books on music. Tiring of the life, he sold-up and blew the proceeds on a ritzy lifestyle. He then arrived in Ireland burnt out and almost penniless, yet determined to write a book that would win the Nobel Prize for Literature. He completed the book and returned to Paris, but then came back again in 1988 for a friend's wedding at which he famously declared: "If you find me a house, I will buy it." A few days later, he bought The Green Gate just outside the tweed town of Adara, converting the thatched cowsheds into comfortable, stylish guest rooms; delicate touches include lampshades made from mother of pearl shells that his teenage son Edouard dived for off Corsica. His amazing life story unfolded during a lamb chop supper cooked over a turf fire as French opera music played in the background. The book remains unpublished but Irish B&B is richer for it. Go with an open mind.

Rooms: 4 doubles, all with en suite bathroom.
Price: IR£20—IR£25 p.p. Sing. supp. IR£10.
Breakfast: Included — Irish fry. 13 home-made preserves.
Meals: Available locally.
Closed: Never.

How to get there: From Ardara, Donegal road for 200yds, then right up winding lane for about 1 mile. Green Gate is signed up lane.

Bruckless House
Bruckless
Dunkineely
Co. Donegal

Tel: 073 37071
Fax: 073 37070
E-mail: bruc@bruckless.com
Web: www.iol.ie/~bruc/bruckless.html

Joan and Clive Evans

Bruckless revels in an extraordinary light from being so close to the sea; the effect seems to make people relax. Life is exceedingly mellow in this handsome Grange Farm in the Georgian style. Joan and Clive have filled its tall, graceful rooms with many lovely things brought back from their years in the Orient; brush stroke paintings from China, beautiful rugs resting on light woollen carpets and a gorgeous rosewood table; Some of the finds were made nearer to home, such as a chunky, Irish oak sideboard, carved with fish and gargoyles, that Joan restored after discovering it in a peat store. The bedrooms are at the back of the house overlooking a delightful cobbled courtyard that dates back to the house's construction in 1745. The garden is an award-winning gem with lawns, flowers, a rockery and paths that meander through bluebells and rhododendrons past old Scots pines and maples to the rocky coast and along to the village of Bruckless. They also run a Connemara pony stud farm on 20 acres, keeping seven horses and some chickens. *Self-catering gate lodge, sleeps 4, IR£135—IR£300 p.w.*

Rooms: 4: 1 twin, 1 double, both with en suite bathroom; 2 singles sharing bathroom.
Price: IR£30—IR£ £35 p.p.
Breakfast: Included — full Irish.
Meals: Not available.
Closed: 1 October—31 March.

How to get there: From Donegal, N56 for Killybegs for 12 miles & go through Dunkineely. House signed on left after 2 miles.

The Gate Lodge and Buncronan Cottage

Salthill House
Mountcharles
Co. Donegal

Tel: 073 35014
Fax: 073 21145
E-mail: etemple@eircom.net

Elizabeth Temple

It is hard to capture the spirit of southern Donegal without resorting to hackneyed clichés. Sure, it is beautiful, unspoilt and sublimely peaceful, but it goes deeper than that. This part of Ireland leaves an indelible memory. The Gate Lodge and Buncronan Cottage are on the remote Doorin peninsula. The 1780 Gate Lodge has a private entrance on the grounds of Salthill House, the Georgian home of the Temple family with its beautiful walled garden and views over bay and mountain. It is a large, well-furnished, carefully thought out self-catering space for those that want to absorb the beauty of the setting and enjoy absolute privacy. Away to the west is Buncronan (translating as "within the sound of the sea"), an 1800s farm cottage close to the more secluded Inver Bay. Inside there is polished timber, a dining room gallery, ball and claw-footed bath, cosy bedrooms and turf fire. Corncrakes have been heard here, and wild orchids and other rare flowers are plentiful. Come here for simple pleasures — to walk, swim, eat and sleep.

Rooms: Gate Lodge: 4 bedrooms, sharing bathroom & 3 toilets, sleeps 6; Buncronan: 2 bedrooms, en suite, sleeps 4.
Price: Gate Lodge: IR£300—IR£550 p.w.; Buncronan: IR£300—IR£400 p.w.
Breakfast: You cook, you choose.
Meals: Available locally or bring a cookbook.
Closed: Never.

How to get there: From Donegal, N56 to Mount Charles, then left at Toyota dealer after village. Down lane, over x-roads, entrance to main house 2 miles on left before road turns left along beach.

Entry no: 6

Map no:1

Portnason House

Portnason
Ballyshannon
Co. Donegal

Tel: 072 52016
Fax: 072 52016
E-mail: portnasonhouse@oceanfree.net
Web: www.sawdays.co.uk

Madge Sharkey

It is always interesting when someone's conviction for design is given rein in a house as grand as Portnason. Originally built as officers' accommodation for the British army in 1750, this Irish Georgian house down a beautiful sycamore-lined drive has been Madge's 'project' for some years; with her formative years spent at art and design school, the results are striking. She likes fresh 'Mediterranean' colours and hates clutter. A mulberry staircase leads to bedrooms with pitch pine floors stripped or painted in pastel shades, tiled and original marble fireplaces, wicker furniture, dhurrie mats and big brass beds with cotton quilts, while spotless bathrooms include re-enamelled claw-footed baths. The Georgian appetite for space and light is typically evident, the old practice of filling in windows to dodge heavy taxation being thankfully absent. White wooden shutters open onto views of the Erne estuary, with its resident seal and, in the distance, miles of sandy beaches at Tullan Strand are accessible by foot or on horseback; the choice is yours as guests' steeds are welcome. Or you could always launch a small sailboat from the private jetty and picnic in the sand dunes. The options are endless and Madge is full of suggestions.

Rooms: 5: 1 kingsize, 1 twin, both with en suite bathroom; 1 twin with en suite bath/shower; 2 doubles with en suite shower.
Price: IR£45—IR£55 p.p. Sing. supp. IR£10.
Breakfast: Included — full Irish.
Meals: Available locally.
Closed: Christmas & New Year.

How to get there: From Donegal, N15 south to Ballyshannon. Through town, over bridge, then right at r'bout to Sligo. Entrance on right down tree-lined avenue by stone gate lodge.

Map no: 1

Ardnamona
Lough Eske
Co. Donegal

Tel: 073 22650
Fax: 073 22819
www.sawdays.co.uk

Kieran and Amabel Clarke

Deep in the rhododendron forest, logs pop contentedly in the hearths at Ardnamona. Amabel is in the kitchen with her two children, working a delicious magic, but Kieran? He maybe in the woods transforming a former arboretum to National Heritage status, or tuning a friend's piano. Or could that be him in the loft-gallery music room, eeking out Beethoven on Paderewsky's Steinway? In the evening, your best bet is to find him relaxing in front of a fire. Kieran likes to sit up late and talk on a range of subjects. "It was a great job tuning pianos in sixties London. Paul McCartney in the morning, Alfred Brendel in the afternoon," he explains. Ardnamona lends itself to long, cosy, convivial evenings; pine floors and gracefully old rugs lead from one room to another, in which fires radiate warmth and dark, heavy, velvet curtains keep the night chill at bay. In the morning, wake up to cheerful, feminine bedrooms with white-painted furniture and patchwork quilts; some have window seats with views over Lough Eske to the heather slopes of the Blue Stack Mountains. Downstairs, the conservatory sparkles with a sea mosaic. After breakfast, stroll down to the lake and take out a boat.

Rooms: 6: 4 doubles, all with en suite bathroom;
1 double, 1 twin, both with private bathroom.
Price: IR£45—IR£50 p.p. Sing. supp. IR£10.
Breakfast: Included — full Irish.
Meals: Dinner, 3 courses, IR£25.
Closed: Never, but advance booking essential.

How to get there: From Donegal, N15 to Letterkenny
for 2.5 miles. Take small turning on left marked
Harvey's Point Country Hotel/Lough Eske Drive.
Straight on for 5 miles. Low wall, then white-gated drive
on right.

Mount Royd Country House

Carrigans
Co. Donegal

Tel: 074 40163
Fax: 074 40400

Josephine Martin

Having lived on a border road just inside the Republic of Ireland for the past 19 years, Josephine remembers the Troubles well. She hung in there through the worst bits with steely optimism, looking after workmen unaccustomed to staying in such comfort. Her cluttered living room is full of gifts they left. As tourism picked up, her reputation grew and then to her surprise she received a nationwide B&B landlady of year award. Josephine is like a professional mum to guests. When I arrived late and tired after a day's driving, she kindly rustled up something. This is an open, friendly house. Later, I ended up at the village pub with two other guests, an Irish airline pilot and a US cop. Mount Royd was built as a farmhouse in the 1940s and it took one man four years to build. Today, creeper softens the edges and curious garden ornaments decorate the front. Boudoir bedrooms are cosy with bolsters on the beds and saloon doors leading to the showers. Every available space has a knick-knack of some sort or another. Agatha Christie wrote several thrillers in a house on a hill opposite in the 1920s. The awe-inspiring Grianán Ailigh prehistoric ringfort is also nearby.

Rooms: 4 doubles, all with en suite shower. Extra bathroom available.
Price: IR£19—IR£20 p.p. Sing.supp. IR£5.
Breakfast: Included — full menu.
Meals: Available locally.
Closed: Winter. Off season by arrangement.

How to get there: From Derry, A40 over border to Carrigans. House signed on left before village.

Map no: 1

Entry no: 9

Croaghross

Portsalon
Letterkenny
Co. Donegal

Tel: 074 59548
Fax: 074 59548
E-mail: jkdeane@croaghross.com
Web: www.croaghross.com

John and Kay Deane

A windy lane leads up past ugly holiday bungalows to the far more civilised climes of John and Kay's carefully-designed, croissant-shaped home; they holidayed in the area for 20 years before moving here, so they knew what they wanted. The three modern patio rooms have wonderful views of Lough Swilly and Ballymastocker Bay, a near perfect crescent of golden sand flanked by a championship standard golf course. There is a little kitchenette, facilities for the disabled and the work of local artists on the walls. John could be described as laid back, unless in campaigning mood against the rampant bungalow blight spreading along the Donegal coast. Kay loves her Aga, exhausting cookbooks and oven gloves to reach yet more culinary peaks. She uses only the best local produce with wild Swilly salmon popular with guests. Both are cheerful and accommodating, and Kay's green-fingered mother, who lives up the hill, makes sure the house is full of flowers from the garden. No one will rush you at breakfast. And for a 19th hole after a round of golf or a good walk, it would be hard to beat the legendary Rita's Bar on the harbour front. They also let a new cottage built near the house.

Rooms: 5: 2 family, 1 double, all with en suite bath; 1 twin, 1 double, both with en suite shower.
Price: IR£20—IR£35 p.p. Sing. supp. IR£5
Breakfast: Included — full menu.
Meals: Dinner, 4 courses, IR£17.50.
Closed: Christmas & New Year. Winter bookings by arrangement.

How to get there: From Ramelton, cross bridge, R246 to Millford for 4 miles. Just before Millford, right to Kerrykeel. In Kerrykeel, left to Portsalon. Carry on, then right at first x-roads for 0.5 miles. House up lane on left, opposite golf club.

Entry no: 10   Map no: 1

Glen House

Straid
Clonmany
Co. Donegal

Tel: 077 76745
Web: www.sawdays.co.uk

Doris Russo

The Inishowen peninsula is one of Donegal's showpieces with its pebbled bays and pristine beaches. Georgian Glen House was built in 1766 by O'Doherty on land given as a dowry after he married a vicar's daughter. It is named after the glen it stands in complete with river and 30ft waterfall. When Doris arrived from New Jersey about a decade ago, she found a "pile of rubble, history and location, and that's it!" Keeping what she could, shutters, thick walls, sash windows, the rest is Doris. The task was made more difficult by the ghosts of a sea captain and a young girl; at least one workman refused to come back. Today, there is a 'ghost corner' for children to play in. The style is American with country pine, recliners, landscape pictures and carpets from the US; as is breakfast, with lashings of maple syrup, pancakes, omelettes, fresh fruit, French toast, and muffins. One Polish woman, who visited, wrote: "I thought I'd died and gone to heaven." High praise indeed. The bedrooms are uncluttered with flowery bedspreads, but you come here for the outdoors. Doris loves walking and will point you in the right direction, whether its mountain or beach.

Rooms: 2: 1 twin, 1 double, both with en suite shower.
Price: IR£20 p.p. Sing supp. IR£5.
Breakfast: Included — American.
Meals: Dinner IR£15, by arrangement. Picnic hampers also available.
Closed: Never.

How to get there: From Derry, A2 to Buncrana. Right in Buncrana, signed to Clonmany. Through village and bear left over bridge then bear right, follow signs to Glen House. House 0.5 miles on left.

Map no: 1

Entry no: 11

McGrory's of Culdaff

Culdaff
Inishowen
Co. Donegal

Tel: 077 79104/79363
Fax: 077 79235
E-mail: mcgr@eircom.net
Web: www.mcgrorys.ie

The McGrory Family

Tucked away in a charming village of 200 people on the remote and spectacular Inishowen Peninsula, and miles from the more traditional haunts of Ireland's folky hipsters, McGrory's seems an unlikely place for one of the most renowned music venues outside Dublin and Galway. Yet every musician worth their fiddle wants to play Mac's Backroom Bar with its unique interior of pine beams salvaged from the old US Navy Docks in Derry. And you will be glad you made the trip with so much culture, unspoilt scenery and good food on your doorstep. Brothers Neil and John and sister Anne are continuing a family tradition that started here in 1924 when their grandparents opened a general store. In the 1960s, their parents, John Joe and Deirdre, started putting on live music and in July 1999, the present generation did the place up and opened a reputable restaurant run by a chef who used to cook at the House of Commons. The bedrooms are done to a high standard in mustard and terracotta colours, with views towards Slieve Snercht — Gaelic for 'snow mountain'. You won't be kept awake as the rooms are well away from Mac's. But this is not the place to go to bed early — not when you can get lost in the best music in Ireland.

Rooms: 10: 4 doubles, 5 double/singles, 1 twin, all with en suite shower.
Price: From IR£30 p.p. Sing. supp. IR£10. Children under 12 sharing parents' bedroom, no charge.
Breakfast: Included — full Irish/buffet.
Meals: In the restaurant IR£15—IR£18. Live music most nights either in Mac's Backroom Bar or the Front Bar at no extra charge to guests.
Closed: Christmas

How to get there: From Derry, A2 to Quigley's Point, then left to Carndonagh. Malin road in Carndonagh for 2 miles then right at x-roads towards Culdaff. House in village on left after tight left hand bend.

Entry no: 12   Map no: 2

Fortsingleton

Emyvale
Co. Monaghan

Tel: 047 86054
Fax: 047 86120
E-mail: fortsingleton@eircom.net
Web: www.fortsingleton.com

Anne and Ray Goodall

Fortsingleton indulges our desire to escape into fantasy once in a while. Ray's resourceful imagination has transformed this 1750s Georgian manor house into one of the only places in Ireland doing 'scene bedrooms'. Stay in a boat-shaped bunk bed, a Victorain train carriage, a Bedouin tent, or a bishop's quarters with a magic wardrobe. Alternatively, those wanting country house style can choose from a variety of elegant bedrooms, with views over hills and fields dotted with sheep. Quirky antique furniture includes a half-tester, a brass bed, a carved frieze, a pianola and an old wireless. Ray, who used to run nightclubs in the UK, has a talent for doing a lot with little, turning a piece of junk into a beautiful standard lamp that looks as though it has been in his drawing room since time immemorial. Outside, overgrown outbuildings are full of stuff waiting to be brought back into use. There is also a small lake, gardens accessible to wheelchair users and a restaurant where candlit dinners use the freshest ingredients grown in Anne's walled vegetable garden. A stylish house with a sense of humour.

Rooms: 10: 6 twins, 2 doubles,1 triple, all with en suite shower; 1 double with en suite bath.
Price: IR£30 p.p. Sing. supp. IR£5.
Breakfast: Included — full Irish.
Meals: Dinner IR£20.
Closed: 23 December—27 December.

How to get there: From Monaghan, N2 towards Derry into Emyvale for 6 miles. Through village, house signed second left after 1 mile (10 minutes from Monaghan).

Glynch House

Newbliss
Clones
Co. Monaghan

Tel: 047 54045
Fax: 047 54321
E-mail: mirth@eircom.net
Web: www.glynchfarmhouse.com

Martha O'Grady

Martha is so open and laid back that even the most trying day melts away over a cup of tea and a few jokes. She and John are a natural double act; both have a finely-tuned sense of humour and their banter can be hilarious. They are genuinely interested in people which probably explains why they are still doing B&B after more than two decades. In that time, the world has beat a path to their door and Martha describes herself as an "armchair traveller". This impressive farmhouse built by Huguenots in 1772 is reached up a long drive. The big drawing room manages to be cosy, with comfortable furniture that's drawn up to an open fire and upstairs bedrooms have good views, wooden beds, white shutters and plenty of space. Guests dine together with John and Martha where possible — dinner is one of Martha's specialities and conversation will flow. You will want to return.

Rooms: 6: 1 twin, 1 family, 1 single, sharing bathroom/shower; 2 twins, each with en suite shower; 1 double with private bathroom.
Price: IR£25 p.p. Sing. supp. IR£5.
Breakfast: Included — full Irish.
Meals: Dinner IR£15. Packed lunch on request.
Closed: October—February. Off season by arrangement.

How to get there: From Clones, R183 Ballybay Rd for 3.5 miles. House signed on left before railway bridge.

Entry no: 14

Map no: 1

Hilton Park

Clones
Co. Monaghan

Tel: 047 56007
Fax: 047 56033
E-mail: jm@hiltonpark.ie
Web: www.hiltonpark.ie

Johnny and Lucy Madden

Hilton Park could be a tourist attraction in its own right. It is one of Ireland's most imposing country houses and guests are lucky on all counts. Built by Johnny's ancestor in 1734, it was remodelled in the Italianate style in the 1870s. Put your bags down by a huge four-poster and admire original wallpaper, a *chaise longue*, and views across lawns to a lake. The bathroom next door is so vast that once immersed in the free-standing bath, you feel as though you have been cast adrift in a boat. Go for a stroll down by the lake, along gravel walkways enclosed by banks of tall trees and rhododendron, to a jetty and watch the swans or fish darting about in the shallows. Dinners are memorable, too. Guests sit down together or separately, as they prefer, in a large wood-panelled dining room, their faces lit by a hearty open fire and candles that create a cosy mood despite the size of the room. Where possible, every ingredient is picked from the garden, minutes before cooking. In the morning, enjoy breakfast basked in sunlight. A special place in every sense. *Children over seven welcome.*

Rooms: 6: 3 doubles, 2 family, 1 twin, all with en suite bathroom.
Price: IR£64—IR£75 p.p. Sing. supp. IR£20.
Breakfast: Included — full Irish.
Meals: Dinner IR£27.50. Wine from IR£15.
Closed: October—March except for groups. Sundays and Mondays during the season.

How to get there: From Cavan bypass, take Ballyhaise turn-off. Through Ballyhaise and Scotshouse. 2.5 miles on, first entrance on left after Clones golf club.

Map no: 1

Entry no: 15

Rockwood House
Cloverhill
Belturbet
Co. Cavan

Tel: 047 55351
Fax: 047 55373
E-mail: jbmac@eircom.net

Susan and Jim McCauley

An enthusiastic westie dog warmly greets guests arriving at Rockwood, with Susan and Jim not far behind. If the weather's good, you will be drinking tea on a sunlit patio before long, chatting away, surrounded by peaceful woodland. This is County Cavan, one of Ireland's best kept secrets. Visitors are drawn to explore the surroundings. A wooden gate leads from the garden to a wood that provides a refuge for the red squirrel and the pine martin. Sightings of both species are frequent, along with a multitude of other wildlife. The McCauleys know their home comforts and that includes real fires for those chilly, inclement days. They were born to entertain and clearly enjoy talking to guests. The house they designed themselves. The immaculate guest rooms are clutter-free, with carpeted floors and pastel blue and yellow interiors. Everything in them seems brand new, and there are lots of well-appreciated extras such as smellies in the bathroom. This is very much a B&B so don't expect mod cons like telephones in the rooms. Good value in a friendly home.

Rooms: 4: 1 double, 3 twins, all with en suite shower. 1 extra bathroom.
Price: IR£20 p.p. Sing.supp. IR£5.
Breakfast: Included — full Irish.
Meals: The Olde Post Inn restaurant 300 yards away. Derragarra Inn at Butlersbridge 2 miles
Closed: One week at Christmas.

How to get there: From Cavan, N3 for Monaghan for 4 miles. Bear right at sign for Monaghan/Butlersbridge onto N54. House 2 miles on left.

Belle Isle

Lisbellaw
Co. Fermanagh

Tel: 028 66387231
Fax: 028 66387261
E-mail: accommodation@belleisle-estate.com
Web: www.belleisle-estate.com

Charles and Fiona Plunket

Belle Isle is the self-catering equivalent of Harrods. This 470-acre estate owned by the Duke of Abercon on nine islands at the northern end of Upper Lough Erne has everything from a mansion to a cottage with a walled garden. The main house with its gorgeous ranging view down the lake dates back to 1750. Here you can stay in the baronial splendour of the Hamilton Wing. In the magnificent drawing, a painting by Sir Edwin Landseer, Queen Victoria's favourite artist, hangs above the fireplace, one of 920 paintings in the house. There is also a Steinway grand piano and a funky drinks cabinet built around the salvaged doors of an 18th-century horse-drawn carriage. Bold, stylish bedrooms were designed by David Hicks, Lord Mountbatten's son-in-law. The lime green room is said to cure a hangover, while Coco Chanel gives her name to another because she once slept there. You can cook for yourself in the Aga kitchen or catering can be arranged. Beyond compare for a large group. Elsewhere, the courtyard apartments have won a prestigious award, while the Bridge House is more secluded with its own mooring. Some of the Annals of Ulster were supposedly written here. I wonder if they mention what a beautiful place it is to stay.

Price: From £150—£2000 p.w.
Rooms: Coach house, apartments, Hamilton wing and cottages sleep from 2-14.
Breakfast: Hamilton wing — £10. Optional.
Meals: Hamilton wing, dinner £25. Lunch £15. Both optional.
Closed: Never.

How to get there: From Enniskillen, B514 Lisnaskea Rd for about 5 miles, then right for 3 miles following signs.

Map no: 1

Rossfad House

Killadeas
Ballinamallard
Co. Fermanagh
BT94 2LS

Tel: 028 66388505
Fax: 028 66388505

John and Lois Williams

Rossfad lies in the heart of Fermanagh's lakelands where the boomerang expanse of Lower Lough Erne and the intricate shape of Upper Lough Erne provide the focal point for this fishing area, with the town of Enniskillen standing sentry between the two. There are so many other smaller lakes and arterial rivers, fringed by forest and the odd castle, that it is easy to lose yourself in Cuchulainn legend. Rossfad itself belongs more to a Georgian fairytale. The house, built in 1776, is separated from the road by a long avenue, so you are completely surrounded by nature; inside, the easy-going lifestyle of the Williams family immediately puts you at ease. The Victorian guest wing, added in 1876, has its own access and the south-facing guest rooms enjoy long views of the garden to Lower Lough Erne and mountains beyond. In the guest living room, the furniture is comfortable with more of those gorgeous views and an open fire for chilly evenings. Big bedrooms are simply decorated and the private bathroom has a big, luxurious bathtub. On bright mornings, the sun floods into the sitting room at breakfast time. There is croquet and badminton in the garden and a lake to swim in if the mood takes you.

Rooms: 2: 1 double/triple with en suite bathroom; 1 double/triple with private bathroom.
Price: From £20 p.p. Sing. supp. £5.
Breakfast: Included — full Irish.
Meals: Available locally.
Closed: December—March.

How to get there: From Enniskillen, A32 to Kesh for 2 miles. At Trory, B82 on left, follow for 3 miles. Avenue opposite road to Whitehill Rd. Look out for trees at the end of unsurfaced road up to house.

Entry no: 18

Map no: 1

The Merchant's House

16 Queen Street
Derry
Co. Londonderry
BT48 7EQ

Tel: 028 71269691
Fax: 028 71266913
E-mail: lucy@fdn.co.uk

Joan and Peter Pyne

That Derry is slowly emerging from the shadows of a turbulent, divided past is welcome news for the traveller because there are places worth visiting in Ireland's best preserved walled city. There's St Columb's Cathedral in the Planter Gothic style, the first cathedral to be built after the English Reformation; the award-winning Derry Tower Museum; and the newly-opened Verbal Arts Centre celebrating the art of Irish storytelling. The real find, however, is Merchant's House, an 1868 townhouse in the Georgian style that has been lovingly restored by Joan and Peter, two of the nicest eccentrics you are likely to meet. After travelling widely in Latin America, the pair came back to Ireland, buying the house in 1993 while Peter was still teaching history at the University of Ulster in Derry. They join a colourful list of previous owners that include a Justice of the Peace, a grocer, two rectors and a butcher. Edward VII is also said to have had tea in the dining room where breakfast is served today around a large wooden table. The bedrooms are full of period furniture, including a gorgeous half-tester bed, and the first floor living room is fabulous. Unforgettable. *Handy for Derry Airport.*

Rooms: 5: 1 double with en suite shower; 1 twin with private shower; 1 double, 1 twin, 1 small single, sharing bathroom with bath and shower.
Price: £25 p.p. Sing. supp. £5.
Breakfast: Included — full cooked breakfast 8am-10.30am.
Meals: Available in Derry.
Closed: Never.

How to get there: From Derry Airport, A2 to Derry over Craigavon Bridge, second road bridge over the river, then right, signed city centre. Over 2 r'bouts, past rear of Tesco, then left into Lower Clarendon Street. First right after traffic lights. Last house on left.

Map no: 1   **Entry no: 19**

Drumcovitt House

704 Feeny Rd
Feeny
Co. Londonderry
BT47 4SU

Tel: 028 77781224
Fax: 028 77781224
E-mail: drumcovitt.feeny@btinternet.com
Web: www.drumcovitt.com

Florence and Frank Sloan

Driving along the small roads that fan out from Londonderry, I saw an intriguing old farmhouse on a hill, with a lovely weeping ash at the front. This 1796 Irish Georgian house has many original features; panes of handblown glass that distort the countryside beyond and a huge 'Christian' door in the front hall with a wooden drop bar that would stop the most determined burglar. Grand rooms have round bays, original pine flooring, gilded pelmets, ancient carpets, dado rails, beehive door knobs, cornices — it is the full Georgian Monty. Stairs sweep up to a wide, creaky, arched landing lined with old books. Large, uncluttered bedrooms have yawning views across fields to the Sperrin Mountains, where hang-gliders jump off the highest spur. On misty mornings, only these peaks and the spire of Banagher church are visible. Climb the glen to the reservoir and filter house, or else, take the back lane from the house to woodland and a prehistoric ring fort. Florence and Frank are friendly, down-to-earth characters, who take great pride in providing a comfortable stay. Exceptional value and a favourite haunt for writers and poets. *Three self-catering cottages, one with full disabled facilities, each sleeps 4, £275—£370 p.w.*

Rooms: 3: 2 twins, 1 family, sharing bathroom & shower room.
Price: £18—£23 p.p. No sing. supp.
Breakfast: Included — full Irish.
Meals: Dinner £7—£18, à la carte. Book by noon the same day. Packed lunch £3.
Closed: Never.

How to get there: From Derry, A6 to Belfast for 10 miles, then right on B74 to Feeny for 5 miles. Through Feeny, house 0.5 miles on left.

Magheramore Courtyard Cottages

59 Magheramore Road
Dungiven
Co. Londonderry
BT47 4SW

Tel: 028 77741942
Fax: 028 77740466
E-mail: info@magheramore.com
Web: www.magheramore.com

Ian and Pamela Buchanan

What makes Ireland so fascinating is the way it gives so little away at first glance. Only when you stop and take a closer look does its rich history and many contradictions begin to unravel. Magheramore is a good example. Ian is the ninth generation descendant of Presbyterian Ulster Scots to live on this 500-acre sheep and cattle farm in the heart of the Sperrin Mountains. Yet delve further and you discover it was also once a safe house for Catholic priests. Today, it is the perfect hideaway for those wanting to escape the congestion of the south. Ian and Pamela have converted three historically listed 17th-century courtyard cottages into outstanding self-catering accommodation. Pamela has a natural talent for colour; fresh, zesty yellows and warm peaches create inviting rooms, while a salt-marsh pink on one landing has the most amazing translucent quality when the sun shines on it. Little details throughout add character, such as the traditional brass trim on mantelpieces above well-designed open fires that draw a good flame. The kitchens have all you need and games and books will keep you occupied in the evening. Two cottages also open onto an enclosed garden where children can play safely.

Rooms: 3 courtyard cottages, all with 2 bedrooms and en suite bath or shower; 2 sleep 4, 1 sleeps six.
Price: £250—£400 p.w. depending on season. Shorter stays available.
Breakfast: You cook, you choose.
Meals: Available locally or bring a cookbook.
Closed: Never.

How to get there: From Belfast, A6 to Dungiven for 50 miles. Left in centre of village before police station, signed Magheramore Courtyard. Entrance on right, about 2 miles on.

Harmony Hill Country House

Balnamore
Ballymoney
Co. Antrim
BT53 7PS

Tel: 028 27663459
Fax: 028 27663740
E-mail: webmaster@harmonyhill.net
Web: www.harmonyhill.net

Trish Wilson

Harmony Hill is so full of surprises that you might think you had arrived at the house of Mr Benn, that cartoon grandmaster of costume changes. The hallway entrance and the lounge and bar area to the left have the feel of a grand country house of restrained good taste. Aromatic turf fires and comfy seats invite you to flop with an aperitif. Stroll across a decked open air walkway with a pretty Mediterranean-style courtyard to the restaurant with its snug, wooden cubicles and the gastronomic pleasures of rural France come to mind. Tantalising dishes, such as 'Beef Welly' and Chocolate Orange Slider, jump off the menu and the home-made ice-cream is gorgeous. Afterwards, let the luxurious log cabin-style bedrooms transport you to the Appalachian Mountains. The bedroom windows look over a tranquil mill pond and Balinamore Mill, a now derelict monument to the village's once prosperous past in cotton. Harmony Hill was built in 1765 by the first mill owner, an outspoken landowner who fled to the US in 1798 to escape charges of treason. Richard and Trish moved here to escape the rigours of running a bigger place. It has done them the world of good.

Rooms: 4: 2 twin/doubles with en suite bath; 2 twin/doubles with en suite shower; 3 rooms have bunk beds for children.
Price: £24.75 p.p. Sing. supp. £15.75. Extra person sharing, £15 p.p.
Breakfast: Included — full Ulster fry.
Meals: Dinner, 3 courses, £20. Restaurant open Wednesdays to Saturdays, 6.30pm — 9.30pm.
Closed: Christmas & New Year.

How to get there: From Ballymoney, A26 for 1 mile, then left signed Balnamore for 1 mile, over railway crossing. Left at T-junc. in village, entrance third right on tight bend, signed. House 400m up gravel drive.

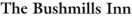

The Bushmills Inn

9 Dunluce Road
Bushmills
Co. Antrim
BT57 8QG

Tel: 028 20732339
Fax: 028 20732048
E-mail: mail@bushmillsinn.com
Web: www.bushmillsinn.com

Roy Bolton

In a past life, Roy Bolton was probably a Victorian illusionist as the inspired partitions, cubicles and hidden doors at Bushmills cleverly retain the cosiness of the original 17th century coaching inn — toast each pleasant discovery with a shot of whiskey made up the road at the world's oldest distillery. The round tower by the main entrance contains a tiny circular library with a secret door to a small conference room; it once foxed a group of businessmen, who began their meeting outside. James McKendry paintings of the Giant's Causeway coastline line the walls of the main staircase that leads to comfortable cottage-style bedrooms, each different from the next, while the newer rooms in the Mill House wing have their own sitting area and small dressing room; mod cons include a baby-listening device. Downstairs, traditional gas lamps, welcoming turf fires, flagstones and whitewashed walls create a cosy atmosphere of relaxed indulgence where friendly staff are always on hand. There is not much to compare at this level.

Rooms: 32: Mill House: 20 twin/doubles, 2 family; Coaching Inn: 4 singles, 4 doubles, 1 twin, 1 family, all with en suite bath or shower.
Price: £44—£64 p.p. Sing. occ. £68—£98. Single room £68—£78.
Breakfast: Included — full menu.
Meals: Dinner £25. Lunch and snacks also available.
Closed: Never.

How to get there: From Antrim, A26 to Ballymoney, then B62 & right on B17 to Bushmills, following signs to Giant's Causeway. Hotel entrance as you cross the River Bush.

Map no: 2

Entry no: 23

Whitepark House

Whitepark Bay
Ballintoy
Co. Antrim
BT54 6NH

Tel: 028 20731482
E-mail: bob@whiteparkhouse.com
Web: www.whiteparkhouse.com

Bob and Siobhán Isles

Whitepark House sits on high ground looking out across the Atlantic Ocean; on clear days, you can see Rathlin lighthouse, Islay and the Paps of Jura. Just the inspiration for a walk along the coast. Bob will drop you off at the Giant's Causeway and the eight-mile cliff walk back to base must be one of the reasons cameras were invented. Entering Whitepark itself will make you blink. You are sure you have just left Co. Antrim on the other side of the magnificent Saxon-style oak front door, yet it feels like you have stepped into the Hindu Kush; Buddha statues sit beatific under lush, leafy houseplants; while it would be no surprise if the carved wooden elephants on the mantelpiece jungle broke into a chorus of "Hup! two, three, four". This is an exotic, sensuous world, teeming with indoor vegetation; ideal for maharajas who want to feel at home while visiting Ireland. Bob and Siobhán created this unique place from trips to India, Sri Lanka and the Far East and they clearly love the business of entertaining, or else it just comes naturally. The original house was built in 1735, then extended in the late Victorian era with mock crenellations. Breakfast is taken in the large open plan hallway near a large bay window, while the big, double rooms ooze luxurious splendour.

Rooms: 3: 2 doubles, 1 twin, sharing bathroom and extra wc.
Price: £25 p.p. Sing. supp. £5.
Breakfast: Included — full Irish.
Meals: Bob and Siobhán will recommend places to eat.
Closed: Never.

How to get there: From Bushmills, A2 coast road to Whitepark Bay. Go past youth hostel entrance, 100yds on right.

The Moat Inn

12 Donegore Hill
Templepatrick
Co. Antrim
BT41 2HW

Tel: 028 94433659
Fax: 028 94433726
E-mail: themoatinn@talk21.com

Rachel Thompson

To my knowledge, this 18th-century inn is the only place in the book that has the blessing of both *Special Places* and the church. Parish records reveal a laid-back clergy quite prepared to allow the local congregation to pop next door for some liquid refreshment at the Moat Inn during an interval in the service. There is no record that the interludes made the parishioners sing with any more gusto but you do wonder. The building lasted as an inn until the 1960s. Now it has been transformed into a modest country house by Rachel and her music teacher husband Robert. They are a young, friendly couple who both play the piano — hence the organ in the library and the Hardman grand piano in the dining room. Built on a slope, some of the building's honeycombed interior is below ground but darker spaces have been turned into cosy snugs with open fires and armchairs — ideal for curling up with a book. One bedroom has a king-size four-poster, while another has a growing collection of lithographs. Dinner is served by candlelight on fine china around an ornate French dining table. *Belfast International Airport is 10 minutes by car. They will collect you.*

Rooms: 3: 1 double, 1 family, 1 twin, all en suite.
Price: £30 p.p. No sing. supp. Extra bed in family room, £15.
Breakfast: Included — full menu.
Meals: High tea £10, 6pm. Dinner £18, 8pm. Book by noon the same day. Packed lunch £5.
Closed: Never.

How to get there: From Belfast airport, A57 towards Belfast, past Templeton Hotel, then left at r'bout. 2 miles on, right signed Donegore, then first right into Moat Rd. Inn up hill on left.

Map no: 2

Entry no: 25

Greenwood House

25 Park Rd
Belfast
Co. Antrim
BT7 2FW

Tel: 028 90202525
Fax: 028 90202530
E-mail: greenwood.house@virgin.net
Web: www.greenwoodhouse.co.uk

Jason and Mary Harris

Jason and Mary have used their love of interior design to create an award-winning B&B that is bright, cheerful, contemporary, and different; reclaimed maple floors, vibrant colours on the walls, Giacometti-style wrought-iron chairs, wooden tables, bold curtains, high ceilings and windows that allow in lots of light. As you climb the stairs there are things to notice all around: brightly-coloured crêpe-paper lamp shades, modern pictures by Ulster artists, and a Big Sleep poster — Jason was a bit sheepish about that. Bedrooms are no less nteresting, with more wrought-iron, comfortable beds and pristine bathrooms with deep, luxurious baths to wallow in. Great breakfasts complete the picture. This late Victorian red brick townhouse overlooks Ormeau Park and a golf course. Belfast city centre is 20 minutes by foot, slightly longer if you walk along the river. Belfast Zoo, the 1894 Grand Opera House and Ulster Museum in the grounds of the Botanical Gardens are just some of the places worth a visit; Jason and Mary have two young daughters and are fun and easy to get on with.

Rooms: 7: 2 twins, 1 double, all with en suite bath/shower; 1 family, 1 double, 2 singles, all with en suite shower.
Price: £27.50 p.p. Sing. supp. £10.
Breakfast: Included — full Irish.
Meals: Available in Belfast.
Closed: Christmas & New Year

How to get there: From city centre, A24 Ormeau Rd towards Newcastle/Downpatrick, over bridge, 500yds further, turn left. House on right.

Carnwood House

85 Victoria Rd
Holywood
Co. Down
BT18 9BG

Tel: 028 90421745
Fax: 028 90421720
E-mail: enquiries@carnwoodhouse.com
Web: www.carnwoodhouse.com

Jenny Foster

Upon arriving at Carnwood, Jenny will take you in hand and give you tea and scones in one of the gigantic drawing rooms with fine Persian carpets, marble fireplaces, ornate plasterwork ceilings and tall windows that overlook the garden. In the morning, she will make you an excellent breakfast that you eat communally. All the bedrooms are a generous size with bed canopies in a couple and a four-poster in the third. They are plushly furnished, with new windows to keep out the chill easterly winds. This large 1840s townhouse lies buried in trees in the lough-side village of Holywood. It is hard to imagine that the city is only a short drive away. You can stroll out for lovely walks in the Craigantlet Hills, while horse riding and fishing are available close by. For those who prefer more sedentary pursuits, painting courses are held across the way. Enjoy the best of town and country in a peaceful, secluded, leafy setting, where a great welcome is guaranteed.

Rooms: 5 doubles, all with en suite shower.
Price: From £30 p.p. Sing. supp. £5.
Breakfast: Included — full Irish.
Meals: Packed lunch £4.50. Excellent restaurants in Holywood.
Closed: Never.

How to get there: From Belfast, A2 to Holywood. At Holywood sign on dual carriageway, go on to third set of traffic lights, turn right & immediately left onto Croft Rd, 250 yds on, first right into Victoria Rd. 50yds on left up small lane.

Map no: 2

Entry no: 27

Beech Hill Country House

23 Ballymoney Rd
Craigantlet, Newtownards
Co. Down
BT23 4TG

Tel: 028 90425892
Fax: 028 90425892
E-mail: beech.hill@btinternet.com
Web: www.beech-hill.net

Victoria Brann

It might surprise you that Beech Hill is only about 30 years old as it feels like a much older house. But then it was built by Victoria's grandmother along the lines of the house she grew up in as a child, which explains everything. Victoria is a natural hostess, the product of years in the catering trade before a friendly doctor told her to slow down. You will be greeted by two dogs, a lurcher called Mistle and a whippet called Swift, and be offered tea and delicious cakes in a long sitting room with fresh flowers and tasteful furniture; the windows look out onto a croquet lawn, and fields with grazing cows. You settle in very quickly here. The whole house is on one floor. Go one way and you come to a lovely wooden conservatory with wicker furniture and hanging baskets filled with geraniums. Go the other way and you come to the bedrooms; they are all immaculate, decorated in plain pale colours with comfortable beds, quality linen, TV, telephone, and demure prints of Belfast on the walls. The house is a welcoming place and Victoria is chatty and friendly. It is a relief to find you have arrived somewhere genuine.

Rooms: 3: 1 twin with en suite bath;
1 double with en suite bath/shower;
1 double with en suite shower.
Price: £30 p.p. Sing. supp. £10.
Breakfast: Included — full Ulster Fry.
Meals: Available in Holywood and Belfast.
Closed: Never.

How to get there: From Belfast, A2 towards Bangor. Bypass Holywood, then right up Ballymoney Rd, signed Craigantlet. House 1.75 miles on left.

Edenvale House

130 Portaferry Road
Newtownards
Co. Down
BT22 2AH

Tel: 028 91814881
Fax: 028 91826192
E-mail: edenvalehouse@hotmail.com
Web: www.edenvalehouse.com

Diane and Gordon Whyte

Diane is one of those people everyone seems to know and like. Exuberant, incredibly friendly and bursting with energy, she will quickly have you settled into this lovely 1780 Georgian house overlooking Strangford Lough. Gordon has a quick humour, too, and is quite prepared to take over welcome duties as the occasion requires. You approach the house up a narrow lane which starts right by the gently lapping waters of the lake. Relax with tea and home-made cakes in the beautifully-furnished drawing room or drift away in the bright sunroom with views of the towering Mourne Mountains. Large, immaculate bedrooms are well-proportioned, with luxuriously big beds, pelmets and hangings. A lot of effort goes into each aspect of the Edenvale experience, including the lovely big flower garden, where roses flourish. Children will love the horse and ponies. The National Trust property of Mount Stewart is close by and a car ferry across the lake leads to Castle Ward and unspoilt coastline. *Only 20 minutes from Belfast City Airport.*

Rooms: 4: 1 family, 1 double, both with en suite bath & shower; 1 double, 1 twin, both with en suite shower.
Price: £27.50 p.p. Sing. supp. £7.50.
Breakfast: Included — full Irish.
Meals: Available in Bangor and Newtownards.
Closed: Christmas & New Year.

How to get there: From Newtownards, A20 Portaferry Rd for 2 miles. Entrance on left up drive.

Sylvan Hill House

76 Kilntown Rd
Dromore
Co. Down
BT25 1HS

Tel: 028 92692321
Fax: 028 92692321

Elise and Jimmy Coburn

Elise and Jimmy like a house to feel lived in, so when the kids had grown up, they started B&B. "We didn't want to grow old staring at each other," says Elise, who also finds time to travel to far-flung corners of the world. Her last trip was to a remote part of Siberia where the only way to get about was by helicopter. She records each trip in meticulous detail and will share her fabulous travels on request. Jimmy prefers his home comforts and is happy seeking adventure over dinner with friends while Elise is away. Horses are a shared passion and the house is full of remarkable racing memorabilia. Guests almost always eat with Elise and Jimmy. She is a self-trained chef and offers wine with the meal at no extra cost — within reason. Breakfasts are a treat, too, with reputedly the best sausages in Ulster from a butcher in nearby Moira. The old house, built in 1781, sits on a hill overlooking the Mourne and Dromara Mountains. In summer, enjoy the view, dining in the plant-filled conservatory. The house is bigger than it seems. The immaculate rooms have comfortable beds on little platforms, while the raised bath in the large en suite bathroom is pure indulgence.

Rooms: 3: 2 doubles with en suite bathroom; 1 double/twin with private shower room.
Price: £28 p.p. No sing. supp.
Breakfast: Included — full Irish.
Meals: Dinner, 3 courses, including wine, £15.
Closed: Never.

How to get there: From Belfast, M1 towards Dublin, then A1 towards Dublin at Sprucefield r'bout. At Hillsborough bypass, Donaghloney Rd to right. 4 miles on, left to Dromore. House 0.25 miles on left at top of hill.

Entry no: 30

Map no: 2

Fortwilliam Country House

210 Ballynahinch Rd
Hillsborough
Co. Down
BT26 6BH

Tel: 028 92682255
Fax: 028 92689608
E-mail: fortwilliam.country.house@ukgateway.net
Web: www.fortwilliamcountryhouse.com

Terry and Mavis Dunlop

Nothing is too much trouble here. Mavis loves to chat with visitors over tea and home-made cakes round a large kitchen table in their lovely country-style Aga kitchen with baskets hanging from oak beams. Fortwilliam is a 300-year-old four-square house; the bay windows were added in the 1930s. Daring carpet colours, hunting prints and bubble glass ornaments contrast with antique furniture throughout. Terry is a busy farmer tending a suckling herd and thoroughbred horses on 70 acres with help from two friendly dogs. Bedrooms are full of restrained good taste and bathrooms have thoughtful extras to pamper yourself with; a window seat in the garden room looks over the daisy-strewn lawn. Curl up beside the log fire in the snug sitting room or relax in the tranquil walled garden and enjoy the view of the hills. The Dunlops deserve their Ulster Guesthouse of the Year award and your welcome could not be more Irish.

Rooms: 3: 1 double with en suite shower; 1 double with private bathroom; 1 double with private shower room.
Price: £25 p.p. Sing. supp. £5.
Breakfast: Included — full Irish.
Meals: Available in Hillsborough.
Closed: Never.

How to get there: From Hillsborough, B177 Ballynahinch Rd for 3.5 miles. House on hill on right, up steep drive.

Map no: 2

Entry no: 31

Dufferin Coaching Inn

31 High Street
Killyleagh
Co. Down
BT30 9QF

Tel: 028 44828229
Fax: 028 44828755
E-mail: dufferin@dial.pipex.com
Web: www.dufferincoachinginn.co.uk

Morris Crawford and Kitty Stewart

They say the law is an ass but at the Dufferin it is a pair of field spaniels called Lord Chief Justice and Queen's Counsel — their wig-like hair and measured stares are very popular with guests at this 1803 coaching inn. Kitty runs the B&B with friendly enthusiasm in one half of the original inn; this part was a bank for many years but they have returned the building to its original use. Classy bedrooms have four-posters in wrought iron and wood, pine furniture, spotless bathrooms and the lovely smell of fresh eucalyptus arranged in vases. Next door, the Dufferin Arms is a real treat. Through the doors with a pair of stain glass mandolin players is a traditional bar with wooden floors and a lovely timeworn atmosphere. On Saturday afternoons, anything from live jazz to Cajun to Irish folk could be playing. The restaurant serves excellent local seafood — it once sparked a famous lobster debate in the bar between celebrity chef Rick Stein and local fishermen — and the pub's monthly wine club makes sure the wine list is equally as good. The 'Siglu' bar outside is a curious addition; imagine having a drink outside in a large tea cosy. Killyleagh Castle is a short walk away and the village is close to Strangford Lough.

Rooms: 6: 4 doubles, 2 twins, all with en suite bathroom.
Price: £32.50 p.p. Sing. supp. £5.
Breakfast: Included — full Ulster fry.
Meals: Dinner from £15 à la carte.
Closed: Never.

How to get there: From Belfast, A22 Downpatrick Rd to Killyleagh for 18 miles. Turn right at mural on wall & follow one-way system. Dufferin Coaching Inn on left, 100yds from castle.

The Narrows

8 Shore Rd
Portaferry
Co. Down
BT22 1JY

Tel: 028 42728148
Fax: 028 42728105
E-mail: info@narrows.co.uk
Web: www.narrows.co.uk

Will and James Brown

The Narrows is sure to become a well-loved institution before long. Brothers Will and James have returned to the birthplace of their father to create a stylish, award-winning shorefront restaurant and guesthouse with a bright, modern, comfortable feel that is all its own. Expect a warm reception and friendly service in the informal restaurant, overlooking Strangford Lough, which has a growing reputation for being one of the best seafood restaurants in Ireland; the dishes are of high quality, good value and not over-elaborate. Just as much effort has gone into well-designed rooms with low beds, coir matting, and white and cream walls — the overall effect is successfully restful on the eye. Window-boxes and paintings by local artists provide splashes of colour amid the stylish minimalism. Rooms look over the mouth of the lough to the pretty village of Strangford, which can be reached by a regular car ferry. The road on the other side leads off down the Co. Down coast through the unspoilt, tree-lined harbour village of Killough to the Mourne Mountains.

Rooms: 13 doubles/twins all with en suite bath or shower.
Price: £42.50-IR£45 p.p. Sing. supp. £15.
Breakfast: Included — full Irish.
Meals: Lunch & dinner in the restaurant, à la carte (main course about £12).
Closed: Never.

How to get there: From Belfast, A20 south for 28 miles to Portaferry. House on shore front.

Map no: 2

Deans Hill
College Hill
Armagh
Co. Armagh
BT61 9DF

Tel: 028 37524923
Fax: 028 37524923

Jill and Edward Armstrong

All those who wisely cross the border into Northern Ireland will want to drop in on historic Armagh, with its stunning Cathedral. They should also stay at Dean's Hill, a wonderful 1770 Georgian house with its own mixed history. It sits on a hill at the end of a steep drive, surrounded by trees looking down over school playing fields. Inside the mood is intriguing, old-fashioned and elegant. Georgian green on the walls, long wooden shutters that block out the night, original cornicing, frayed drapes on old sofas and piles of rugs on the floor. The bedrooms are extraordinary. One has the tallest double bed I have ever seen and all the rooms are colossal with wooden floors, pretty wallpaper and views onto a wild garden. The most impressive has an old fireplace, wooden beds and huge rugs overlapping on the wooden floor. Bathrooms are commensurately large. This is an old-world family home where creaky floorboards and antique furnishings lend the house a feeling of relaxed grandeur.

Rooms: 3: 1 four-poster with en suite bathroom;
1 twin with en suite bathroom;
1 single with private bath.
Price: £19—£25 p.p. No sing. supp.
Breakfast: Included — full Irish.
Meals: Available in Armagh.
Closed: Christmas & New Year.

How to get there: From Armagh centre follow signs for the Planetarium. Dean's Hill is next stone entrance on left after Planetarium, with stone balls on pillars. If you reach Shell petrol station you've gone too far.

Entry no: 34

Map no: 2

Grange Lodge

Grange Rd
Dungannon
Co. Tyrone
BT71 7EJ

Tel: 028 87784212
Fax: 028 87784313
E-mail: grangelodge@nireland.com
Web: www.sawdays.co.uk

Norah and Ralph Brown

Grange Lodge's original foundations were laid in about 1698 but the house has been extended to ever since; the result is a harmonious whole, although tell-tale creaks from floorboards, and ceilings that vary in height point to different eras. The house sits in three acres of attractive gardens and manicured lawns; and with 17 more acres surrounding the property, guests feel secluded and at peace here. Norah and Ralph are natural hosts, with Ralph front of house, spinning yarns as he serves up the breakfast special of Irish whiskey and porridge, and Nora in the kitchen, producing memorable food that has won her a hatful of awards; a gold 'Salon Culinaire' and the Galtee Breakfast to name just two. Many of the vegetables, herbs and fruit are home-grown and served in season; and after an evening meal that would satisfy a giant, coffee is taken either in a large drawing room decorated in pale greens and pinks, or on wet, wintry evenings, around an open fire in the cosy 'den'. Upstairs, the bedrooms are all different, with thick carpets, feminine frills, pot pourri and ivy-clad windows. This is a house full of character in beautiful surroundings with outstanding food and a warm welcome.

Rooms: 5: 3 doubles, 1 twin, 1 single, 3 with en suite shower, 1 with en suite bath/shower, 1 with hip-bath & shower.
Price: £39 p.p. Sing. supp. £16.
Breakfast: Included — full Irish.
Meals: Dinner from £25, à la carte.
Closed: 20 December—1 February.

How to get there: From junc. 15 on M1, A29 towards Armagh/Moy. 1 mile on, left at Grange, then first right. House on right through white-walled entrance.

Co.Mayo
•

Co. Galway
•

Co. Roscommon
•

Co. Leitrim
•

Co. Sligo
•

Connacht

"A good holiday is one spent among people whose
notions of time are vaguer than yours."
J B Priestley

The Crooked Cottage

Terrybawn
Pontoon
Co. Mayo

Tel: 01 6765011
Fax: 01 6762929

Noel Comer

Could this possibly be the best self-catering retreat in Ireland? You are tucked down a small lane in 10 acres on the shores of Lough Conn; close the door of this 300-year-old thatched cottage and you are blissfully detached from the outside world. Beautifully decorated in a simple, chintz-free style, Crooked Cottage got its name because nothing inside is symmetrical. There are painted floorboards, stripped doorways, exposed stonework, white walls, mounted candle holders, comfy sofas, a turf fire and central heating. The name befits its history, too. About 100 years ago, the then owner did a roaring trade in poteen, an illegal alcohol made from potatoes. The fierce brew was made on an island out on the lake and then stored in a secret compartment in the thatch. The authorities apparently knew it was being produced but could never find where it was hidden because every time they raided the place, a small tap that stuck out of a wall was covered with a hat. Noel, the present owner, has yet to find the secret store so it is anyone's guess what might be tucked under the eaves. Stock up before you arrive because the nearest village is five miles away, but a nearby hotel serves good dinners. Come here to unburden yourself.

Rooms: 2 doubles sharing bathroom.
Price: IR£250—IR£500 p.w.
Breakfast: You cook, you choose.
Meals: Available locally or bring a cookbook.
Closed: Never.

How to get there: From Foxford, R318 Pontoon Road for 5 miles, then right at Healey's Hotel, signed Latherdaun. After about 1 mile, right signed Terrybaun Pottery, into small lane, then left at Y-junc. House 300m through red gates.

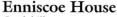

Enniscoe House

Castlehill
Nr. Crossmolina, Ballina
Co. Mayo

Tel: 096 31112
Fax: 096 31773
E-mail: mail@enniscoe.com
Web: www.enniscoe.com

Susan Kellett

Imagine an 19th-century landscape painting with the tiny figures of a couple dwarfed by the beautiful scenery and to one side, an elegant Georgian mansion. Such a picture exists of Enniscoe, which is set in parkland surrounding Lough Conn and the towering presence of Mount Nephin. This splendid Heritage House has a relaxed, well-worn grandeur that exudes history. Susan is a descendant of the original family who arrived here in the 1660s and family portraits grace the walls. Some of the finest features are the oval landing, stairs that lead off in all directions and a drawing room full of antiques. Cosy bedrooms have four-posters that require a ladder to get into, sash windows that extend from floor to ceiling, paintings by Susan's mother and the spectacular lake view. Take time to explore the grounds, with five acres of restored Victorian gardens, trails through woodland, boats to fish or navigate the lake and a Heritage Centre that traces family trees. How does Susan manage to run all this and remain such good company? Energy and brains, perhaps. One of my favourite places to stay. *Four self-catering apartments, sleep 4-6, IR£250—IR£400 p.w.*

Rooms: 6: 2 family suites, 1 twin, 2 double/twins, 1 double, all with en suite bathroom.
Price: IR£54—IR£66 p.p. Sing. supp. IR£10. Special rates available.
Breakfast: Included — full Irish.
Meals: Dinner IR£28. Packed lunch from IR£6.
Closed: Mid-October—March. Groups in January by arrangement.

How to get there: From Ballina, N59 to Crossmolina, then left on R315 Castlebar Rd for 2 miles. House entrance first of two on left.

Entry no: 37   Map no: 3

Rosturk Woods
Rosturk
Mulranny, Westport
Co. Mayo

Tel: 098 36264
Fax: 098 36264
E-mail: stoney@iol.ie
Web: www.rosturkwoods.com

Louisa and Alan Stoney

A big surprise is in store when you go down to Rosturk Woods. It is only when you reach the end of the long, wooded drive that you realise how close the sea is. It is a beautiful setting. Along the headland, the turrets of a castle poke above trees — it is where Alan was born. At high tide, the sea laps at the garden gate. At low tide, you can walk to an island. This is a good-looking modern house on five acres, employing the Georgian principle that if windows are taller than they are wide, a house can be pleasing to the eye. A long sitting room leads to a huge kitchen cluttered with the paraphernalia of cooking and children. Double doors open onto a long veranda which looks straight onto Clew Bay, home to otters and a host of birdlife. This part of Mayo is not well known except to sailors. Alan is a qualified sailing instructor and they organise boating and fishing in their own boats. There is also a tennis court and a stream with three little waterfalls. Louisa is naturally good company with a great sense of humour. This is a warm, family home with lots of laid-back style. *Self-catering in main house or an adjacent house with wheelchair access, sleeps 8, IR£450—IR£695 p.w.*

Rooms: 3: 2 double/twins, with en suite bathroom; 1 double/twin with en suite shower.
Price: IR£35 p.p. Sing. supp. IR£15.
Breakfast: Included — full Irish.
Meals: Dinner IR£25. Give 24 hours notice. Picnic lunches from IR£5.
Closed: December—February.

How to get there: From Newport, N59 Mulranny/Achill Rd for 7 miles. Big blue sign for house on left.

Map no: 3

Entry no: 38

Clare Island Lighthouse

Clare Island
Westport
Co. Mayo

Tel: 098 45120
Fax: 098 45122
E-mail: clareislandlighthous@eircom.net
Web: homepage.eircom.net/~clareislandlighthous

Monica and Robert Timmermans

I was filled with a mixture of excitement and wonder as one of Robert's old Landrovers pitched and swayed over the rough road that crawls the mile or so from the pier up to this incredible fortress of luxurious solitude. Every fixture, every ingredient, every ounce of comfort here came up the same way. This Belgium couple have achieved the impossible at the edge of civilisation. The lighthouse perches on 380 ft cliffs at the northern end of Clare Island and Robert explained how the wind dictates what they can do each day. Monica's meals are exquisite and the dinner table is beautifully laid. Centrally-heated bedrooms are all unique and different in style. Robert jettisoned a career in banking and opened a fishing lodge in Co. Cavan, but his true quest was this lighthouse that was decommissioned in 1965. He strikes you as a man finally at peace — and hugely entertaining with it — while Monica has the sweet stoicism of someone who never stopped believing the dream. The island covers 27 square miles and is home to 160 inhabitants and one of only three abbeys in Ireland with frescos. There is nowhere else like it in the world, so take your time.

Rooms: 5 doubles, all with en suite bathroom.
Price: IR£60 p.p. for 1 night; IR£50 p.p. for 2 nights or more.
Breakfast: Included — Continental.
Meals: Dinner IR£20.
Closed: Never.

How to get there: From Westport, R335 to Louisburgh, then signed to Roonagh Pier for Clare Island passenger ferry. Leave car in secure car park. Robert may collect you from pier on island or taxi available in harbour. For ferry times, contact Ocean Star ferry on 098 25045 or Clare Island ferry on 098 26307 or 25212.

Entry no: 39

Map no: 3

Delphi Lodge
Leenane
Co. Galway

Tel: 095 42222
Fax: 095 42296
E-mail: delfish@iol.ie
Web: www.delphilodge.ie

Peter Mantle

The photograph above gives a good idea of what to expect at Delphi Lodge. It had been recommended from Rosslare round to Galway; even Prince Charles has stayed here. Originally built in the mid-1830s by the The Marquis of Sligo who wanted a fishing lodge in the heart of Connemara, the estate covers 600 acres of land and 1,000 acres of mountain, water, and bogland. Fly-fishing is still a top priority with courses available to the raw novice. Fisherfolk provide the colour here, while the rest try and stop them talking of nothing else. Guests dine together in the evening at a long table with Peter at the helm; conversation, wonderfully fresh food and atmosphere make these occasions hard to beat though no-one is obliged to eat in. The bedrooms are uncluttered with long mirrors, proper bathrooms and no gimmicks, and most come with a wonderful view of Fin Lough. Take a walk in this beautifully unspoilt region then come back to friendly faces and a medicinal whiskey in front of a cosy fire. Delphi does it well whatever the season and most leave knowing it is only a matter of time before they return.

Rooms: 12 doubles, all en suite.
Price: IR£40—IR£80 p.p. Sing. supp. 50%.
Breakfast: Included — full Irish.
Meals: Dinner IR£27. Lunch IR£10. Packed lunch IR£10.
Closed: Mid-December—mid-January.

How to get there: From Clifden, N59 to Leenane. 3 miles on, left onto R335 signed Delphi, along coast for 6 miles. House in woods on left, 0.5 miles after Delphi Adventure Centre.

Map no: 3

Entry no: 40

Rosleague Manor Hotel

Letterfrack
Connemara
Co. Galway

Tel: 095 41101
Fax: 095 41168
E-mail: rosleaguemanor@eircom.net
Web: www.connemara.net/rosleaguemanor

Mark and Edmund Foyle

Where other self-styled country house hotels can fall short of expectations, Rosleague delivers. From the moment you see the view over the front lawn of Bearnaderg Bay and the Twelve Pins of Connemara National Park, this delightful 200-year-old Regency manor house looks, feels, even smells like a country house hotel should. With just 21 rooms, it doesn't feel impersonal, either. Snug drawing rooms have an unstuffy elegance with open fires, comfortable seats and private cubby holes. Across the hallway, the long, pristine dining room draws in the view — ideal for a leisurely breakfast by the window. In the evening, it had the buzz of a dinner party despite the separate tables. Friendly staff orchestrated each course with little fuss, serving dishes that have won many plaudits. Bedrooms either have the view or compensate by being absolutely enormous. My room was strictly a double but the giant bed and palatial bathroom made it feel more like a suite. And if you can pull yourself away from all this laid-back luxury, visit Inishboffin Island, play tennis, take a sauna, or climb one of those mountains.

Rooms: 20: 4 junior suites, 16 double/twins & triples, all with en suite bathroom.
Price: IR£40—IR£80 p.p. Sing. supp. IR£20.
Breakfast: Included — full menu.
Meals: Dinner from IR£30. Lunch from IR£5.
Closed: November—Easter.

How to get there: From Clifden, N59 Westport Rd for 7 miles, through Moyard. Entrance signed on left as road dips into Letterfrack.

Entry no: 41

Map no: 3

Crocnaraw Country House

Moyard
Co. Galway

Tel: 095 41068
Fax: 095 41068
E-mail: lucyfretwell@eircom.net
Web: homepage.eircom.net/~lucyfretwell

Lucy Fretwell

This place had an other worldliness before I learnt Crocnaraw meant 'hill of the fairy fort'. Perhaps it was the bizarre lampshades, a throwback to when Lucy's mother started B&B in the 1960s. Perhaps it was the bamboo wardrobe and sky-blue bathroom. Maybe it was the beautiful garden that hides this Georgian fishing lodge from view. Or maybe it was the untroubled, almost ethereal quality about Lucy that completely dismantled my plans for the day. I sat talking with her and a well-spoken gentleman in the timeworn Aga country kitchen for what seemed like ages. This is a house that can't be hurried. The rooms are eclectic period pieces fossilised somewhere between the '60s and the '80s and are a lot of fun. The drawing room is lovely and airy, ideal to kick back in on a summer's day, while the warm snug with its turf fire would be just the place for a good book and a whiskey in winter. The wooden-floored dining room feels part teashop, part conservatory with lovely views of the garden planted by her mother from scratch. Lucy looks after it today, decorating the house with fresh flowers. She also looks after four special donkeys that live in a field next door. Here the magic of Ireland is alive and well.

Rooms: 4: 2 doubles, 2 twins, all with en suite bathroom.
Price: From IR£25 p.p.
Breakfast: Included — full menu.
Meals: Dinner IR£25. Give 24 hours notice.
Closed: November—February.

How to get there: From Clifden, N59 Westport Rd for 6 miles. Small sign on left 200m before entrance on left. Drive slowly or you will miss it.

Map no: 3

Entry no: 42

Dolphin Beach House

Lower Sky Road
Clifden, Connemara
Co. Galway

Tel: 095 21204
Fax: 095 22935
E-mail: dolphinbeach@iolfree.ie
Web: www.connemara.net/DolphinBeachHouse/index.html

Billy and Barbara Foyle

What if you could lie in bed watching dolphins play in the bay from your bedroom window, then walk to a private sandy cove for a swim, collecting breakfast eggs on the way back? But then Dolphin Beach is no ordinary place. This modified early 19th-century farmhouse lies at the edge of Europe, surrounded by wild fuchsia, a muster of peacocks, windswept scenery and the Atlantic ocean. You are in good hands. Billy and Barbara belong to a family whose hotel pedigree is almost without equal in Ireland. The bedrooms are big and full of luxurious fun and eccentric detail; sleigh beds, mosaic tiles, portholes, underfloor heating and Swedish patio doors that open with smooth precision onto quiet courtyards. Only seasonal local produce is used in the kitchen — Connemara lamb, organic garden vegetables, wild salmon, fresh lobster — and meals are served in a raised dining room with views over Clifden Bay. After dinner, visit busy, bustling Clifden by taxi or return to your room, open the windows and let the sound of the sea lull you to sleep.

Rooms: 8: 4 doubles, 3 twin/doubles, 1 single; 4 with en suite shower, 4 with en suite bath and shower.
Price: IR£30—IR£45 p.p. Sing. supp. IR£10.
Breakfast: Included — full menu.
Meals: Dinner, 3 courses, IR£25 at 7.30pm — book in advance. Snacks also available.
Closed: Mid-November—early March.

How to get there: From Clifden, Sky Road for 2 miles. At Y-junc., left on Lower Sky Road, following signs for 1.5 miles. House on left overlooking bay.

Entry no: 43   Map no: 3

The Quay House

Beach Road
Clifden
Co. Galway

Tel: 095 21369
Fax: 095 21608
E-mail: thequay@iol.ie
Web: www.thequayhouse.com

Julia and Patrick Foyle

Everyone should visit the Quay House once in their life. Imagine the best bits of the nicest houses you've ever seen under one roof and you begin to get the picture. Paddy has a magician's touch for mixing the remarkable and the elegant with casual style. The tiger's skin draped over the sofa in the drawing room is an abiding memory. The house was built in 1820 for the harbour master and overlooks Clifden Bay and working fishing boats moored at the quayside. Rooms have fantastic mirrors, white-shuttered windows and painted wooden walls; some have views, others four-posters. Next door, six themed studio rooms, four with open fires, have little balconies and the lovely view — a safari room has zebra skins and African shields, a French Regency room ornate furniture. Long breakfasts are taken in a leafy conservatory where birds chirp cheerily with amazing regularity! Julia is English, Paddy Irish, and both are full of natural bonhomie. Nearby Clifden is full of life and nearby Connemara is inspiring. Hard to beat in every sense.

Rooms: 14: 2 triples, 2 family, 10 double/twins, all with en suite bathroom.
Price: IR£45—IR£50 p.p. Sing. supp. IR£10.
Breakfast: Included — full Irish.
Meals: Available locally.
Closed: November—mid-March.

How to get there: In Clifden, beach road down hill from centre of town. House 500m on right, on quayside.

Emlaghmore Lodge

Ballyconneely
Connemara
Co. Galway

Tel: 095 23529
E-mail: marquis@eircom.net

Nick Tinne

Emlaghmore Lodge lies just inland from some of the most beautiful and sparsely populated shoreline in Ireland; its remoteness brings to mind the raw atmosphere of an Ingmar Bergman film. The Tinne family have lived on and off in this 1862 fishing lodge since the 1920s. Nick first came here as a child in 1946, returning for good when his parents passed away a few years ago. He has redecorated the house in a simple country house style, with the exception of the grand dining room where imperious portraits of the Tinne dynasty cover deep vermilion walls. Nick fondly recalled their triumphs and occasional indiscretions over a wonderful candlit dinner cooked by his partner Janet – salmon has never tasted so good. Food plays a big part here as Nick used to run a restaurant in Dublin called Snaffles where the shakers and movers of the time clamoured for a table. Bedrooms with few frills have views over lakes to mountains or out across the Atlantic — it was a joy to lie in bed listening to the sea. Go for long walks past fishing boats listing idly at low tide or explore rock pools full of sealife. You might even sail in Nick's own Galway hooker or fish on private lakes. Whatever you choose, do it at a leisurely pace.

Rooms: 3: 1 double, 1 twin, both with en suite bathroom; 1 double with private bathroom.
Price: IR£40 p.p. Sing. supp. IR£10.
Breakfast: Included — full Irish/Continental.
Meals: Dinner IR£25.
Closed: November—March.

How to get there: From Roundstone, R341 Clifden Rd for 6 miles, then right at white 2-storey gabled building and before bridge. Follow narrow lane to house.

Entry no: 45

Map no: 3

Ballynahinch Castle Hotel

Recess
Connemara
Co. Galway

Tel: 095 31006
Fax: 095 31085
E-mail: bhinch@iol.ie

Patrick O'Flaherty

This beautiful estate with several thousand acres of fishing and shooting rights once boasted the world's longest driveway — its entrance was in Galway City, 41 miles away. Today, after a 700-year absence, the house is back in the hand of the O'Flaherty family. Their predecessors may have been labelled 'ferocious', but Patrick is friendly, a dapper presence in Irish tweed who personally looks after guests with genuine warmth. The present house was expanded from an inn in 1813 by Richard Martin, a famous duellist and former MP for Galway, who was nicknamed 'Humanity Dick' after proposing a bill that led to the formation of the Society for the Prevention of Cruelty to Animals. In 1924, a Maharaja and world class cricketer known fondly to locals as Ranji bought the castle, landscaping the gardens to the present state and keeping elephants and bears on a nearby island. The late Sir Alec Guinness stayed, as did guitarist Eric Clapton who caught his first salmon here. It was probably paraded in the timeworn bar where fishermen bring their catch to be weighed. Rooms are luxurious, comfortable and varied. Ballynahinch is unique in every sense.

Rooms: 40: Main hotel: 10 superior, 18 standard, all en suite; Luxury wing: 3 suites, 9 luxury, all en suite.
Price: Standard from IR£55; Superior from IR£65; Luxury from IR£85; Suite from IR£125.
Breakfast: Included — full menu.
Meals: Dinner IR£27.50. Snacks available in bar.
Closed: Never.

How to get there: From Galway, N59 Clifden Rd to Recess. 6.5 miles on, left down small lane, signed to hotel.

Currarevagh House

Oughterard
Connemara
Co. Galway

Tel: 091 552312
Fax: 091 552731
E-mail: currarevagh@ireland.com
Web: www.sawdays.co.uk

Harry and June Hodgson

The great attraction of Ireland is you are never quite sure what to expect next. I arrived at this graceful early Victorian manor in bright sunshine and went inside to find English afternoon tea laid out in the drawing room. Cucumber sandwiches, home-made fruit cake, tea in delicate bone china. Then without warning the heavens opened like a tropical monsoon, drenching two guests who had gone out to play croquet. Currarevagh, pronounced 'Curra-reeva', lies at the edge of Lough Corrib surrounded by 150 acres of woodland and rhododendrons brought back from India by earlier Hodgson generations who built the house in 1842. Harry or June will meet you on arrival and show you to your room, explaining there are no rules except turning up for dinner at 8 o'clock sharp. June cooks beautifully and has won many accolades for her creative flair. Afterwards, guests come together for coffee by the fire in the drawing room. Bedrooms vary; three have great lake views. You can boat and fish on the lake from their private jetty but stay awake because it is 30 miles long.

Rooms: 15: 14 double/twins, 12 with en suite bath, 2 with en suite shower; 1 single with en suite bath.
Price: IR£55—IR£60 p.p. Sing. supp. IR£20. Half-board for 3-6 days IR£75 p.p. per day. Half-board for 1 week IR£470 p.p.
Breakfast: Included — full Irish.
Meals: Dinner, 5 courses, IR£24 at 8pm. Complimentary afternoon tea if taking dinner that night. Picnic lunch available.
Closed: Mid-October—Easter.

How to get there: From Oughterard, Glann Lakeshore Rd for 4 miles. Entrance on right.

Camillaun

Eighterard, Oughterard
Connemara
Co. Galway

Tel: 091 552678
Fax: 091 552439
E-mail: camillaun@eircom.net
Web: homepage.eircom.net/~camillaunfishing

Deirdre and Greg Forde

Greg and Deirdre pinpointed where they wanted to live, bought a plot of land and built a warm, modern, family home with real fires next to the River Owenriff. Camillaun means 'hidden island' and to know its secret cross the garden past the new hard tennis court to Greg's floating jetties where seven boats are moored in season. Fisherfolk take the boats a mile or so down river and out onto Lough Corrib to fish for brown trout, salmon, perch and pike; a ghilly can be arranged. A more leisurely alternative is a boat trip to Inchagoill Island — take a picnic and explore its two monasteries. Upstairs bedrooms look over the garden of azaleas and rhododendrons to the burbling river — you can hear its soothing sounds with the windows open. Attractive rooms are simply done with polished wooden floors and plain-coloured rugs, bright colours, the odd antique; nothing is overdone. This is a lively, cheerful, involving household and only a short stroll from the village down a leafy lane. B&B in the truest sense.

Rooms: 4: 1 twin with en suite bath; 1 twin with en suite shower; 2 family (double plus single), both with en suite shower.
Price: IR£17—IR£21 p.p. Sing. supp. IR£6. B&B, packed lunch, dinner: IR£36—IR£38 p.p.
Breakfast: Included — full Irish.
Meals: Dinner IR£18.
Closed: November—15 March.

How to get there: From Galway, N59 to Oughterard, then right in centre & first left over bridge. House signed 200m on right down side road.

Map no: 3

Entry no: 48

Railway Lodge

Canrower
Oughterard
Co. Galway

Tel: 091 552945
E-mail: railwaylodge@eircom.net

Carmel Geoghegan

Carmel has returned to her native Galway after a successful career in retailing that took her all over the world. She found a plot of land outside Oughterard near a disused railway line that carried passengers from Galway city to Connemara's 'wild west' up to 1936. There she commissioned an L-shaped cottage-style house with a steep gabled roof and pretty dormer windows. It is an exceptionally attractive modern house, unlike many of Ireland's shapeless, utilitarian bungalows and Dallas-style ranches that seem at odds with their surroundings. Inside and out, she has done a wonderful job. Attractive bedrooms have polished wooden floors, decorative stitched bedspreads, Oxford pillowcases and old Irish pine furniture. The ones upstairs make a feature of the sloping roof with charming Gothic-style shuttered windows and views of the Cloosh hills. The snug living room with open fire and comfy armchairs feels old and settled and leads to a conservatory overlooking a developing garden with newly-planted trees. Carmel's father breeds Connemara ponies locally and is the inspiration behind much of the railway memorabilia dotted about

Rooms: 4: 1 family, 3 doubles, all with en suite shower.
Price: IR£25 p.p. Sing. supp. IR£5.
Breakfast: Included — full menu.
Meals: Available locally.
Closed: Christmas week.

How to get there: From Galway, N59 Clifden Rd to Oughterard. Through town, then left after Corrib House Hotel and immediately right. Follow signs to house.

Fermoyle Lodge

Casla (Costelloe)
Connemara
Co. Galway

Tel: 091 786111
Fax: 091 786154
E-mail: fermoylelodge@eircom.net
Web: www.fermoylelodge.com

Nicola Stronach & Jean-Pierre Maire

The road between Oughterard and Costelloe tapers to a single lane as you climb above farmland and forestry to the rocky wilderness of Connemara's lakelands. Save for the odd sheep, there seems to be little else around, but keep going because you will eventually see a parcel of trees and rhododendrons; hidden among them is Fermoyle Lodge and an incredible view across an expanse of lakes and bog that stretches west to the mountainous horizon of Connemara National Park. Dinner here at sunset has few equals. The view changes before your eyes like a painting in progress, blue sky melting into yellows, oranges and purples. Guests can eat on a gravel terrace outside if the weather allows. Jean-Pierre's French cuisine delivers as well, with locally sourced ingredients used in season, and Nicola, who is English, looks after you with charm and wit. They bought and restored this 19th-century fishing lodge to raise a family and do B&B. Comfortable rooms in the main house have the spectacular views, while two elegant rooms in a converted outbuilding are blissfully quiet. The garden has some curious Victorian follies, including a dolmen and Inca-style stone staircase, while a path leads to a lake. Perfect.

Rooms: 6: Main house: 2 twins, 2 doubles, all with en suite bathroom; Mews: 2 doubles, both with en suite bathroom.
Price: IR£45—IR£55 p.p. Sing. supp. IR£20.
Breakfast: Included — full menu.
Meals: Dinner IR£25. Picnic lunch IR£7 for fisherfolk.
Closed: Mid-October—mid-March. Groups off season by arrangement.

How to get there: From Galway, N59 to Oughterard. Left in town along minor road to Costelloe for 11 miles. Entrance on right among trees.

Map no: 3

Entry no: 50

Man of Aran Cottage

Inishmor
Aran Islands
Co. Galway

Tel: 099 61301
Fax: 099 61324
E-mail: manofaran@eircom.net

Maura and Joe Wolfe

Maura and Joe are so relaxed and friendly, people visibly unwind as they stoop through the low front door of Man of Arran Cottage. A visiting US senator was so moved by the welcome, he sent back an official certificate praising their contribution to Irish-American relations. The house was built in the 1930s for the interior shots of Robert Flaherty's documentary film on the islands, *Man of Aran*. It is right by the sea, surrounded by wild roses, gentian, maidenhair fern and saxifrage. All their food is home-spun and Joe is an enthusiastic organic gardener, not afraid to use what nature provides. His salad was a riot of colour with nasturtium flowers, pansies, even young nettle leaves. "It's the only artistic inclination I have," he says. Maura cooks the hot stuff; delicious soups, stews, home-made cakes. Thick, white-painted stone walls enclose three small rooms with lots of character and the restaurant. The Aran Islands get very popular in summer so it is best to visit on a wild winter's day or better still, in the spring or autumn. This is the perfect little hideaway. Go there and write your first novel. They let the whole place out in winter.

Rooms: 3: 1 twin, 1 double, sharing bathroom; 1 double with private shower.
Price: IR£22—IR£25 p.p. Sing. supp. IR£7, in high season.
Breakfast: Included — full Irish.
Meals: Dinner IR£17. Lunch from IR£2, 12.30pm-3pm. Packed lunch available.
Closed: November—February.

How to get there: From Galway, take the Spiddal Road to Rossaveen. Take a ferry and hire a mini-bus or bike on arrival.

Entry no: 51   Map no: 3

Iverna Cottage
Salahoona   **Tel:** 091 553762
Spiddal
Co. Galway

Patricia and Willy Farrell

A book on Ireland wouldn't be complete without a leprechaun but as these mischievous sprites belong to Irish folklore, we've found the next best thing. According to Patricia, husband Willy is "a lot of people's idea of a leprechaun". The Abraham Lincoln beard that travels under his chin and the infectious smile do bear an uncanny resemblance and judging by the warmth of the welcome at Iverna, you've found the legendary crock of gold, too. The Farrells built this stone-clad house from scratch after courageously giving up careers in London to return home and start a B&B overlooking Galway Bay in the mid-1990s. They brought the huge oak corner posts, salvaged from Canary Wharf in London, with them. Its distinctive look is a welcome sight on the coast road west of Galway, breaking a necklace of anonymous white bungalows. Inside, Chinese slate floors and wooden beams create a warm homely atmosphere. Bedrooms with wrought iron beds and patchwork bedspreads have a lovely cottage feel and I liked the cosy living room with its comfy sofas, open fire and shelves of books. Patricia is an avid reader and loves to chat. Good beaches nearby.

Rooms: 4: 2 doubles, 2 family, all with en suite shower. Bathroom also available.
Price: From IR£20 p.p. Sing. supp. IR£5—IR£10.
Breakfast: Included — full menu.
Meals: Available locally.
Closed: November—March.

How to get there: From Galway, R336 coast road to Spiddal for 12 miles. Through village, house 1 mile on left.

Map no: 3   **Entry no: 52**

Norman Villa

86 Lower Salthill
Galway
Co. Galway

Tel: 091 521131
Fax: 091 521131
E-mail: normanvilla@oceanfree.net
Web: www.sawdays.co.uk

Dee and Mark Keogh

It is not easy to find a city address with a personal touch and the feel of a country house but Norman Villa manages both. Dee and Mark have the ability to create a friendly, chatty atmosphere from nothing. Their cheerful *bonhomie* clearly rubs off on guests; a hearty breakfast was marked by laughter rather than the sepulchral sound of cutlery tinkling on crockery. They are also masters at making the most of limited space. The subtly-designed bedrooms are not big, but you will be too busy admiring the pine floors, brass beds, floral quilts, high ceilings and elegant lithographs to notice. The windows fitted with working shutters let in lots of light and the showers, behind slatted wooden doors, deserve an engineering award. The contemporary style of this relaxed house continues downstairs with the Keogh's collection of modern Irish art. The house was built in 1855 and you enter through a narrow tunnel to park securely in a small courtyard. Views of oak trees and a field at the rear are a welcome surprise in the middle of busy Galway. Let the Keoghs advise you on what to do, where to eat, and how to get there. *B&B in converted coach house, sleeps 4, from IR£100 per night.*

Rooms: 5 double/triples, all with en suite shower.
Price: From IR£37.50 p.p. Sing. supp. from IR£7.50.
Breakfast: Included — full Irish.
Meals: Available in Galway.
Closed: December—January.

How to get there: In Galway City, follow signs to Salthill, then Lower Salthill. House on right.

Killeen House

Killeen
Bushypark
Co. Galway

Tel: 091 524179
Fax: 091 528065
E-mail: killeenhouse@ireland.com

Catherine Doyle

Like many of the best Galway houses, Killeen House looks over a lake; in this case, Lough Corrib. The water's edge is a short walk from Catherine's immaculate garden past some stone ruins. The 1840s house was recently extended to create large rooms and a suite that overlooks colourful shrubs and a baize-smooth lawn. Each bedroom is themed — English Victorian, Edwardian, and Regency — and the furniture and furnishings reflect this. The retro antique radio sets were a quirky bonus. Thick, locally-made hand-woven rugs stretch luxuriously over wooden floors, while huge, comfortable beds — some strapping seven-footers — tempted me to take a short siesta. Catherine has a magpie's love of shiny objects; the house sparkles with antique silverware. Expect proper tea on arrival, served in the finest china as you relax in regal high-backed armchairs in the formal drawing room. A wonderful setting and ideal for exploring Connemara by day and the buzz of nearby Galway City by night.

Rooms: 5 doubles, 4 with en suite bathroom, 1 with en suite shower.
Price: IR£45—IR£55 p.p. Sing. supp. IR£20.
Breakfast: Included — full menu.
Meals: Available locally or in Galway City.
Closed: Christmas week.

How to get there: From Galway, N59 towards Clifden for 4 miles. House signed on right.

Map no: 3

Cregg Castle
Corrandulla
Co. Galway

Tel: 091 791434
E-mail: creggcas@indigo.ie
Web: indigo.ie/~creggcas

Ann Marie and Pat Broderick

Cregg Castle must be one of the most laid-back places in Ireland. It is in a grand setting in 165 acres of farm and parkland but Ann Marie and Pat are hands on owners. They were relaxing on the large stone-stepped entrance, soaking up some late afternoon sun when I arrived. Before long we were sitting in big old worn sofas in the huge drawing room, drinking tea. This is where music is played most evenings. Both play a variety of traditional Irish instruments and guests are welcome to join in; some travel great distances just to jam in these fireside sessions which can last long into the night. The Brodericks are unstuffy, down-to-earth characters who prefer what money can't buy — take music, long walks and human communion as examples. The castle was built in 1648 for the Kirwan family. Eccentric bedrooms vary in size and design; some are enormous with lovely views. There are no rules here, only the hope you will kick back and enjoy the pace of life here. Children will love the animals and the freedom to explore and adults the peace, music and conversation.

Rooms: 9: 2 triples, 2 doubles, 1 twin, 1 single, all with en suite shower; 2 twins, both with en suite bath; 1 twin with private bathroom.
Price: IR£35—IR£45 p.p. Sing. supp. IR£15.
Breakfast: Included — full Irish.
Meals: Dinner IR£20. Wine IR£12—IR£16.
Closed: Never.

How to get there: From Galway, N17 towards Sligo. After 7 miles, left signed Corandulla. 3 miles on, gates and sign on left.

Lisdonagh House

Caherlistrane
Co. Galway

Tel: 093 31163
Fax: 093 31528
E-mail: cooke@lisdonagh.com
Web: www.lisdonagh.com

John and Finola Cooke

Lisdonagh is a magical find in every sense. Tiny lanes through avenues of trees take you to this gorgeous 1707 house on the shores of Lough Hackett. Before you step inside, consider the view for a moment. Legend says Finvarra, King of the Fairies, held court on nearby Knockma Hill, while St Patrick converted the King of Connaught to Christianity in 427 on a *crannóg* (a man-made island) in the middle of the lake, to which you can row. John and Finola have restored the whole house with style and five-star comfort. 18th-century trompe-l'oeil murals of the four virtues greet you in the oval entrance hall, its shape mirrored in a lovely bedroom above. Rooms are uncluttered and luxurious, some with views of the lake, while the pavilion suite in a converted rent house with pyramid roof and Venetian window is unique. Enjoy peace and quiet in snug basement rooms reached by a staircase that winds down in satisfying arcs. The Cookes are charming, relaxed hosts and Finola creates fabulous dinners with organic produce. They say the philosophy here is home from home. If only! *Self-catering in Victorian gate lodge, sleeps 4, IR£300—IR£400 p.w. and two courtyard apartments, both sleep 4, IR£1,200 p.w.*

Rooms: 10: Pavilion suite, 1 family, both with en suite bathroom; 8 doubles/twins, 3 with en suite shower, 5 with en suite bath.
Price: IR£50—IR£90 p.p. Sing. supp. IR£30.
Breakfast: Included — full Irish.
Meals: Dinner IR£30 at 8pm. Packed lunch for fisherfolk.
Closed: Mid-November—mid-March.

How to get there: From Galway, N17 to Sligo for 16 miles, then left on R333 to Caherlistrane. Right at Queally's pub, then left down narrow lane after 2 miles. House signed.

Map no: 3

Entry no: 56

Gardenfield House

Tuam
Co. Galway

Tel: 093 24865
Fax: 093 24601
Web: www.sawdays.co.uk

Michael and Esther Mannion

Esther's children make great tour guides at Gardenfield and their enthusiasm is catching. They want to show you everything; the mob of sheep doing their bit mowing the front lawn, the hens that provide the eggs for breakfast, and we must not forget the two ponies. The house, built in 1860, is a busy family farm on 56 acres of pastureland raising sheep and cattle. Upstairs, the bedrooms are clean, light and homely with slate fireplaces, warm, dark colours, wooden shutters, and the odd teddy bear; there is a lived-in feel that permeates the whole house. Everything for dinner is home-made and Esther uses her discretion about communal dining. If you want to cater for yourself, the converted stables at the back of the house are very comfortable, with stone flagstones, exposed walls and nicely finished wooden interiors. Fishermen head down to the River Clare that runs through their land, and pets are welcome. Good value, great conversation and ideal for children.

Rooms: 3: 1 twin with private bathroom; 1 twin with private shower room; 1 double with en suite shower.
Price: IR£18—IR£20 p.p. Sing. supp. IR£4.
Breakfast: Included — full Irish.
Meals: Dinner IR£16. Packed lunch IR£4.
Closed: Never.

How to get there: From Galway, N17 Sligo Rd to Tuam for 20 miles. Through town, house signed 1 mile after traffic lights. Follow signs for about 1.5 miles.

Entry no: 57

Map no: 3

Castle ffrench

Ballinamore Bridge
Co. Galway

Tel: 0903 22288
Fax: 0903 22003
E-mail: castleffrench@eircom.net
Web: www.castleffrench.com

Bill and Sheila Bagliani

The Castle, as it is known locally, lies a mile up a drive and appears suddenly round a curve, a huge solid block built in 1779 by Sir Charles ffrench on the site of an earlier castle. Blazing turf fires, huge bedrooms and good food are the hallmarks of this listed Georgian house set in rolling parkland. The refurbished rooms are delightful and full of eye-catching features — the vaulted semi-basement, ornate cornicing, marble fireplaces, wooden floors, flagstoned hallway and barrel-ceilinged corridors. Bedrooms have thick rugs and the odd tapestry; the bathrooms are enormous. The house is surrounded by its own woods and paddocks and the views improve as you climb to higher floors. Horses are important at Castle ffrench. Bill, who is American, is a keen carriage driver and breeds Arabian horses. Sheila is Irish and as keen on horses. She also runs painting courses. There is good trout fishing in nearby rivers, or you might prefer a walk through a genuine Irish bog. Refined luxury. *Two self-catering cottages, each sleeps 2, IR£350 p.w.*

Rooms: 4: 2 doubles with en suite bathroom; 1 twin with private bathroom; 1 double with private shower.
Price: IR£75 p.p. Sing. supp. IR£20.
Breakfast: Included — full Irish.
Meals: Dinner IR£30. Give 24 hours notice.
Closed: November—mid-April. Groups off season by arrangement.

How to get there: From Ballinasloe, R358 Tuam Rd to Ahascragh. Through village, past Statoil garage for 1 mile to school, then right signed Ballygar. Entrance 3 miles on right. House 1 mile up drive.

Clonalis House

Castlerea
Co. Roscommon

Tel: 0907 20014
Fax: 0907 20014
E-mail: clonalis@iol.ie

Pyers and Marguerite O'Conor Nash

The history of the O'Conor family runs through this historic building like a supporting wall. The clan has been linked to this land for an estimated 2000 years. Approached up a mile-long drive, Clonalis sits aloof in its 700 acres, 250 of which are wood and parkland. Pyers is an engaging, down-to-earth host and the resident expert on the house's history which is fully Irish, a rarity among houses of this stature. It was built in 1878 by Charles Owen O'Conor Don in the Victorian Italianate style with 45 rooms. One of the highlights of the ground floor is the wonderful library lined with shelves of ancient tomes. The bedrooms are impressive, a four-poster here, a half-tester there, gilt-framed mirrors, elegant fireplaces, massive bathrooms, all full of old family furniture and looking out over the formal front gardens. Marguerite and Pyers have worked hard on the grounds, opening up old woodland walks. There are two brown trout rivers on the property and a walled garden. The O'Conor Nashs are hugely energetic and welcoming. Breakfast in the fabulous dining room surrounded by the family portraits and palm-tree silverware felt like a scene from an old black and white movie. Pinch yourself, then act the part in absolute splendour.

Rooms: 4: 3 doubles, 1 twin, all with en suite bathroom; 1 double has a separate toilet.
Price: IR£52p.p. Sing. supp. IR£6. 10% discount for 3 nights or more.
Breakfast: Included — full Irish.
Meals: Dinner IR£24 Tuesday to Saturday. Give 24 hours notice.
Closed: October—mid-April.

How to get there: From Athlone, N61 to Roscommon, then bypass to N60 and Castlerea. House well signed in town. Entrance up long drive through fields and woodland.

Entry no: 59   Map no: 4

The Old Rectory

Ardcarne
Boyle
Co. Roscommon

Tel: 079 67149
Web: www.sawdays.co.uk

Bernie and Jim Reynolds

The atmosphere at the Old Rectory is charged with energy. Jim and Bernie and their three boys are all exceptionally friendly. Bernie seems to do everything at once without fuss and the first thing you notice about her is her obvious enjoyment of other people. Kids will love the pony, which slowly mows the buttercupped field in front of the house. The house is decorated in plain colours with pretty bedrooms, wooden floors, huge zip-and-link beds, pot plants and timber-framed windows that look onto the paddock. Downstairs is an amazing bathroom with wooden posts and miniature bottles crowding the shelves. Breakfast is served with the best silver and everything is home-cooked. Down the road is Lough Key Forest National Park, while those looking for more rigorous exercise should consult Jim who is mad on hill-walking — not quite what you would expect in an area more famous for its lakes, but you are not far from the Arigna Mountains. Down-to-earth, Irish country hospitality at its best.

Rooms: 3: 1 double, 1 family, both with en suite bathroom; 1 double with private bathroom.
Price: From IR£20 p.p.
Breakfast: Included — full Irish/Continental.
Meals: Available locally.
Closed: Christmas.

How to get there: From Carrick-on-Shannon, N4 west for about 5 miles, then right on R285 Knockvicar/Keadue Rd. Entrance immediately left opposite Ardcarne Garden Centre.

Map no: 4

Entry no: **60**

Glencarne House

Carrick-on-Shannon
Co. Roscommon

Tel: 079 67013
Fax: 079 67013
Web: www.sawdays.co.uk

Agnes and Pat Harrington

Agnes has been doing B&B for about thirty years and still loves it. She is always there to greet you when you arrive. For her, a comfortable, welcoming environment is of paramount importance. Flowers are fresh, butter is curled on a plate, all her ingredients are completely farm-fresh, open fires are laid. No detail is overlooked and the house is a dangerous place for dust and dirt. The house sits on a hill that looks down over fields from the front and is surrounded by a tangly garden and the 100-acre farm. Although carpets are a bit bold on occasion, bedrooms are very comfortable with plain-coloured walls, warm rugs, brass beds, lovely wooden windows and lots of light. Carrick-on-Shannon sits on 40 lakes, a major attraction for boaters and fisherfolk. Opposite Glencarne is Lough Key forest park with its walks and bog gardens. You will be very well looked after by Agnes — breakfast was a feast.

Rooms: 4: 2 double/twins with en suite shower; 1 double with en suite bath; 1 twin with en suite shower.
Price: IR£25 p.p. Sing. supp. IR£5.
Breakfast: Included — full Irish.
Meals: Dinner IR£20.
Closed: November—February.

How to get there: From Dublin, N4 towards Sligo for 100 miles, past Carrick-on-Shannon. After 4.5 miles, house signed on left up drive.

Hollywell

Liberty Hill
Carrick-on-Shannon
Co. Leitrim

Tel: 078 21124
Fax: 078 21124
E-mail: hollywell@esatbiz.com
Web: www.sawdays.co.uk

Rosaleen and Tom Maher

Rosaleen and Tom used to run the busy Bush Hotel in town before moving to this tranquil setting on the far bank of the River Shannon. They are far happier for it, having more time to give guests their individual attention. The house is late 1700s with 1850s add-ons and brims with the flair of these experienced hoteliers. Arise from your white delicately-embroidered duvet and the crisp sheets of a Victorian brass twin or draped queen, throw back the shutters upstairs and gaze at the riverboats that ply their trade along this reed-banked stretch of the River Shannon. You are looking at one of the last surviving habitats of the rare corncrake. It is easy to imagine yourself drifting along the Shannon — Lough Erne waterway. This is the beauty of Hollywell. It has turned its back on the town, thanks to a driveway which is something of a magic wardrobe. You are still close enough for a drink in lively pubs full of weekending Dubliners, but when you return 100 yards across the bridge, the town disappears, the bustle is a memory, and any moment now it will be time for breakfast laid out on beautiful burr walnut table.

Rooms: 4: 2 doubles with en suite bathroom; 1 twin, 1 double, both with en suite shower.
Price: IR£30—IR£39 p.p. Sing. occ. IR£35—IR£49.
Breakfast: Included — full Irish.
Meals: Available in Carrick-on-Shannon.
Closed: Christmas & New Year.

How to get there: From Dublin, N4 to Carrick. Cross bridge over River Shannon, then first left past Ging's Pub up lane. Entrance first left, signed.

Map no: 4

Arrow Lodge
Kilmactranny
Boyle
Co. Sligo

Tel: 079 66298
Fax: 079 66299
E-mail: rob@arrowlodge.com
Web: www.arrowlodge.com

Rob and Steph Maloney

Arrow Lodge is literally a stone's throw away from Lough Arrow, one of the few remaining wild brown trout lakes in Europe and probably the best dry-fly fishing lake in Ireland. Rob is an approved ghillie and will take out the experienced or the novice; he has two boats. You enter the lodge via a small yard with an old stable, some outbuildings and colourful plants. A horse leant over the gate and a pretty cat hastened off into the wild green yonder where the odd hen could be glimpsed between overgrown bushes. The house is 1840 outside but completely modern inside as the Maloneys bought a derelict shell and restored most of it themselves. The guest dining room has an old wooden floor, lovely lavender walls, paintings, an amazing old range that now holds plants rather than heat and a long table that comfortably seats eight. The tackle room where you dump your fishing gear has character, while comfortable bedrooms do what is asked of them. In the evening, Steph cooks a delicious dinner and there is a sitting room to flop in afterwards. The pair moved here from Guernsey in 1998 where Rob had been an engineer and Steph a lawyer. Both are enthusiastic, good-humoured and easy to get on with.

Rooms: 4 twins, all with en suite shower.
Price: From IR£27 p.p. Sing. supp. IR£8.
Breakfast: Included — full Irish.
Meals: Dinner IR£19 p.p. Book in advance. Packed lunch IR£7 p.p.
Closed: December—January.

How to get there: From Dublin, N4 Sligo Rd to just north of Boyle, then right signed Corrigeenroe & Arigna Scenic Drive for 3.2 miles through x-roads. Go left at fork for 1.2 miles, then first right. House on left.

Ross House

Ross
Riverstown
Co. Sligo

Tel: 071 65787
Fax: 071 65140
Web: www.sawdays.co.uk

Oriel and Nicholas Hill-Wilkinson

When I first met Nicholas, his overalls and face were smattered with mud and tractor oil as if to illustrate that while some may merely *claim* to be working farmers, there was absolutely no doubting him. Both he and Oriel are infectious smilers; they seem to rejoice in life, obviously fascinated by people from other walks of life as they travel without leaving their sitting room. It seems hard to imagine that Oriel only planned to B&B for one year. That was 20 years ago. "Last Wednesday we had one Tongan, one St Lucian and two Indians staying," said Nicholas with amazement. This 1890s farmhouse has always been in Oriel's family home. Enter through a lovely flower-bedecked porch with flagstones outside. You are surrounded by cow fields and byres and the mellifluous sounds of nature going about its business. Great for children. Rooms of varying sizes are decorated in plain colours with modern furniture and brass beds. It is exactly what you want from down-to-earth farmhouse accommodation. Nearby lies the well-kept secret and archaeological site of Carrowkeel with its amazing passage tombs. Unpretentious peace and quite on a proper Irish farm.

Rooms: 6: 1 family with en suite bathroom; 2 family, 1 twin, all with en suite shower; 1 double, 1 single, sharing bathroom.
Price: IR£23 p.p. Sing. supp. IR£3.
Breakfast: Included — full Irish.
Meals: Dinner IR£16. Packed lunch on request.
Closed: Never.

How to get there: From Sligo, N4 Dublin Rd to Drumfin for 8 miles. Left signed Riverstown, then follow signs in village for about 1 mile. House on left.

Map no: 1

Entry no: 64

Coopershill House

Riverstown
Co. Sligo

Tel: 071 65108
Fax: 071 65466
E-mail: ohara@coopershill.com
Web: www.coopershill.com

Brian and Lindy O'Hara

Coopershill is a fantastic place that never ceases to delight and amaze from the moment you finally arrive, having wound up and around the long parkland drive through gardens where a muster of peacocks roam resplendent. For a house so handsome and distinguished, you might expect a formal welcome but Brian, in his baggy cords and sweater, greeted me with a friendly wave when I arrived. The warm welcome softens the somewhat intimidating grandeur of the stone-floored double height entrance hall with its hanging flags, stag heads, white marble figurines in primrose alcoves and a fine 19th-century parchment map of Ireland. They know how to make you feel at home. No pomp here. "If a job's worth doing," is their credo and it shows. Everything is exemplary; fresh flowers, beautiful pictures, a chaise longue in every room and amazing old beds with brand new mattresses. The king-sized bedroom on the top floor looks out over copper beeches and the River Unsin, but their favourite room is a four-poster with huge corner windows. The bathrooms don't disappoint, either; the pristine 1900 canopied bath in its cool green-tiled grotto, will knock your socks off.

Rooms: 8: 6 doubles, 1 twin, all with en suite bathroom; 1 double with private bathroom.
Price: IR£56—IR£73 p.p. Sing. supp. IR£10.
Breakfast: Included — full Irish.
Meals: Dinner IR£29—IR£32.
Closed: November—March.

How to get there: From Sligo, N4 towards Dublin for 11 miles, then left at Drumfin x-roads, signed Coopershill. Entrance on left after 1.25 miles, before sharp turn.

Entry no: 65   Map no: 1

Temple House

Ballymote
Co. Sligo

Tel: 071 83329
Fax: 071 83808
E-mail: guests@templehouse.ie
Web: www.templehouse.ie

Deb and Sandy Perceval

Temple House is one of the most imposing and idiosyncratic places you are likely to stay anywhere in the world. Approached up a long parkland drive, passing the three ruins of previous Temple houses on your left, one medieval, one Tudor, one Jacobean, the great bulk of today's version sits ponderously on higher ground looking down on the lake. The yawning outer and portrait-galleried inner hall evoke a glittering past culled from the Far East. Before a wonderful wild salmon supper, take a glass of wine in a fireside sitting room where Deb ministers with engaging and reassuring ease. The bedrooms exude the air of past grandeur; one is even called the half-acre room. The feeling of space is reinforced in the museum-like drawing room which is adorned with wonderful Victoriana and is still shaded by the gilt pelmetry, silk folds and gold braid of the original curtains. The stunning lakeside parkland has the greenest grass and fattest lambs. Sandy grows all their vegetables organically in a big walled garden, but is "allergic to perfumed products and sprays so please avoid". *Call for advice.*

Rooms: 6: 2 family suites, both with en suite bathroom; 1 double with en suite shower; 1 double with private shower; 1 twin with en suite bathroom; 1 single.
Price: IR£42—IR£45 p.p. Sing. supp. IR£10.
Breakfast: Included — full Irish.
Meals: Dinner IR£20. Children's high tea (under 5s) at 6.30 p.m.
Closed: December—March.

How to get there: From Sligo, N4 towards Dublin, then N17 towards Galway. Left signed Temple House 0.25 miles after Ballinacarrow.

Map no: 1

Entry no: 66

The Glebe House
Collooney
Co. Sligo

Tel: 071 67787
Fax: 071 30438
E-mail: glebehouse@esatbiz.com
Web: www.glebehouse-restaurant.com

Brid and Marc Torrades

This is a country house full of personality. Brid and Marc have been restoring what was left of this old glebe house, transforming it into both a family home and an award-winning restaurant, for which they are justly renowned. They use the finest local ingredients fruit, vegetables and herbs from the old walled garden and seafood direct from Atlantic ports together with an unusual selection of wines. The restaurant is charming and informal, with painted wooden floors, red tablecloths, wood panelling, attractive wallpaper and French doors that look onto a garden. Country-style bedrooms are large with wooden beds, the odd sofa, magazines and views onto surrounding meadows. At the end of the garden the River Owenmore completes a pleasant rural scene — good for canoeing or fishing. A great place to relax and enjoy excellent food in a home from home. You will have no trouble settling in.

Rooms: 4: 2 doubles/twins with en suite bath;
1 double/twin, 1 double, both with en suite shower.
Price: IR£30 p.p. Sing. supp. IR£5.
Breakfast: Included — full Irish.
Meals: Dinner, 5 courses, IR£23. A la carte also
available. Lunches for groups by request.
Closed: Christmas.

How to get there: From Sligo, N4 towards Dublin for
5 miles. Right at r'bout, signed Collooney, then first
right & follow road round. Left after Quigleys Pub,
entrance second turning on left after 400m.

Entry no: 67   Map no: 1

Markree Castle

Collooney
Co. Sligo

Tel: 071 67800
Fax: 071 67840
E-mail: markree@iol.ie
Web: www.sawdays.co.uk

Charles and Mary Cooper

There is quite a story to how Charles ended up back in the family castle after it had lain empty for 36 years. Fifteen generations of Coopers are in the hall's stained-glass family tree and five more since the glazier stopped work. The fantastic Victorian Gothic detail was added later, but the 15th-century heart remains. Charles and Mary started out seven years ago with three bedrooms and have now inventively reclaimed 30 — some high up and split-levelled in a surreal roofscape of lead, buttressed chimneys and crenellations. Others, vaulted and panelled with exotic woods, look out through arched and mullioned windows. There is an extravagance of features: galleries, long, luxuriously carpeted passageways, deep carved panelling and angel corbels hanging from a soaring atrium ceiling. The dining room is a rococo feast of heavily-ornamented plaster, gilt cherubs and mirrors. The cosy lounge paced out to a mere 23 yards and the fireplaces hold whole smouldering chunks of wood. Charles, the boyish-looking chap casually dressed at the reception computer, eschews formality, rules or signs. The result is a remarkable, pleasantly familiar ease about the place. The park is beautiful and the river runs close by.

Rooms: 30 doubles/twins, all with en suite bathroom.
Price: IR£54—IR£69 p.p. Sing. supp. IR£12.
Breakfast: Included — full Irish.
Meals: Dinner IR£23 or IR£28.50. Light lunch and Sunday lunch IR£14.50.
Closed: Christmas.

How to get there: From Sligo, N4 towards Dublin for 7 miles, then left at first r'bout. Entrance at top of hill on right. Castle 1 mile up avenue.

Map no: 1

Entry no: 68

Ardtarmon House

Ballinfull
Co. Sligo

Tel: 071 63156
Fax: 071 63156
Web: www.sawdays.co.uk

Charles and Christa Henry

What a setting. From Ardtarmon's top-floor parapets you can see the sea and mountains in three counties — the Mayo Mountains, Knocknarea mountain in Sligo and the Yeats country mountains in Leitrim. The house is surrounded by a labyrinth of walls and outbuildings, containing established gardens and old orchards. They are a friendly couple with a young family and are just finding their way in B&B. Relaxed and quick to laugh, they ensure that the atmosphere here is wonderfully hospitable. Charles does the cooking, producing meals in a solid country Irish style, and he will encourage you to walk up an appetite beforehand. A short stroll through woods, down a lane and across a field takes you to a beach which you will probably have all to yourself, it's so secluded here. Guest rooms have lots of space, huge beds, fluffy pillows, thick carpets, duvets to sink into and views of the garden. This is a great find. *Five self-catering cottages in grounds, sleep 2-6, IR£85—IR£300 p.w.*

Rooms: 4: 1 double with en suite bath; 2 doubles, 1 double/single, all with en suite shower.
Price: IR£25—IR£35 p.p. Sing. supp. IR£5.
Breakfast: Included — full Irish.
Meals: Dinner IR£15.
Closed: Christmas & New Year.

How to get there: From Sligo, N15 north towards Donegal for 5 miles to Drumcliffe. Left towards Carney for 1 mile. In village, follow signs to Raghley for 4.5 miles, left at Dunleavy's shop. Gate lodge and drive on left after 1.5 miles.

Entry no: 69   Map no: 1

The Old Rectory

Easkey
Co. Sligo

Tel: 096 49181
E-mail: adlib@eircom.net

Robert and Lorely Forrester

This area of Sligo and north Mayo remains fairly undiscovered to all but the international surfing community which rates Easkey as one of the wave capitals of the world. Through the bedroom windows of this lovely 1790s rectory, you can see the church, the River Easkey and even the sea. Lorely's interior design skills have created rooms that completely surprise; starry ceilings, gold curtains, wooden shutters and pink walls with gold suns give each their own individual character. The house is surrounded by a high wall, enclosing lovely mature gardens where bamboo and subtropical plants grow happily. In the creeper-covered coach house, the Forresters run short courses, ranging from stone-wall-building to investing in the stock market, while the lovely stone courtyard with working hurricane lamps is perfect for barbecues, jugs of Guinness and musical evenings. You won't forget the animals either which are everywhere — dogs, cats, sheep, lambs, hens, donkeys. Lorely and Robert are a young, friendly, creative couple with lots of energy.

Rooms: 3: 2 doubles, 1 family, sharing bath & shower.
Price: IR£25 p.p. Sing. supp. IR£8.
Breakfast: Included — full Irish.
Meals: Available locally.
Closed: Christmas & New Year.

How to get there: From Dublin to Sligo, exit N4 dual carriageway at Coolooney, then old Sligo Rd to Ballisodare. Before bridge, left onto N59 to Ballina. Continue to Dromore West, then right signed Easkey 5 miles. House next to church.

Map no: 3   **Entry no: 70**

Co. Louth
•

Co. Meath
•

Co. Westmeath
•

Co. Longford
•

Co. Kildare
•

Leinster

"A house can't be kept without talk."
Irish proverb

Ghan House

Carlingford
Co. Louth

Tel: 042 9373682
Fax: 042 9373682
E-mail: ghanhouse@eircom.net
Web: www.ghanhouse.com

Paul, Cairlinn and Joyce Carroll

Pure serendipity led me to Ghan House. I was looking for somewhere else that turned out to have closed. Some first-time guests were having lunch outside and rarely have I met such enthusiasm for a place. This early 18th-century house is enclosed within the ancient walls of Carlingford, probably the best preserved medieval town in Ireland. Lying at the base of Slieve Foy which rises impressively behind, the house looks over Carlingford Lough and the Mourne Mountains in the distance. It is a beautiful setting. Some guests prefer the bedrooms in the creaky timeworn atmosphere of the house, while others prefer the peace and the quiet of the dairyhouse next door. There are arched doorways, corbelled ceilings, a half-tester bed, proper bathrooms — everything is impeccably done. Behind the house is a herb garden for their cookery school that includes a course on how to cook the perfect barbeque. Dinners are just as special. The Carrolls know what they are doing and are very friendly with it — I was introduced to everyone. You won't be short of things to do, either. Restaurants, pubs, watersports, hill-walking, or the simple pleasure of sitting by a turf fire.

Rooms: 12: Main house: 1 double,
2 doubles/twins, all with en suite bathroom;
1 single with en suite shower. The Dairyhouse:
5 doubles/twins, 1 double,
2 family, all with en suite bathroom.
Price: IR£35—IR£45 p.p. Sing. supp. IR£10.
Breakfast: Included — full menu.
Meals: Dinners from IR£15. Restaurant open Fridays
and Saturdays. Book in advance. Other good restaurants
in Carlingford.
Closed: Christmas & New Year.

How to get there: From Dublin, N1 north for 53
miles, then right at first r'bout after Dundalk, signed
Carlingford. House first on left entering village.

Map no: 5

Entry no: 71

Cooley Lodge

Mountbagnal
Riverstown, Dundalk
Co. Louth

Tel: 042 9376201
Fax: 042 9376201
E-mail: cooley1@gofree.indigo.ie

Geraldine and Freeman Lynn

There is something democratic about Cooley that disorientated me at first. The farm has no natural focal point, only a series of converted outbuildings and stone walls around a field. Geraldine and Freeman explained all: the main farmhouse was burnt down in the troubles in the 1920s. Today, they live in a stone barn where shire horses used to be kept and guests stay in a series of elegant ground — and first-floor bedrooms in a long cow shed. Original arched entrances lead to walled patios where children can play safely. A sunny dinning room has a wooden staircase leading to a gorgeous bannistered gallery where you can sit in front of a turf fire. At the other end of the building is a conservatory with Lloyd Loom-style chairs and potted plants that leads to a 25m indoor heated pool. The Lynns are friendly former mushroom farmers with a bohemian reluctance to tart the place up too much. You are in a wonderful setting framed by the distant Cooley Mountains and Slieve Nagloch ('lake on top of a mountain') — both are well worth the walk. In the other direction, visit an unspoilt beach and pretty Carlingford with its excellent restaurants. *Four self-catering cottages available, sleep 2-6, IR£280—IR£350.*

Rooms: 9: 6 doubles, 3 twins, all with en suite bathroom.
Price: IR£35 p.p. Sing. supp. IR£10.
Breakfast: Included — full menu.
Meals: Available in Carlingford.
Closed: October—May. Special arrangements for groups.

How to get there: From Dublin, N1 to Dundalk, then right at first r'bout after town, signed Carlingford, for 7 miles. Left after old graveyard, entrance 400m on left.

Red House

Ardee
Co. Louth

Tel: 041 6853523
Fax: 041 6853523
E-mail: redhouse@eircom.net
Web: homepage.eircom.net/~redhouse

Linda Connolly and Fred Bereen

The drawing room-cum-library has huge French doors that give onto a lawn sheltered by Ireland's biggest Cedar of Lebanon tree — there can be few better places to rest on a hot summer's day. Red House is a Georgian house with a tennis court and a pool surrounded by 40 acres of woodland, garden and paddock; whatever the attractions of nearby Newgrange and the Boyne Valley, it is hard to dislodge yourself. The house was built by the Fortescues in about 1800 and the bedrooms are very special. Mine was *massive*. Despite sharing the room with two armchairs, a round table, a huge chest of drawers, a full-length mirror, a wardrobe, a dressing table and a beautifully ornate light of winged Sphinxes, I still had acres of thick carpet to pad around on. The bathroom was nearly as big. Linda seems to look after you without putting herself out. You feel at home almost immediately. Meals are taken together unless otherwise requested. Good for horse-owners. *Ask about children.*

Rooms: 3: 1 twin, 1 double/twin, both with private bathroom; 1 double with en suite bathroom.
Price: IR£40—IR£47.25 p.p. Sing. supp. IR£12.
Breakfast: Included — full Irish.
Meals: Dinner by arrangement. Please enquire when booking.
Closed: Mid-December—mid-January.

How to get there: From Dublin, N2 to Ardee, then right on N52 Dundalk Rd. House 0.5 miles on left.

Netterville Manor

Dowth
Co. Meath

Tel: 041 9844624
Fax: 041 9844624
E-mail: cormacandann@eircom.net
Web: www.netterville.i.am

Ann and Cormac McIvor

If history turns you on, come to Netterville and the surrounding Boyne Valley — there are centuries of it. Start in the Neolithic period as you come up the drive with Dowth passage grave on your right, thought to be the oldest burial site of it kind in Ireland at around 5,000 years. A group of English Israelites searching for the Ark of the Covenant once tried to blow it up with dynamite in the 1930s. As you approach the main house, the well-preserved 13th-century medieval tower house was the baronial seat of the Netterville family until the sixth and childless Viscount Netterville asked that the estate become a home for widows and orphans of "prosperous families" on his death in 1812. From the top of the castle, you can see the famous Newgrange burial site and the hills of Tara and Slane, both powerful centres in Celtic times. The seven-bay redbrick almshouse was built in 1877 by the Netterville Trust. In the mid-1980s, it was bought by the sister of US media mogul Randolph Hearst, who left it to a Buddhist order on her death. Finally, the McIvors came here in 1995 and opened a B&B, serving breakfast in the old chapel. Ann and Cormac clearly love it here. A place steeped in warm welcomes.

Rooms: 4: 2 doubles, 1 twin, all with en suite bathroom; 1 family suite with private bathroom.
Price: From IR£30 p.p. Single supp. IR£5.
Breakfast: Included — full breakfast.
Meals: Dinner from IR£15 p.p. available on request.
Closed: Never.

How to get there: From Drogheda, N51 towards Slane for 3 miles, then left at brown sign to Dowth. Entrance 1 mile on left. House up drive.

Entry no: 74

Map no: 5

Annesbrook
Duleek
Co. Meath

Tel: 041 9823293
Fax: 041 9823024
E-mail: sweetman@annesbrook.com
Web: www.annesbrook.com

Kate Sweetman

There is an incredible stillness about this haven on the busy east coast that will unravel even the most tightly-sprung car journey. You enter through a narrow gatehouse known locally as 'the pockets', so named because the two sides look like the pockets of a pair of trousers, then up a drive enclosed by dense undergrowth and through a walled entrance. Suddenly the view opens out over green fields and this large, slightly eccentric Georgian house comes into focus. There are basically two main rooms downstairs; a nicely proportioned dining room and a drawing room with soft sofas, a lovely carved marble fireplace, gilt mirror and yellow plasterwork. Above each entrance, carved heads of Voltaire and Shakespeare eye each other. Modern paintings by contemporary Irish artists crowd the walls; some are by Kate's daughter. Bedrooms are enormous, uncluttered and full of light; one has a wonderful German Art Nouveau sleigh bed. Those at the front look over rolling countryside, while others look onto a courtyard with a rare surviving stone meat-safe. Kate is a great advert for the house, calm, thoughtful and a gracious host at the dinner table. Ideal for the historic Boyne Valley, or to just switch off for a few days.

Rooms: 5: 2 family, 1 twin, all with en suite bath; 1 double, 1 twin, both with en suite shower.
Price: IR£30—IR£40 p.p. Sing. supp. IR£10. Reduction for more than 1 night.
Breakfast: Included — full Irish.
Meals: Dinner IR£23 except Tuesdays & Wednesdays. Give 24 hours notice. Groups of 6 or more anytime by arrangement.
Closed: October—April.

How to get there: From Dublin, N2 to Derry through Ashbourne. 4.5 miles on, right on R152, signed Drogheda/Duleek. Annesbrook 4.5 miles on left.

Map no: 5

Entry no: 75

The Old Workhouse

Dunshaughlin
Co. Meath

Tel: 01 8259251
Fax: 01 8259251
E-mail: comfort@a-vip.com
Web: travel.to/oldworkhouse

Niamh Colgan

The Old Workhouse has a big reputation in Ireland and it is all down to Niamh. This friendly professional puts in a huge amount of effort to ensure guests will want to come back and they do. And so do their friends. Naturally, much has changed here since the building's austere beginnings in the 19th century and its later use by 500 Belgian refugees. Rooms are very comfortable, with antiques and thoughtful little extras such as a decanter of sherry, bowls of fruit and sweets, and when you turn in, the blinds will have been closed and the bed folded neatly back. Relax in a large beamed hall with dark blue walls, a long dining table and an open fire surrounded by armchairs — Niamh, pronounced 'Neeve', lights fires wherever you go; she is a wizard in the kitchen and holds the title 'Best Breakfast in Ireland' — the spread that awaits you in the morning is truly amazing. An ideal introduction to Ireland and often the preferred last port of call on the way back, too. *Dublin airport 20 minutes by car.*

Rooms: 4: 1 twin with en suite bathroom; 1 double with private bathroom; 1 double/twin, 1 double, both with en suite shower.
Price: IR£30—IR£50 p.p. Sing. supp. IR£10—IR£15.
Breakfast: Included — full Irish/buffet.
Meals: Available locally.
Closed: Christmas week.

How to get there: From Dublin, N3 north towards Navan for 16 miles. House on right on main road, 1 mile before Dunshaughlin.

Killyon

Dublin Rd
Navan
Co. Meath

Tel: 046 71224
Fax: 046 72766

Michael and Sheila Fogarty

You might find this modern house on the main Navan/Dublin road a slightly unprepossessing place on arrival but a pleasant surprise lies in store. On the other side is a balcony with comfy chairs and sun-loungers that looks straight onto the historic River Boyne and parkland on the far bank which is protected from development. It is a wonderful place to have breakfast on a sunny day. And what a breakfast — Sheila makes everything, including the yoghurt. The house is larger than it looks, with four floors and efficient double-glazing that shuts out any noise from the road. Comfortable rooms are cool in the summer and snug in the winter. Down by the river, swans, otters, foxes and kingfishers have been spotted during walks along the towpath to old castles and ruins. In good weather, choose a sheltered spot and have a picnic. The crystal clear water is safe for swimming and children will love spotting fish in the shallows. Sheila and Michael are an unpretentious, easy-going couple who insist there are no rules or regulations. Just lay back and float downstream.

Rooms: 4: 3 doubles, 1 triple, 2 with en suite bath, 2 with en suite shower.
Price: IR£25—IR£30 p.p. Sing supp. IR£5.
Breakfast: Included — full Irish.
Meals: Dinner IR£14. Give 24 hours notice.
Closed: Christmas.

How to get there: From Dublin, N3 north for 25 miles. Enter Navan with river on right, house is opposite Ardboyne Hotel.

Mountainstown House

Castletown-Kilpatrick   **Tel:** 046 54154/54195
Navan   **Fax:** 046 54154
Co. Meath   **E-mail:** pollock@oceanfree.net
                                  Web: www.sawdays.co.uk

John and Diana Pollock

Mountainstown is a Dutch Wren and early Georgian house on 800 acres. Generations of Pollocks have lived here since 1796. Grand rooms lead from one to another, servants' corridors running obediently behind the scenes. Original pine floors have been restored and huge bay windows and massive mirrors give the whole house a bright, airy feel. The drawing room with coral wallpaper is beautiful, while enormous bedrooms with wooden floors and antiques are spectacular; one has a huge antique four-poster, while windows run from floor to ceiling, opening up views over fields. This is an animal-friendly place with horses, cows, donkeys, ducks, peacocks, turkeys, geese and dogs wandering about. Mountainstown is presided over by the busy, vigorous Diana, while John is the perfect gentleman, quietly-spoken and a pleasure to talk to. Breakfast in the basement kitchen overlooking a sunny terrace, then go and explore. The house is available for wedding receptions. *Self-catering cottage overlooking Bear Island in Co. Cork, sleeps 6-8, IR£300—IR£400.*

Rooms: 5: 3 doubles, all with en suite bathroom; 1 double, 1 single, sharing bathroom.
Price: IR£25—IR£55 p.p. Sing. supp. 10%. Children under 10 in cots or camp beds IR£10.
Breakfast: Included — full Irish or make your own.
Meals: Dinners IR£20. Give 24 hours notice.
Closed: Christmas & New Year.

How to get there: From Navan, R162 Kingscourt Rd for 7 miles through Wilkinstown, 1.5 miles on, left at x-roads after 2 Burmah garages. 1 mile to church, then right, entrance 200yds on left, signed Mountainstown Stud.

Entry no: 78   Map no: 5

Lennoxbrook

Kells (Ceanannas Mor)
Co. Meath

Tel: 046 45902
Fax: 046 45902
E-mail: lennoxbrook@unison.ie
Web: www.sawdays.co.uk

Pauline Mullan

You enter the grounds through a full and low tunnel of foliage. The 18th-century house is sheltered from the main road by trees and a stream that Pauline struggles to keep visible through vigorously regenerative undergrowth. The house has been in the family for five generations and it has an old-style feel, with the odd creaking stair, wooden slatted ceilings, old floorboards, oak furniture and proper bathrooms. Pauline has a real feeling for old houses and shuns the idea of breaking up this fine house, so bathrooms are not always next door; three steps lead down to one, with a beautiful turn-of-the-century free-standing bath and lots of plants. Low, narrow doorways lead to bedrooms and some have bay windows overlooking the garden. This is a lively family house. Pauline's three daughters, Louise, Sally and Anna, all help out as their respective ages allow. Pauline is great fun, enormously relaxed and a mine of local information on historic Kells and its megalithic heritage.

Rooms: 4: 1 triple, 1 twin, sharing 2 bathrooms; 2 doubles with en suite shower. Upstairs can be used for self-catering, too.
Price: IR£18—IR£25 p.p. Sing. supp. IR£7.
Breakfast: Included — full Irish.
Meals: Dinner, 3 courses, IR£16. B.Y.O wine. Packed lunch on request.
Closed: Christmas.

How to get there: From Kells, N3 towards Cavan for 3 miles. House signed on right after Burmah petrol station.

Map no: 5

Entry no: 79

Boltown House

Kells
Co. Meath

Tel: 046 43605
Fax: 046 43036
Web: www.sawdays.co.uk

Jean and Susan Wilson

Jean loves having people to stay, though finding her was problematic. Each time I wound down the window to ask the way, it was clear everyone knew and liked her but didn't quite know how to get there, proving perhaps the Irish are better at liking people than giving directions. Boltown is well away from the main tourist areas, set back from the road among fields. As you pull up to the house and the lovely horse chestnut in the garden, look out for the back legs of a terrier digging in a flowerbed — then see if it moves. The farmhouse was built in the 1740-60s and its marble fireplaces, thick faded rugs and creaking floorboards recall times past. The staircase splits to a double landing, with a concave ceiling, that leads to three big, old-fashioned bedrooms, with wooden shutters, deep baths and views of the garden. Jean and her daughter Susan clearly love the place, as do the friendly terriers that curl up by the Aga. Susan cooks delicious dinners, using fresh ingredients that concentrate on quality rather than elaboration. A leisurely breakfast reading old copies of the *New Yorker* was a true pleasure. The rest of the day lay ahead but I was in no hurry.

Rooms: 3: 2 doubles with en suite bathroom; 1 double with private bathroom.
Price: IR£35 p.p. Sing. supp. IR£10.
Breakfast: Included — full Irish.
Meals: Dinner IR£25 at 8pm or by special arrangement. Book by noon on the same day.
Closed: Christmas week.

How to get there: From Kells, R163 Oldcastle Rd for 4 miles, second left after petrol station, signed Kilskyre. House 0.75 miles on right. First 2-storey building with a short drive.

The Gate Lodge

Clonleason House
Fordstown
Co. Meath

Tel: 046 34111
Fax: 046 34134
Web: www.sawdays.co.uk

Sinead Connelly

The Gate Lodge sets the standard for self-catering in Ireland. Sinead was an interior designer for many years and she has converted this Georgian cottage just the way she wants. The end result indulges the senses and yet despite the apparent luxury and attention to detail, it doesn't feel too oppressively perfect. Here, country house elegance meets cosy cottage. The Lodge lies at the end of her drive, secluded by trees, and backs onto a small country lane with only the odd tractor to break the peace and quiet. You enter by the kitchen with hand-printed Brunschwig and Fils wallpaper, a Welsh dresser storing patterned Portmeirion china, red deal cupboards distressed to create a limewash effect and a hob but no oven. Left is the sitting room with books, paintings and a comfy cream sofa in front of an open fire. The sabre is purely for decoration. French doors open on to a terrace and a beautiful secret garden that leads to a small stream. The double bedroom has wooden cupboards, fresh white linen, coir matting and a pretty shower room. If you can drag yourself away, there are lots of fabulous public gardens to visit, too. Enchanting.

Rooms: Gate Lodge: 1 bedroom with en suite bathroom, sleeps 2.
Price: IR£260—IR£360 p.w. depending on season. Weekend rates available.
Breakfast: You cook, you choose.
Meals: Available locally or bring a cookbook.
Closed: Christmas.

How to get there: From Dublin, N3 to Kells, then N52 towards Mullingar for 6 miles, left at x-roads on R154. Keep left through 2 juncs. House 2nd on right after sharp bend.

Map no: 5   Entry no: 81

Woodtown House

Athboy
Co. Meath

Tel: 046 35022
Fax: 046 35022
E-mail: woodtown@iol.ie
Web: www.iol.ie/~woodtown

Colin and Anne Finnegan

This is one of my favourite houses in Ireland. Gorgeous on the outside, gorgeous on the inside. Built in 1725, Woodtown is a beautiful example of early Irish Georgian. It also has a secret passage from the troubles of the 1920s. The house is tucked away in remote countryside, so getting there down a series of long lanes makes the discovery all the more enjoyable — I arrived as a setting sun turned the stone golden. The rear of the house has a bowed middle with stone steps leading into the garden from the dining room where dinner is served surrounded by antiques and an Art Deco marble fireplace. Colin and Anne are zealous collectors of social history — signs, implements, books, bottles, tins, anything with a curiosity value is lovingly arranged to take you down memory lane. Even the biscuits with my tea were old favourites: Cafe Noir and Lemon Puffs.; Everything has been restored, including servants' bells with a different chime for each room. Large bedrooms painted in period colours have views and either morning or afternoon sun. Breakfast is in a lovely cellar room off the kitchen. Colin and Anne are a relaxed and engaging couple. He teaches agricultural science and she manages the B&B.

Rooms: 3: 2 family, both en suite; 1 double with private bathroom.
Price: IR£20—IR£30 p.p. Special weekend rates available.
Breakfast: Included — full Irish.
Meals: Dinner IR£12, 7.30pm, B.Y.O wine. Book by noon the same day.
Closed: October—March. Off season by arrangement.

How to get there: From Trim, R154 to Athboy, then left on N51 to Mullingar. 1.5 miles on, left signed Woodtown House, follow signs for 2.5 miles. House through gates at end of road.

Entry no: 82

Map no: 5

Mornington House

Mornington
Multyfarnham near Mullingar
Co. Westmeath

Tel: 044 72191
Fax: 044 72338
E-mail: info@mornington.ie
Web: www.mornington.ie

Anne and Warwick O'Hara

Seclusion here is absolute. With the shutters closed on your bedroom windows you could sleep all day, provided the jackdaws do too. You approach Mornington through a gap in a barrier of trees, the manifold guardians of the property that protect it on all sides. Follow the drive round, past fields, to the entrance of this splendid house. The central section was built in 1710, the front in 1897 and the wing in 1906, combining the concerted efforts of the founders, the Daly Family and the original O'Haras who took up residence in 1858. Most of the bedrooms are large, in bright colours, with big bathrooms, oval baths, brass beds and views that include the wonderful solitary oak tree on the front lawn. A path has been cut through the meadow to Lough Derravaragh with Knock Eyon in the distance. Downstairs, carpets fade as they approach long ranks of park-facing windows and a huge potted lime tree in the dining room catches the sunlight in the morning. Warwick and Anne are genuinely dedicated hosts and produce the most delicious meals, growing much of their vegetables in the walled garden behind the house. *Children by arrangement.*

Rooms: 5: 1 double, 1 double/twin, both with en suite bathroom; 2 doubles, both with private bathroom; 1 single with private shower.
Price: IR£40 p.p. Sing. supp. IR£7.50. Three-day rates available.
Breakfast: Included — full Irish.
Meals: Dinner, 4 courses, IR£25.
Closed: November—March.

How to get there: From N4/Mullingar bypass, R394 towards Castlepollard for 5 miles. Left at Wood Pub in Crookedwood, then 1.25 miles to first junc. Turn right, house 1 mile on right, down long drive.

Map no: 4

Entry no: 83

Lough Owel Lodge

Cullion
Nr Mullingar
Co. Westmeath

Tel: 044 48714
Fax: 044 48771
E-mail: aginnell@hotmail.com
Web: www.angelfire.com/tx/aginnell

Martin and Aideen Ginnell

So often in Ireland, you only need to turn off a main road to immediately find yourself in beautiful countryside. Lough Owel Lodge is just off a dual carriageway north of Mullingar, yet is far enough away that you quickly forget the road is there. Nothing spoils the view from this 1940s house. The open-plan sitting/dining room has full-length, wood-framed windows that seem to draw in the countryside. In winter you can also see writer J.P. Donleavy's house through the trees. There is literally nothing that spoils this view for miles. The Lodge's land stretches past a terraced garden and a tennis court to the lake below. Unusually-shaped rooms are scrupulously clean with some lovely beds, including a four-poster and a 150-year-old half-tester. Walkers will appreciate the library of books on the region known as the 'Land of Lake and Legend'. Trout fishing can be arranged with ghillies and boats. Aideen and Martin are easy-going hosts — this a good-natured family home and ideal for children. *Pets not allowed in the house.*

Rooms: 5: 1 family suite with en suite bathroom; 1 twin, 2 four-posters, 1 double, all with en suite shower.
Price: IR£20—IR£25 p.p. Sing. supp. IR£6.50.
Breakfast: Included — full Irish.
Meals: Available in Mullingar. Packed lunch IR£5.
Closed: December—mid-March. Off season by arrangement.

How to get there: From Dublin, N4 for 50 miles, past Mullingar follow signs. As lake comes into view, left, signed Lough Owel Lodge. Entrance on right.

Entry no: 84

Map no: 4

Mearescourt House

Rathconrath
Mullingar
Co. Westmeath

Tel: 044 55112

Brendan and Eithne Pendred

The approach to Mearescourt must be one of the most beautiful in Ireland. A lovely avenue of trees cup the drive like gnarled fingers as it curves to the front of this large Georgian mansion. Spend a moment looking over meadows dotted with magnificent horse chestnuts, a restored 18th-century lake and a walled garden with monkey-puzzle trees to one side. Bedrooms are huge, with brass beds and plain walls, bay windows and graceful views. Brendan and Eithne, pronounced 'Etna', are a gentle, easy-going couple who have created a homely environment in this big old house. They didn't even like the idea of leaving brochures on the hall table for fear of introducing the feel of a hotel until constant requests finally made them succumb. Brendan is a thoughtful man with measured opinions and a dry sense of humour, while Eithne is instantly likeable. This is a green leafy country area in the sleepy Midlands where you will find peaceful seclusion.

Rooms: 4: 1 family, 2 doubles, all with en suite bathroom; 1 twin with private bathroom.
Price: IR£30—IR£35 p.p. Sing. supp. IR£10.
Breakfast: Included — full Irish.
Meals: Dinner IR£20—IR£23.
Closed: Christmas week.

How to get there: From Mullingar, R392 Ballymahon Rd for 6 miles through Rathconrath. Turn right 2 miles past village at bottom of steep hill, then first left, signed. House on right up drive.

Map no: 4

Entry no: 85

Cornaher House
Tyrellspass
Co. Westmeath

Tel: 044 23311
Fax: 044 23311
E-mail: rrtreacy@eircom.net

Nowell Treacy

If Dr Doolittle was ever recast as a woman, I'd nominate Nowell for the part. This remarkable woman literally walks and talks with the animals. One visiting organic farm inspector said he had "never seen happier cows". Her cattle are treated like good friends. Many have pet names and her favourites are on stroking terms, rare for the usually timid cow. Her coup de grace is captured below when she took a pew on the back of a surprisingly tolerant Hereford bull – I was as far away as my zoom lens would allow. Cornaher is up a long drive surrounded by acres of lush pastureland, woodland and glacial bog. Nowell opted for the good life after becoming bored of selling real estate in Dublin. She has furnished this Georgian house in a style that can only be described as eclectic bordering on the psychedelic. The walls of the large drawing room are crammed with paintings; the good, the bad and the ugly are all here, reflecting Nowell's warm, non-judgemental slant on life. Bedrooms continue in a similar vein with crazy-patterned carpets and wild fabric designs mixing chaotically with French furniture, a four-poster and painted floorboards. Funky, comfortable and unique, the world according to Nowell is well worth a visit but go with an open mind.

Rooms: 5: 4 doubles, 1 twin, all with en suite bathroom.
Price: IR£20 p.p. Sing. supp. IR£10.
Breakfast: Included — full Irish.
Meals: Dinner IR£20. Give 24 hours notice.
Closed: Never.

How to get there: From Dublin, N6 Galway Rd to Tyrellspass. 1 mile after village, left down lane, signed to house. Entrance at end of lane. Long drive leads to house.

Entry no: 86

Map no: 4

Temple Country House and Spa

Horseleap
Moate
Co. Westmeath

Tel: 0506 35118
Fax: 0506 35008
E-mail: templespa@spiders.ie
Web: www.spiders.ie/templespa

Declan and Bernadette Fagan

The idea here is to provide relaxing breaks away from the in-tray-out-tray demands of modern life, to smooth out those knots in the neck and induce some much-needed calm. Guests are not encouraged to jump in their cars at 7am every morning to charge round significant chunks of Ireland and return exhausted just in time for dinner; take out a house bike, or explore on foot is the credo here. Temple provides massages, places to read and think... or not to think, depending on your mood. They have added a relaxation annexe complete with sauna, steam room, massage, beauty rooms and the jewel in the crown is a miraculous hydrotherapy bath. It is a lovely 200-year-old house with surprisingly large bedrooms, big brass beds, proper bathrooms, thick carpets and views over lawns and fields. Guests eat excellent food together in an atmospheric, candlelit dining room. Declan and Bernadette, who is a self-trained cook, dedicate themselves to helping people de-stress; their easy-going hospitality influences the mood of the whole place. Great for those who have grown weary of the city.

Rooms: 8: 2 doubles/twins, 2 doubles, 1 family, 3 twins, all with en suite bathroom. 1 single en suite.
Price: IR£40—IR£50 p.p. Sing. supp. IR£10—IR£20. Inclusive weekend and midweek spa programmes available.
Breakfast: Included — full Irish.
Meals: Dinner IR£20, Tuesday to Saturday. Packed lunch on request.
Closed: December—January.

How to get there: From Moate, N6 towards Dublin for 4 miles. Left, signed to house, which is 0.5 miles further on left.

Map no: 4

Entry no: 87

The Bastion

2 Bastion Street   **Tel:** 0902 94954
Athlone   **Fax:** 0902 93648
Co. Westmeath   **E-mail:** bastion@iol.ie

Vinny and Anthony McCay

Athlone more than justifies its claim to being the culinary capital of the Midlands, but why isn't this historic staging post between Dublin and Galway on the banks of the River Shannon more well known? Walk through the Left Bank district next to King John's Castle built in 1210 and you find a place buzzing with life. The narrow streets on the site of the old medieval town are full of good restaurants and swinging pubs; Sean's pub is so old it is mentioned in the 9th-century Clonmacnoise Annals. I discovered The Bastion by accident — it was recommended by a waitress where I was eating dinner. Brothers Vinny and Anthony have turned an old draper's shop into a cool B&B. Their laid-back style has a following among more worldly travellers but it deserves wider recognition. Bedrooms where apprentice tailors would have lived have a clean, spartan elegance with crisp, white linen, wooden floorboards and the odd modern print. A healthy buffet-style breakfast in the snug subterranean dining room is a welcome alternative to the Irish fry. Ask about trips down river to prehistoric Clonmacnoise and unspoilt Banaher village. You may even spot the rare corn-crake.

Rooms: 5: 2 family, 2 doubles, all with en suite shower; 1 double with private bathroom.
Price: IR£19 p.p. Sing. supp. IR£6—IR£8.
Breakfast: Included — buffet.
Meals: Available in Athlone's Left Bank district.
Closed: Never.

How to get there: From Dublin, N6 Galway Rd to Athlone for 78 miles. Follow signs to town centre, cross bridge to Left Bank, then left round castle. Follow street round, house 100m on right.

Entry no: 88   Map no: 4

Viewmount House

Dublin Road
Longford
Co. Longford

Tel: 043 41919
Fax: 043 42906
E-mail: viewmt@iol.ie
Web: www.viewmounthouse.com

Beryl and James Kearney

It is always a pleasure to find owners with the enthusiasm and ideas to bring a period Georgian house back to life. Beryl and James have spent the past decade restoring this country house built in 1840 by the Cuffe family and later used as a base to administer the Earl of Longford's estate. Climb the elegant white spiral staircase surrounded by walls of warm red to magnificent bedrooms with big antique beds, wooden floors, woven rugs and views over gardens and fields. Each has its own character. Breakfast is served in a dinning room with beautiful vaulted ceilings and Georgian blue walls. James does the cooking, having given up a pedestrian life as an accountant to devote himself full-time to the house and grounds. He has restored the terraced flower beds at the back and is now working on an ambitious Japanese garden. There are plans to convert outbuildings into a restaurant; James may do the cooking, realising a long-held dream. The Kearneys are a sincere, friendly couple who laugh easily. An ideal staging post for Co. Mayo and Co. Donegal, or a good base to explore historic Carriglas Manor and award-winning Ardagh village. *Self-catering apartment, sleeps 8, IR£200—IR£300 p.w.*

Rooms: 5: 4 doubles, 1 twin, all with en suite shower.
Price: IR£25—IR£35 p.p. No sing. supp.
Breakfast: Included — full menu.
Meals: Available locally.
Closed: Never.

How to get there: In Longford, R393 to Ardagh for 0.7 miles, then right up sliproad following signs to house. Entrance 200m on right.

Griesemount

Ballitore
Co. Kildare

Tel: 0507 23158
Fax: 0503 40687
E-mail: griesemount@eircom.net
Web: www.sawdays.co.uk

Robert and Carolyn Ashe

This well-proportioned Georgian house sits on top of a hill overlooking the Quaker village of Ballitore, which sprung up in the early 1800s after two Quakers, resting in the valley as they made their way to Cork, decided it was the perfect place to start a community. Even the bathrooms in this 1817 house have lovely views which look over a walled garden to the River Griese and a ruined water mill. Paddocks that run down to the river remind you this is horse country and Carolyn can organise riding to suit all abilities. The sunny breakfast room matches Carolyn's warm, loquacious personality. She enjoys people so much she claims never to have disliked anyone who has stayed. The house is full of creaky stairs and floorboards and quirky memorabilia such as the soldier sculpture in the front hallway and the bookshelves tucked under window sills. The bedrooms are all interesting; one has a great half-tester. And try the library bathroom for an inspirational wallow. The drawing room is well lived-in with low, worn in furniture that crowds round the fireplace and a piano which is there to be played. The Ashes hope you will enjoy the house as you find it, in true bed and breakfast tradition. *Shaker furniture for sale in village.*

Rooms: 3: 1 double with en suite bathroom; 1 double, 1 twin, both with private bathroom.
Price: IR£30—IR£35 p.p. Sing. supp. IR£5.
50% discount for third night.
Breakfast: Included — full Irish.
Meals: Available locally.
Closed: December—mid-February.

How to get there: From Dublin, N7 off M50 towards Naas for 20 miles, then N9 towards Carlow for 12 miles. Second right after Texaco garage down small road, signed to house. First entrance on left.

Martinstown House
The Curragh, Kildare
Co. Kildare

Tel: 045 441269
Fax: 045 441208

Meryl and Thomas Long

Martinstown is something very different for Ireland. Originally part of the huge estates of the Dukes of Leinster, the house was completed by the Burrowes family in the Gothic style as a *cottage orné* between 1832 and 1840. The place is a flight of fancy with many surprises — the ceiling in the drawing/ballroom is twice as high as the rest of the ground floor and has wonderful painted garlands and a 'sky ceiling'. The hallway has more trompe-l'oeil with pastoral scenes and stone columns. Then there is Meryl, full of great energy, drive and character, who settles easily into conversation with guests. The house bubbles with vitality, is beautifully decorated and the overall style is informal and elegant. Guests all eat together and whenever possible, Meryl joins them. Dinners are often centred on big roasts. Food is sourced locally or grown in their walled garden. A perfect combination of old-fashioned hospitality and modern comfort. *Horse racing nearby. Unsuitable for young children.*

Rooms: 4: 1 twin, 1 double, both with en suite bathroom; 1 twin with private bathroom; 1 double with private shower.
Price: IR£55—IR£70 p.p. Sing. supp. IR£10.
Breakfast: Included — full Irish.
Meals: Dinner IR£30, at 8pm. Book by noon the same day.
Closed: Mid-December—mid-January.

How to get there: From Dublin, N7/M7 south past Naas, then M9 Kilcullen exit for about 3 miles. Right on N78 Athy Rd for 1 mile, then right signed Martinstown for 1.5 miles. Left opposite Ballysax Church. Entrance 0.5 miles on left.

Map no: 5

Entry no: 91

Pine Lodge

Ross Rd
Screggan, Tullamore
Co. Offaly

Tel: 0506 51927
Fax: 0506 51927
Web: www.sawdays.co.uk

Claudia Krygel

Pine Lodge fits my idea of a health farm as Claudia's philosophy is to pamper rather than keep guests on a strict diet of lettuce and lengths. This secluded spot comes fully equipped with sauna, steambath, sunbed and an indoor heated swimming pool. Massage, yoga and reflexology are also available as are special diets if you really need a good cleanse. Claudia only has a maximum of four people to stay at a time, so the attention is personal. Heaven. Breakfasts are award-winning and the house is well ordered with wood everywhere. It's a well-ordered house with wood everywhere, particularly stripped pine which Claudia adores — the house name is a happy coincidence. The main part of the house is the open-plan kitchen, breakfast area and cordoned-off snug for watching TV or reading on sofas in front of the fire. Bedrooms lie off a single corridor and have low wooden beds, duvets, pine ceilings, excellent showers, wooden windows and good-sized towels. Claudia is intelligent, direct, fun and assiduous in keeping a tight ship. You feel healthier just being here. *Minimum stay 2 nights.*

Rooms: 4: 1 double with en suite bath; 1 double,
2 twins, all with en suite shower.
Price: IR£25 p.p. Sing. supp. IR£10. Health break rates available.
Breakfast: Included — full Irish.
Meals: Available in Tullamore.
Closed: Mid-December—mid-February.

How to get there: In Tullamore, N52 towards Birr. Keep right on main road as road forks 1 mile out of Tullamore. Left 2 miles on, signed to house.
Lodge 0.5 miles on left.

Spinner's Town House

Castle Street
Birr
Co. Offaly

Tel: 0509 21673
Fax: 0509 21673
E-mail: spinners@indigo.ie
Web: www.spinners-townhouse.com

**Seamus Merrigan and
Liam Maloney**

What do an airline pilot, a dressage instructor and a showjumper have in common? They own an old woollen mill and a terrace of five houses that enclose one of the most beautiful courtyard gardens in Ireland. Liam, the charming and extrovert dressage instructor, and Seamus, the calm and collected showjumper, run the day-to-day stuff, while Tim drops in now and again between flying 747s. Spinner's is in the heritage town of Birr, a well guarded secret in the heart of the Irish Midlands. Well laid out Georgian streets and squares back onto Birr Castle with its famous grounds and historic telescope. But the garden by Irish landscape designer Rachel Lamb is the real treasure here. Stone and gravel paths divide manicured parterres and mopstick ash trees, creating a magical setting which you appreciate from so many different angles, whether eating in the converted grain store bistro, walking to your room or sitting in the garden itself watching live theatre. Clean, uncluttered bedrooms come in either contemporary style, with pine floors, wooden mirrors and pastel colours, or modern Gothic, with forged iron fittings and handmade ceramic tiles. Great fun. *Self-catering cottage, sleeps 7, IR£200—IR£550 p.w.*

Rooms: 13: 4 doubles, 2 doubles/twins, all with en suite bathroom; 4 family with en suite shower; 3 doubles/twins with private shower.
Price: IR£22.50—IR£35 p.p. Sing. supp. IR£5—IR£10.
Breakfast: Included — full menu.
Meals: Dinner from IR£12.
Closed: Never.

How to get there: From Dublin, N7 to Mountrath, the right on R440 to Birr. From Emmet Sq, down Main St to Market Sq, right at monument, house 500m on right, opposite Birr Castle.

Map no: 4

Entry no: 93

Ballaghmore Castle
The Manor House
Borris-in-Ossory
Co. Laois

Tel: 0505 21453
Fax: 0505 21195

Grace Pym

I can't make up my mind whether it is the castle or Grace that makes this place so special, but then one could not exist without the other. This former gilder and restorer, with a gallery of 18th-century Irish paintings, left the good life in Dublin for an even better life in the country converting a 15th-century tower house into a medieval fantasy. Here you can be King Arthur or Lady Guinevere, staying in the baronial bed chamber with its heavily carved half-tester, tapestries, thick rugs and a freestanding ball-and-claw bath. Below is a split level banqueting hall with heavy oak tables, torchères and a throne complete with makeshift crown. Above is a well-lit hall with an open fire and spectacular views. This is as authentic as it gets and comes with all your creature comforts. Concerts are also held here by hoisting instruments up past the stone *sheila-na-gig* using a car in low gear. Next door is the Manor House which does B&B in a country house setting with four-posters, stripey wallpaper and lots of oil paintings. And amid it all, the remarkable Grace. *Groups can rent the castle for IR£1,000 p.w. Self-catering cottage, sleeps 4, IR£250 p.w.*

Rooms: Castle: 1 double/single with en suite bathroom; 4 singles, sharing bathroom; Manor House: 1 double, 1 twin, both with en suite bathroom; 1 family suite with private bathroom.
Price: House: IR£25—IR£35; Castle: IR£75 p.p. No sing. supp.
Breakfast: Included — full Irish.
Meals: Available locally.
Closed: Never.

How to get there: From Dublin, N7 Limerick Road to Borris-in-Ossory. 3 miles after village towards Roscrea, house and castle signed. Entrance on right.

Entry no: 94

Map no: 4

Ivyleigh House

Bank Place
Portlaoise
Co. Laois

Tel: 0502 22081
Fax: 0502 63343
E-mail: dinah@ivyleigh.com
Web: www.ivyleigh.com

Dinah Campion

Dinah means it when she says you are going to get the best of everything in this 1850 townhouse built in the Georgian style. Every item has been carefully chosen for your greater comfort: the Italian Frette towels, which I was assured would dry you properly, the Piubelle linen from Brown Thomas, the pocket-sprung mattresses, the Mason tableware, the Newbridge silver cutlery, the Osborne and Little wallpaper and the lovely Chippendale double bed. Nothing falls short. The big drawing room is full of antiques collected over the past 20 years; my favourite piece was the Chippendale dining table with its beautifully-carved ball and claw feet. Dinah's breakfast is more than a match. Choose from a dizzy array of delicious breakfast alternatives including surprises such as yoghurt with geranium jelly and Cashel Blue cheesecakes. Port Laoise has good restaurants and a theatre all within walking distance. Dinah and husband Jerry are friendly, down to earth people who work hard for you. The ideal staging post en route to the south-west of Ireland.

Rooms: 5: 3 twins/doubles, 1 double, 1 single, all with en suite bathroom.
Price: IR£36 p.p. Sing. supp. IR£10.
Breakfast: Included — full menu.
Meals: Available in Port Laoise.
Closed: Christmas.

How to get there: From Dublin, N7 Limerick Rd, then Port Laoise turn-off on M7 bypass into town. Right at church, signed railway station, next left, then keep right at following junc. House 25m on right.

Map no: 4

Entry no: 95

Preston House
Main St
Abbeyleix
Co. Laois

Tel: 0502 31432/31662
Fax: 0502 31432

Allison and Michael Dowling

Allison is warm, smiley and instantly draws you into the friendly atmosphere of this former Georgian house on the main road out of historic Abbeyleix. It's the old schoolhouse and breakfast is served in what used to be the head teacher's study. No doubt generations of children have knocked and entered with some trepidation, but it couldn't be more welcoming nowadays. The house is both a family home and a busy café by day with wooden tables, a piano, attractive lighting, creaky pine floorboards, a big old school cupboard and an open fire in winter. There are plans to do something with the beautiful beamed hall upstairs, with its bannistered gallery, where many a child would have learnt to read and write. Even the bare space at present is worth a peek. Bedrooms are large with big comfortable wooden beds, sofas, magazines, quirky showers and pine floors scattered with rugs. The sitting room is a quiet space in this bustling house.

Rooms: 4 doubles/twins, all with en suite shower.
Price: IR£26 p.p. Sing. supp. IR£5.
Breakfast: Included — full Irish.
Meals: Dinner from IR£15, Thursday to Saturday. Suppers on request other times. Lunch from IR£7.
Closed: Christmas & New Year.

How to get there: From Dublin, N7 to Port Laoise for 65 miles. Then N8 south to Abbeyleix. House on right on main road through town.

Entry no: 96

Map no: 4

Sherwood Park House

Ballon
Co. Carlow

Tel: 0503 59117
Fax: 0503 59355
E-mail: info@sherwoodparkhouse.ie
Web: www.sherwoodparkhouse.ie

Patrick and Maureen Owens

Sherwood Park would grind to a halt without Maureen; as I was leaving, Patrick bounded down the stone steps at the front to hurry her up. "They need you in there, Maureen," he said, and she was led away, one arm raised in farewell. The only rule she seems to lay down is that you enjoy yourself; with her boundless generosity and Paddy's gift for hilarious one-liners, it is not hard to have a good time here. Sherwood is a fine example of early Irish Georgian approached through an original stone entrance. Its four storeys are unusual for the simple reason that houses from this period were never built on foundations, so the higher you went, the more likely the building would sink; as a result, the house has subsided six feet since it was first built in 1730. There are some interesting sloping floors but the graceful design remains intact with high ceilings and big, welcoming rooms. In the main hallway past the well-played piano is an elegant staircase that leads to comfortable bedrooms with half-testers and four-posters. Downstairs, breakfast is served round a large dining table that must take weeks to polish. An enchanting house and popular with Dubliners.

Rooms: 4: 2 suites, 1 double, 1 family, all with en suite bathroom.
Price: IR£30 p.p. Sing. supp. IR£6.50.
Breakfast: Included — full Irish.
Meals: Dinner IR£20.
Closed: Never.

How to get there: From Naas, N9 south to Carlow, then N80 towards Wexford to Ballon. Through Ballon, up hill, then left at second x-roads, signed to house.

Map no: 8

Entry no: 97

Lorum Old Rectory

Kilgreaney
Bagenalstown
Co. Carlow

Tel: 0503 75282
Fax: 0503 75455
E-mail: info@lorum.com
Web: www.lorum.com

Bobbie and Don Smith

An honest-looking house and a lovely family — you feel at home as soon as you step through the front door of Lorum. The atmosphere is delightfully Irish. Don is from New Zealand but adapted to the way of life a long time ago. Dinner is a feast taken round a big old dining table. Bobbie uses local organic produce and has won awards for her cooking. A highlight is the vast Irish cheeseboard at the end; worth leaving room for. In the big living room, thick rugs and comfy sofas surround a beautiful marble fireplace with an open fire. Bobbie and Don have three musical daughters so the piano and flute are not there for show; expect impromptu renditions or sing-alongs. Up the creaky stairs, warm, cosy bedrooms with four-posters, antiques and views over the Blackstairs Mountains are all different and full of character. Don keeps Jacob sheep and horses and grows Christmas trees on 18 acres, while Bobbie has turned her hand to stained glass art. They will also arrange cycling tours to other equally lovely houses and your luggage travels separately for hassle-free cycling.

Rooms: 5: 4 doubles, 1 double/twin, all with en suite shower.
Price: IR£37.50-IR£40 p.p. Sing. supp. IR£15.
Breakfast: Included — full Irish.
Meals: Dinner, 6 courses, IR£27.50.
Closed: Christmas & New Year.

How to get there: From Bagenalstown, R705 towards Borris for 4 miles. House signed on left.

Entry no: 98   Map no: 8

Kilgraney Country House

Bagenalstown
Co. Carlow

Tel: 0503 75283
Fax: 0503 75595
E-mail: kilgrany@indigo.ie
Web: www.kilgraneyhouse.com

Martin Marley and Bryan Leech

Designers Martin and Bryan have breathed life into the Irish country house genre. Uncluttered rooms make each bold touch more startling and enjoyable as familiar blends with exotic. Wooden floors, lush house plants, huge mirrors, comfortable beds and immaculate bathrooms mix with fabrics, furniture and art collected from extensive travels abroad. The Marilyn chairs and marble-topped furniture with brass inlay were both designed by Martin and made in the Philippines, while diaphanous cotton and gold 'Jamdani' curtains in one bedroom took a weaver in Bangladesh two months to make. Every aspect of the house has received the designer's attention and your mild-mannered hosts will happily share the story of how each piece found its way into this late Georgian house. Meticulously-prepared dinners are served in the enveloping atmosphere of the candlelit dining room. Breakfast in an east-facing room received the same care; the crepes with sour cream are superb. One guest said she was reluctant to spread the word about Kilgraney because this was where she came to escape. Amen to that. *Plans for self-catering apartments.*

Rooms: 6: 3 doubles, all with en suite bathroom; 3 doubles, all with en suite shower.
Price: IR£35—IR£55 p.p. Sing. supp. IR£15.
Breakfast: Included — full menu.
Meals: Dinner IR£28. Book by noon the same day.
Closed: Please check with owners.

How to get there: From Bagenalstown, R705 towards Borris for 3.5 miles. House signed on right at x-roads. Entrance on left down lane.

Map no: 8

Entry no: 99

Berryhill

Inistioge
Co. Kilkenny

Tel: 056 58434
Fax: 056 58434
E-mail: info@berryhillhouse.com
Web: www.berryhillhouse.com

George and Belinda Dyer

This is an area you will want to visit: a blissful green valley frames the River Nore in a wedge, so clean-cut as it meanders mazily through meadows and under old stone bridges. And there is nowhere better perched for viewing it than Berryhill. Built on a hillside in 1780, the house lies in 250 acres of farmland with wonderful walks — "each field has an even more stunning view than the last", as the brochure says. The land has river frontage for picnics or fishing and there is a mirthful cross-country croquet course on the front lawn. Bedroom suites are animal-themed and decorated accordingly: Frog with a veranda? Pig or Elephant? Actress Mia Farrow brought her children here. Each has its own dressing/sitting area with the latest glossy mags and a collection of novels. Comfort is a priority. The honesty bar for the drinks trolley in the elegant drawing room is typical of George and Belinda's attitude to their guests. Sheep, fantails, and chickens potter about the place, adding to the cosy farmyard atmosphere of this most hospitable place. *Children over 10 welcome.*

Rooms: 3 suites, all with bathroom & dressing room/sitting area.
Price: IR£45 p.p. Sing. supp. IR£10. Minimum two nights.
Breakfast: Included — full Irish.
Meals: Available locally.
Closed: 1 November—1 May.

How to get there: From Thomastown, R700 to Inistioge. Through village, cross bridge keeping right, then next left on Graiguenamanagh Rd. First right, second entrance on left at gate lodge.

Ballyduff House

Thomastown
Co. Kilkenny

Tel: 056 58488
E-mail: ballyd@gofree.indigo.ie

Breda Thomas

Ballyduff is B&B heaven. The big white gates, the graceful curved drive, the Georgian architecture fringed with wisteria and the big lawn surrounded by mature woodland are all so inviting. Ring the bell and Breda will arrive all smiles and enthusiasm to welcome you in. This human dynamo runs the show single-handed along with managing 240 acres of farmland, running a pony club for youngsters and bringing up two children. She has genuine warmth, the product of 10 years working in the restaurant business in the US, while the house is the epitome of Anglo-Irish refinement. The library was my favourite room with books and ancient tomes arranged on shelves in four corners and comfy lived in sofas — just the place to "kick back in" she says. You'll see what she means. Lovely bedrooms are all generously big and different with beautiful antiques, Colefax & Fowler wallpaper and linen from the White Company in London. Two have views over the River Nore that runs right past the house — you can fish here and Breda can organise children's pony rides. A perfect retreat.

Rooms: 4: 1 double, 1 family suite, both with en suite bathroom; 1 double, 1 twin, sharing bathroom.
Price: IR£30 p.p. Sing. supp. IR£5.
Breakfast: Included — full Irish/buffet.
Meals: Available in Thomastown.
Closed: November—February.

How to get there: From Thomastown, R700 New Ross Rd for 3 miles. After Brownsbarn Bridge, immediately right, then right at x-roads. Entrance on right after 200yds. No sign.

Map no: 8

Entry no: 101

Belmore
Jerpoint Church
Thomastown
Co. Kilkenny

Tel: 056 24228

Rita and Joe Teesdale

This old hunting lodge built for Lord Belmore in 1790 overlooks the beautiful Nore Valley. Local folklore says the secret of eternal happiness was discovered here by a monk at nearby Jerpoint Abbey who sat down in the abbey garden one day to listen to a songbird. On returning to the abbey, he found that no-one recognised him except an old man who told him he had been sitting outside for 100 years. Belmore feels so completely detached from the outside world. Joe and Rita are a warm, friendly couple who keep busy running two sheep and barley farms on either side of the valley; guests are free to fish their two miles of salmon and trout fishing on the River Nore with more extensive waters available at the local club at very reasonable rates. Unusual bedrooms with vaulted ceilings and views over the valley are matched by excellent breakfasts. Downstairs feels part castle, part country house, with flagstones and more vaulted ceilings. From the house, there are walks to a ruined church and an abandoned medieval village, while the now ruined abbey is just a short stroll down the road and St Nicholas is said to be buried nearby.

Rooms: 3: 1 twin, 2 doubles, all with en suite shower.
Price: IR£25 p.p. Sing. supp. IR£5.
Breakfast: Included — full Irish.
Meals: Available locally.
Closed: Never.

How to get there: From Kilkenny, R700 to Thomastown. Cross bridge onto N9 Waterford Rd, then first right after Jerpoint Abbey. House signed on right.

Cullintra House

The Rower   **Tel:** 051 423614
Inistioge   **Fax:** 051 423614
Co. Kilkenny   **E-mail:** cullhse@indigo.ie
                                       Web: indigo.ie/~cullhse

Patricia Cantlon

Cullintra is something of a B&B legend in Ireland. This is for those who enjoy the
unprescribed. Let Patricia's eccentric whimsy lead you through an unforgettable
experience. If time allows, stay two nights and expect to eat a truly fabulous dinner
late — no going into town for supper, but who would want to? Wonderful breakfasts
don't start much before 9.30am, though Continental breakfasts are available for
early birds. Tell Patricia the night before if you *are* in a hurry. The rooms are
astonishing. From the stunning conservatory/studio to the gallery rooms converted
out of old barns, this is Accommodation Art. Patricia loves her cats and won't stand
for blood sports — foxes come to the garden to feed. The 250-year-old house stands
at the foot of Mount Brandon in 230 acres with gorgeous views and woodland
walks. Come with an open mind. *Cullintra is 50 minutes from Rosslare ferry port
and 2 hours from Dublin Airport.*

Rooms: 6: 3 doubles, en suite; 1 family room with
shower and separate wc; 2 doubles sharing bathroom.
Price: IR£23—IR£30 p.p. Sing. supp. IR£10.
Breakfast: Included — full Irish.
Meals: Dinner IR£18, B.Y.O wine. Guests must book
dinner.
Closed: Never.

How to get there: From Rosslare ferryport, N25 to
New Ross, then R700 Kilkenny road for 6 miles. House
signed up lane on right.

Map no: 8   **Entry no: 103**

Ballaghtobin

Callan
Co. Kilkenny

Tel: 056 25227
Fax: 056 25712
E-mail: gabbetts@indigo.ie
Web: www.ballaghtobin.com

Catherine and Mickey Gabbett

From the fertile agricultural region of Kilkenny springs a brand of hospitality that celebrates life with warmth and generosity. Nowhere is this more the case than at Ballaghtobin. Catherine and Mickey are renowned for entertaining friends, colleagues and guests, at this impressive Georgian house on 450 acres of cereals, blackcurrants, Christmas trees and woodland. Everyone is treated with the same easy-going courtesy. Mickey farms in between driving at classic car rallys; he will show you his prized motors if you ask, while Catherine is the kind of person who puts you in a good mood. When I visited, an impromptu smoked salmon lunch was prepared and we had a grand time in the conservatory. It is a beautiful home with lots of charm and understated elegance — they started collecting the Herend china in the drawing room when they got married. A dining room with parkland views is the setting for meals that are second to none and gorgeous bedrooms are all different; the east-facing Barrack room is our favourite.

Rooms: 3: 1 twin/double, 1 family, 1 double, all with en suite bathroom.
Price: IR£35 p.p. Sing. supp IR£10 in high season.
Breakfast: Included.
Meals: Dinner or supper from IR£15, by arrangement.
Closed: Never.

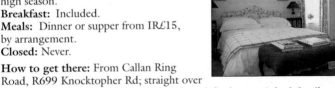

How to get there: From Callan Ring Road, R699 Knocktopher Rd; straight over x-roads at bridge, past Callan Golf Club on left, then straight 2.3 miles, bear left. 0.3 miles, left at Y-junct. Entrance 0.3 miles on left opposite lodge.

Entry no: 104   Map no: 7

Tuckmill

Danesfort Rd
Bennettsbridge
Co. Kilkenny

Tel: 056 27620

Des and Maureen Kennedy

Maureen is irrepressible, full of chat and concerned for her guests' welfare, while Des is more demure, but equally friendly. They own a modern house in a lovely area of Ireland. Culture and countryside is on your doorstep. Historic Kilkenny town is a couple of miles away, while the gorgeous River Nore valley is even closer. The rooms at Tuckmill are simple in design, not frilly, with good-sized showers and a big bath. The emphasis is on comfort. I slept like a log here after relaxing in front of a coal fire. The Kennedys work hard to ensure they only get satisfied customers. They will drop you off in Kilkenny for dinner if you want to leave your car and get a taxi back. Breakfast is next to the kitchen, a bustling, chatty affair, and the fry is delicious. Maureen and Des offer very good value in a friendly home. *Children by arrangement.*

Rooms: 3: 1 double with en suite shower;
1 double & single with en suite shower;
1 twin with en suite bath/shower.
Price: IR£20—IR£22 p.p. Sing. supp. by arrangement.
Breakfast: Included — full Irish.
Meals: Available locally.
Closed: Never.

How to get there: From Kilkenny, road signed Thomastown/New Ross. 5 miles on, enter Bennettsbridge. Right before the bridge, then immediately right again up hill. House 400m on left.

Map no: 8

Entry no: 105

Danville House

New Ross Rd
Kilkenny
Co. Kilkenny

Tel: 056 21512
Fax: 056 21512
E-mail: treecc@iol.ie
Web: www.sawdays.co.uk

Kitty Stallard

You would never know this old Georgian farmhouse was on the outskirts of historic Kilkenny. Tucked down a drive surrounded by ancient trees, it is a rural haven; many of the oaks were planted around the time the house was built in the 1765. At the back of the house is a lovely walled garden festooned with shrubs and climbers and the apple orchard is full of fragrant blossom in the spring. Cromwellian armour and a grandfather clock greet you through the arched front door and a pretty staircase leads up to a big landing with an unusual antique conversation seat. The four bedrooms are immaculate in pale colours, floral covers that are pretty rather than garish, firm beds and timber windows overlooking the paddock; the largest room has a half-tester, windows on both sides and lots of space. Kitty is a gentle, softly-spoken soul who is adamant the house keeps its country feel. The Stallard family has farmed the 100 acres of dairy cattle to the south and west of the house since 1905. Friendly, unpretentious and full of old-style charm, Danville is an ideal base for exploring the region.

Rooms: 4: 2 triples/twins, 1 twin, 1 double, all with en suite shower.
Price: IR£20 p.p. Sing. supp. IR£10.
Breakfast: Included — full Irish.
Meals: Available in Kilkenny.
Closed: November—mid-March.

How to get there: From Kilkenny, R700 towards New Ross. House 1 mile on right from city centre, just after big r'bout.

Entry no: 106

Map no: 8

Blanchville House

Dunbell
Maddoxtown
Co. Kilkenny

Tel: 056 27197
Fax: 056 27636
E-mail: info@blanchville.ie
Web: www.blanchville.ie

Monica and Tim Phelan

Monica would cringe if I said she was the perfect hostess, but it has to be said. This large Georgian farmhouse is the epitome of relaxed sophistication. It has absolutely no airs or graces as I discovered when Monica handed me a can of Guinness in the graceful drawing room, with gold pelmets, early 19th-century wallpaper and a portrait of the house's creator Sir James Kearney, giving his beatific approval. Monica cannot bear the thought that guests might feel neglected and yet she looks after you with such unfussy ease. Large bedrooms have half-testers and thick carpets but the luxury is in the detail — enamelled taps in one of the modern bathrooms warranted a photograph, while glorious pastoral views over Carlow and Kilkenny belong in an oil painting. Breakfast around a gigantic dining table beautifully laid with silver and white linen was a delight. A ruined clocktower without a clock stands outside, a legacy of the last owner. Blanchville is a place that lives long in the memory. *Three self-catering apartments available in converted coach houses, one with wheelchair access. Sleep 4-6, IR£250—IR£350 p.w.*

Rooms: 6: 4 doubles, 2 twins, all with en suite bath or shower.
Price: IR£32—IR£40 p.p. Sing. supp. IR£8.
Breakfast: Included — full Irish/buffet.
Meals: Dinner IR£25. Book by noon the same day.
Closed: November—February.

How to get there: From Kilkenny, N10 towards Carlow/Dublin for 2.5 miles, past Pike Inn, then right signed Blanchville House. Follow signs, turning left at Connolly's pub. House on left up drive with ruined clocktower on right.

Map no: 8

Entry no: 107

Swift's Heath

Jenkinstown   **Tel:** 056 67653
Co. Kilkenny   **Fax:** 056 67653

Brigitte Lennon

You drive through swaying cornfields to discover the cosmopolitan grandeur of
Swift's Heath that has attracted the rich and famous for the past 350 years; royalty,
artists, writers, they all came here. It is one of Ireland's Historic Houses and once
home to Jonathan Swift (1667-1745), author of *Gulliver's Travels*; it was built by his
uncle, Godwin, in 1651 and remained in the family until the Lennons took it over
in 1970. Today, Japanese scholars of Swift visit regularly — one bookcase proudly
displays their published work. Brigitte, a German interior designer, has put a
refreshingly clean, uncluttered stamp on the massive bedrooms and bathrooms,
which show off the ornate architectural features to perfection. You can sense the
history of the place just sitting quietly in the magnificent living room; the
conversations, the laughter, the intrigue, they seem to linger in the air. Brigitte is an
irrepressible talker interested in practically everything, from architecture to zen. The
more active can play grass court tennis, or walk in the 200 acres of park and
farmland, with cedar of Lebanon and weeping beech trees. A unique experience.
Children over 12 welcome.

Rooms: 3: 1 double, 1 twin, both with en
suite shower; 1 twin with en suite shower
and bath.
Price: IR£35 p.p. No sing. supp.
Breakfast: Included — full Irish.
Meals: Dinner IR£20. Not always available
so ask in advance.
Closed: Christmas & January.

How to get there: From Kilkenny, N77 for
3 miles. Left signed Swift's Heath. Entrance
3 miles on right through big gates.

Entry no: 108   Map no: 8

Kilrush House

Freshford
Co. Kilkenny

Tel: 056 32236
Fax: 056 32588
E-mail: stgeorge@gofree.indigo.ie

Richard and Sally St George

The St Georges have lived in Freshford since the mid-17th century, moving out of the now ruined castle next door into this elegant early 19th-century Irish Georgian house. Richard and Sally have modernised the house without sacrificing historic detail. Experts regularly come to admire the wallpaper in the dining room which has not changed since 1830 and many of the treasured family heirlooms, including the Irish furniture, were designed specially for the house. Large bedrooms have free-standing old-fashioned baths and long views over paddocks dotted with mature beech. Richard and Sally are passionate horsebreeders. Ignorant to such things, I was shown Wetherby's stallion book which breeders use to choose suitable mates for their thoroughbred mares. In theory, the right pairing could produce the next Desert Orchid. In practice, the right breeding is no guarantee of producing a horse with the will to win. Richard is naturally friendly and easy-going and an expert on Irish history and architecture. Sally's interests are horses, dogs and gardening but she still finds time to produce delicious evening meals. Roam in mature garden and 250 acres, play tennis and croquet, or visit the foals. All refined pleasures.

Rooms: 3: 2 twins, 1 double, all with en suite bathroom.
Price: IR£45 p.p. Sing. supp. by arrangement.
Breakfast: Included — full Irish.
Meals: Dinner IR£15—IR£25 p.p. for groups of 4 or more. Give 24 hours notice.
Closed: October—March.

How to get there: From Dublin, N7 to Port Laoise, then N8 Cork Rd to Johnstown. Left, signed Freshford. Entrance on right after 6.5 miles.

Map no: 7

Entry no: 109

Kilmokea Country Manor and Gardens

Great Island
Campile
Co. Wexford

Tel: 051 388109
Fax: 051 388776
E-mail: kilmokea@indigo.ie
Web: www.kilmokea.com

Mark and Emma Hewlett

Georgian Kilmokea is one of those rare places where it is hard to find a chink in the armour. Book ahead though, because rooms are few and precious. Mark and Emma could not be nicer. Every room in the house has been made over with flair, taste and humour. Colours throughout are mellow and warm, carpets are thick, showers are luxurious, bath towels big and beds wonderful. In the evening, food picked from their walled garden is enjoyed at one table, in dinner-party style. The house is on Great Island in the Barrow Estuary and is surrounded by seven acres of award-winning gardens; from the walled garden you go through a heavy wooden door into the magical woodland garden. They offer private trout fishing and horse riding nearby. Emma is an aromatherapist. Have a massage then indulge yourself further with cream tea in the Georgian conservatory. Perfect. *Two self-catering apartments, each sleeps 4, IR£210—IR£385 p.w.*

Rooms: 4: 1 twin with private shower; 2 doubles with en suite bath; 1 four-poster with en suite shower.
Price: IR£45—IR£80 p.p.
Breakfast: Included — full Irish.
Meals: Dinner IR£28.
Closed: 4 November—1 February.

How to get there: From Waterford to Passage East, then R733 north past Dunbrody Abbey. After 1.5 miles road swings sharp right — straight on signed Great Island. Left at T-junc. 1.25 miles to house. From Newross, R733 for Campile. Before village, right signed Kilmokea Gardens.

Glendine Country House

Arthurstown
Co. Wexford

Tel: 051 389258
Fax: 051 389677
E-mail: glendinehouse@eircom.net
Web: www.glendinehouse.com

Tom and Annie Crosbie

Glendine sits on a hill with views over the Barrow Estuary to the hills of Co. Waterford on the other side. Tom and Annie have put a huge amount of effort into renovating this 1830 house, adding comfort while retaining the old style. Large bedrooms are decorated in warm, bright colours with Victorian bedsteads and wooden floors. Relax in the big drawing room with family photographs dating back to when the Crosbie clan first moved here in 1948. Across the hallway is the dining room which doubles as a tearoom during the day serving home-cooked food. They have three young boys who are always on the look-out for new friends and children will love the dogs and ponies. Tom runs a busy farm with sheep, beef cattle and arable produce; their corn crop is used in a well-known beer. This is a lively household run by a relaxed and friendly couple who will thoroughly look after you. Just ask. Hearty breakfasts use organic produce where possible and provide the sustenance for a spectacular coastal walk to the Hook Peninsula, whence came Cromwell's expression 'By hook or by crook' after his forces were determined to land here or at Crookhaven further up the coast. *Two self-catering stone cottages, each sleeps 5, IR£300 p.w.*

Rooms: 5: 1 family with en suite
bathroom; 1 family, 1 double, 2 twins,
all with en suite shower.
Price: IR£25 p.p. Sing. supp. IR£10.
Breakfast: Included — full Irish.
Meals: Snacks from IR£4 in tearoom.
Open 11am-6pm. Dinner available locally.
Closed: Christmas.

How to get there: From Rosslare, N25
north for 5 miles, then left at first r'bout
and left at second r'bout onto R733 towards Wellington Bridge for 20 miles.
Entrance on right as road dips into Arthurstown.

Map no:

Entry no: 111

Dunbrody Country House

Arthurstown
Co. Wexford

Tel: 051 389600
Fax: 051 389601
E-mail: dunbrody@indigo.ie
Web: www.dunbrodyhouse.com

Kevin and Catherine Dundon

Anyone in Ireland interested in food talks about Kevin's cooking. And what a place to showcase his talent. This late Georgian mansion built by Lord Donegal in 1830 lies in 20 acres with sea frontage overlooking Waterford Harbour; a new wing completed in 1999 is an exact replica of the original Georgian wing knocked down in the 1950s. Kevin, a former head chef at the Shelburne Hotel in Dublin and 'double gold' winner at the culinary Olympics, moved here with his wife Catherine and set about converting it into a luxurious country house hotel. Strong colours, striped wallpaper and antique furniture suits the Regency period, while the large dining room mixes the traditional elegance of white tablecloths and wooden floors with bold rug designs and modern paintings. Bedrooms are all different and done to hotel standard. There is something playful and down to earth about Dunbrody. When I visited, they were recovering from a Christening party for their child. Kevin took me into the garden and proudly showed me a snug bar built in time for the celebrations. Meals are prepared with organic vegetables grown in the kitchen garden and meat and seafood are sourced locally. There is a Blue Flag beach nearby and clay pigeon shooting can be arranged.

Rooms: 20: 7 suites, 8 superior,
5 standard, all with en suite bathroom.
Price: IR£59—IR£120 p.p. Sing. supp.
IR£20.
Breakfast: Included — full menu.
Meals: Dinner, 4 courses, from IR£30.
Closed: Christmas & January.

How to get there: From Wexford, R733 to Duncannon and Arthurstown. Entrance sharp left before Arthurstown.

Entry no: 112

Map no: 8

Churchtown House

Tagoat
Rosslare
Co. Wexford

Tel: 053 32555
Fax: 053 32577
E-mail: churchtown.rosslare@indigo.ie
Web: www.churchtown-rosslare.com

Austin and Patricia Cody

The genuine warmth of a family home with all the comforts of an hotel — a perfect combination for many. Patricia and Austin have pulled off something special here. Pristine rooms decorated in bright colours have a cosy elegance that provide a welcome antidote to the most bitter winter's day, while tall windows and an atrium draw in the sunshine. Big bedrooms vary greatly; some have bay windows, some views over the countryside, others are suitable for wheelchair users. The windows of the hallway look onto an open courtyard where a Mexican brazier called a chiminea gives off a haze of heat in cooler evenings. The Codys are relaxed, generous hosts who pull each other's leg to amusing effect. Nothing is too much trouble for them; they will find somewhere for your bike, your trailer, even your boat — just ask when booking. Ideal for the Rosslare ferry and worth stopping off for a couple of days to walk along unspoilt beaches before continuing your journey.

Rooms: 12: 1 suite, 1 mini-suite, 5 doubles, 4 twins, 1 single, all with en suite bathroom.
Price: IR£45—IR£70 p.p. Sing. supp. IR£15.
Breakfast: Included — full Irish.
Meals: Dinner IR£27.50 including sherry. Packed lunch IR£5, on request.
Closed: Mid-November—March. Bird watcher groups welcome off season by arrangement.

How to get there: From Rosslare ferryport, N25 to Tagoat for 3.5 miles, then right on R736. House 0.5 miles on left.

Map no: 8

Entry no: 113

Ballinkeele House

Ballymurn
Enniscorthy
Co. Wexford

Tel: 053 38105
Fax: 053 38468
E-mail: info@ballinkeele.com
Web: www.ballinkeele.com

Margaret and John Maher

Every part of this grand 19th-century house has a sense of easy-going, lived-in grandeur. The columned portico entrance sets the tone. Ballinkeele was designed with space and light in mind. All the rooms are massive and adorned with Margaret's paintings mixed in with old family pictures. Bedrooms are named by colour and are exquisite; some have two windows on different walls overlooking the park and one has an extended balcony. But the jewel in the crown is the master bedroom with its superb four-poster. Outside, John supervises the corn and forestry on the surrounding farm. Inside, Margaret presides over mouth-watering meals. The result is a meeting of the elegant and the down-to-earth. A splendid place to relax and go for long walks around the ponds and lakes in 360 acres of grounds. It genuinely matters to this couple that you are completely at ease.

Rooms: 5: 1 twin/double with en suite bathroom; 3 doubles with en suite shower; 1 twin with en suite bath.
Price: IR£45—IR£60 p.p. Sing. supp. IR£12.
Breakfast: Included — full Irish.
Meals: Dinner IR£26. Wine list. Book by noon the same day.
Closed: November—February.

How to get there: From Rosslare ferryport, N25 to Wexford, then N11 to Oilgate. Right at traffic lights in village, signed to Ballinkeele, for 4 miles. Left in Ballymurn, first black gates on left.

Entry no: 114   Map no: 8

Salville House

Enniscorthy
Co. Wexford

Tel: 054 35252
Fax: 054 35252
E-mail: salvillehouse@eircom.net

Gordon and Jane Parker

Salville is one of those places where you could imagine spending the rest of your days in quiet contentment, working your way through the books you always meant to read but never got round to. The house sits on top of a hill with views across fields to the River Slaney. Sit back among the croquet hoops on the rambling front lawn and watch a warm summer's evening dissolve into a purple-orange sunset before a candlelit dinner that has won many plaudits, including the Irish Food Guide. Gordon is a maestro in the kitchen, using only organic produce from the garden or local producers. Jane, a practising doctor, likes to do front of house, chatting to guests and suggesting things to do. The house itself started life in the 17th century and was added to up to the late 19th century. There is a comfortable and cosy sitting room with deep armchairs and a log fire in winter. Bedrooms are homely; one pink, one blue and one with yellow stripey wallpaper, and beds have good mattresses and linen. After a leisurely breakfast, take a stroll down lovely country lanes or pick up a book where you left off. Above all, come to rest in this cosmopolitan retreat. *Self-catering apartment, sleeps 4, IR£220—IR£250 p.w.*

Rooms: 3: 1 double with en suite bathroom; 1 double with en suite shower; 1 double with private bathroom.
Price: IR£25—IR£30 p.p. Sing. supp. IR£5 (2001).
Breakfast: Included — full Irish.
Meals: Dinner from IR£22.50, B.Y.O wine.
Closed: Never.

How to get there: From Enniscorthy, N11 Wexford Rd past sign to hospital on left, then next left signed to house. Bear left up hill. Entrance 0.25 miles along windy road on left.

Map no: 8

Entry no: 115

Woodbrook House

Killanne
Enniscorthy
Co. Wexford

Tel: 054 55114
Fax: 054 55671
Web: www.sawdays.co.uk

Giles and Alexandra FitzHerbert

Woodbrook lies in a parkland setting worthy of an Old Master. You sweep down a long drive surrounded by mature woodland to a pillared entrance flanked by two marble lions. So far, so Anglo-Irish, but walk inside the hallway with its painted frieze and the mood changes. Rooms feel like they were designed with a hotter climate in mind. Giles and Alexandra are no strangers to the rest of the world. She is half-Italian and he capped a career in the diplomatic service as UK ambassador to Venezuela; they lived through two attempted military coups, one by the country's now elected president, Hugo Chavez. They travelled to Italy and India before starting the restoration work on this enigmatic 1770s Georgian house which has Ireland's only 'flying staircase' — it quivers as you walk on it. Alexandra has used paint techniques picked up in Rome to transform the interior with subtle washes and trompe-l'oeil. Painted furniture from Rajasthan and a Regency-striped claw-foot bath add distinctive style. Giles is a seasoned character, well travelled, well read with strong convictions and a wry humour, while Alexandra and their four young children lend youth and vitality to this memorable family home.

Rooms: 4: 2 doubles and 1 twin, all with en suite bathoom; 1 family room with private bathroom.
Price: IR£50 p.p. Sing. supp. IR£15.
Breakfast: Included — full menu.
Meals: Simple supper IR£20.
Closed: November—May. Events/groups off season by arrangement.

How to get there: From Enniscorthy, R702 to Kiltealy, through village towards Rathnure for 1.7 miles, then left down small lane with tall trees. Entrance 300m on left down drive.

Rathsallagh House

Dunlavin
Co. Wicklow

Tel: 045 403112
Fax: 045 403343
E-mail: info@rathsallagh.com
Web: www.rathsallagh.com

The O'Flynn Family

Somehow, despite the bustle, the 29 rooms, the 18-hole championship golf course, the heated indoor swimming pool, *somehow* this manages to feel like a home from home. Staff are friendly, open fires crackle in hearths between carved elephants, it even smells homely. Food at Rathsallagh is done to a T. Organic vegetables and fruit are plucked from the beautiful mature walled garden, home to a full-grown sequoia and the courtyard walls are full of herbs. The O'Flynns have recently added 12 huge rooms in a courtyard wing behind the main courtyard. The two are connected by an orangery with a spa room and sauna. Every room is a delight. Often wide and short with many windows, they either have a long-distance view over parkland, or the equally lovely courtyard shot for the more myopic. No two are the same; some have their own access to the garden, one its own sitting room, one a Tardis-shower which gives you a foot massage. All the O'Flynns have their own field of expertise which they exercise with easy-going friendliness.

Rooms: Inner Courtyard: 17: 6 twins, 11 doubles, all with en suite bathroom; Outer Courtyard: 12 twin/doubles, all with en suite spa bathroom.
Price: IR£55—IR£105 p.p. Sing. supp. IR£30—IR£55.
Breakfast: Included — full Irish.
Meals: Dinner from IR£36-IR£45.
Closed: Christmas (3 days) & 2 weeks of January.

How to get there: From Dublin, N81 south to Blessington. 6 miles on, right at Toughers petrol on R756 to Dunlavin. Through village towards Colbinstown for 2.5 miles. Hotel signed. Entrance on left.

Map no: 5   Entry no: 117

Barraderry House

Kiltegan
Co. Wicklow

Tel: 0508 73209
Fax: 0508 73209
E-mail: jo.hobson@oceanfree.net
Web: www.barraderrycountryhouse.com

Olive and John Hobson

Life at Barraderry hums along to a cheery tune amid a peaceful, bucolic setting in the shadow of Lugnaquilla, Ireland's second highest mountain. The television series *Ballykissangel* was filmed nearby and there are numerous opportunities to ride in the stunning countryside. The main house is early Georgian with Victorian additions and is approached along a drive that dips and curls through an avenue of trees — at the rear of the house is an amazing grafted beech tree. Olive decided to spruce up the farmhouse after the last of six daughters left home; she has done a wonderful job. The large hallway is spare of ornament and warm in colour with a lovely black and white tiled floor. It leads to a dining room with gleaming silverware where breakfast is served around a huge oval table. The drawing room has beautiful porcelain, a rosewood grand piano that's over 100 years old and a bay window that looks onto the garden. In the unfussy bedrooms there are pretty bedspreads, good prints on the walls and the odd fireplace. Olive is so friendly and easy-going, while John likes to sing to piano accompaniment when the mood is right.

Rooms: 4: 1 twin/double, 1 double,
1 twin, 1 single, all with en suite bathroom.
Price: IR£25 p.p. Sing. supp. IR£5.
Breakfast: Included — full menu.
Meals: Available locally.
Closed: Mid-December—mid-January.

How to get there: From Dublin, N81 Blessington to Baltinglass for 35 miles, then left on R747 Kiltegan Rd. Entrance on right just before village.

Derrybawn House

Glendalough
Co. Wicklow

Tel: 0404 45134
Fax: 0404 45109
E-mail: derrybawnhouse@hotmail.com

Donald and Lucy Vambeck

You approach Derrybawn House along the rollercoaster roads that wind through the forested Wicklow Mountains. Built in 1780 as part of a sporting estate, the house has a panoramic backdrop of wooded hills and is surrounded by paddocks, lawns, a lake and mature trees. There is a wonderful sense of peace here. You enter through a trellised porch covered in vines. On hot days, floor-to-ceiling windows downstairs are opened up to let in the view. The house is far larger than you imagine when you first arrive. The full tour seemed to go on and on past a billiards room and down a corridor to rooms with views over a courtyard. Bedrooms are all interesting, with pretty windows, mirrors and good showers; one has a Belmore-barrelled ceiling, another a jacuzzi bath, though the overall style is resolutely country cottage. Two grander rooms at the front have high ceilings, armchairs, a four-poster and a lovely view beyond the walled flower gardens.

Rooms: 6: 2 doubles, both en suite bathroom; 2 doubles and 2 twins, each with en suite shower.
Price: IR£27.50—IR£35 p.p. Sing. supp. IR£12.50.
Breakfast: Included — full Irish.
Meals: Dinner IR£20, for groups by arrangement.
Closed: Christmas.

How to get there: From Dublin, N11 to Kilmacanoge, then R755 to Laragh, following signs to Glendalough. Through village keeping on R755. Entrance 0.5 miles on right.

Map no: 5

Entry no: 119

Laragh Lodge
Laragh
Glendalough
Co. Wicklow

Tel: 0404 45302
Fax: 0404 45235
E-mail: laraghlodge@yahoo.com

Len and Lisa De La Haye

The story of Len and Lisa's purchase of Laragh Lodge illustrates why 'serendipity' was recently voted as one of the most popular words in the English language. They only found this converted stone schoolhouse because they stopped to buy an ice-cream for their two young sons. It was a sunny day and Lisa immediately fell in love with the setting overlooking Laragh village and the wooded valley behind. The sale was completed within days. Laragh Lodge used to be Mitchell's Restaurant and Guesthouse. Though they look one and the same from the outside, it is a different story inside. Lisa has turned it into a lodge in the true sense, replacing the modern restaurant furniture with antiques and Len's assorted collection of sea-related memorabilia accumulated from travels worldwide as an airline pilot. Bedrooms are also in an old-style and most have a village view. Len is from Jersey, Lisa is Irish and the family moved to Ireland after three years in Mauritius and 12 in the Middle East. Len has many exotic tales of derring-do, while Lisa is realising a long-held dream of running a B&B; themed dinner parties and 'murder weekends' are planned for the winter. Prehistoric Glendalough is a short walk.

Rooms: 5: 1 double, 2 twins, 2 family, all en suite shower;
Price: IR£25—IR£35 p.p. Sing. supp. IR£10. Weekend rates available.
Breakfast: Included — full menu.
Meals: Dinner IR£20. Book by noon the same day.
Closed: Never.

How to get there: From Dublin, N11 to Kilmacanoge, then R755 to Laragh, following signs to Glendalough. In village, turn right. House 50m on right.

Entry no: 120

Map no: 5

The Manor Cottages

Manor Kilbride
Blessington
Co. Wicklow

Tel: 01 4582105
Fax: 01 4582607

Margaret Cully

The Manor Cottages lie hidden from the outside world in the grounds of a wonderful 1820s Heritage House at the foot of the Wicklow Mountains. The drive here is one of the nicest in Ireland through thick woodland, rhododendron, bamboo and over river. The film *Widow's Peak*, starring Mia Farrow, was shot in the main house which has been lovingly restored by the present owners. Herds and Wood Cottages are at opposite ends of the pretty mid-18th-century courtyard. Anvil Lodge and River Lodge are dotted about the 40-acre estate with views over pastureland and the river. All have little gardens and open plan interiors that are tastefully done with exposed stonework, wooden beams, stone floors, four-posters and comfy sofas around an open fire. Kitchens are fully equipped with hob, microwave, dishwasher and washing machine. The local village shop is a five-minute walk away and good restaurants and pubs are nearby. Take long walks with mountain views around two lakes well stocked with trout. A tranquil base to explore Dublin and Wicklow. *Swimming can be arranged in owner's pool. French and Spanish spoken.*

Rooms: 4 cottages: 3 with 2 bedrooms and 2 bathrooms each (1 en suite), each sleeps 4; 1 with 1 bedroom and en suite bathroom, sleeps 2.
Price: IR£280—IR£500 p.w. depending on season.
Breakfast: Self-catering.
Meals: Available locally or bring a cookbook.
Closed: Never.

How to get there: From Dublin, N81 to Brittas, then left 2 miles after village on R759, signed Kilbride. Left at T-junc, signed Sallygap. Entrance 50m on right.

Map no: 5

Entry no: 121

Dublin

"May you live all the days of your life."
Jonathan Swift

Druid Lodge
Killiney Hill Rd
Killiney
Co. Dublin

Tel: 01 2851632
Fax: 01 2848504
Web: www.sawdays.co.uk

Ken and Cynthia McClenaghan

The Dalkey/Killiney area of County Dublin has been compared to the French Riviera with its corniche roads winding round blue bays and all those nice houses. Druid Lodge is one of the best of them. On a beautiful day there is not much that doesn't catch the eye, inside or out. This 1832 house and its tangled garden look straight out to sea and the views from the upstairs bedrooms and the first-floor with its balcony and creeper are mesmerising. There is an eclectic eye at work: the unusual, the arcane and the merely beautiful grab the attention from all sides — amazing overmantles in ebony with bevelled glass mirrors, Africana from Ken's long years as a sociologist there, figurines, leather masks and modern paintings for contrast. But this is not some museum to ponder in silence. Ken and Cynthia love to talk to guests and have gone to great lengths to create wonderful bedrooms. The largest first-floor rooms with the views are spectacular, though none disappoint. A really entertaining house.

Rooms: 4: 2 doubles, 2 doubles/twins, all with en suite shower.
Price: IR£35—IR£45 p.p. Sing. supp. IR£10.
Breakfast: Included — full Irish.
Meals: Available in Dalkey.
Closed: 24 December—28 December.

How to get there: Follow signs for Dun Laoghaire ferry. From ferry, follow signs for Killiney via Dalkey. Entrance to lodge between Druid's Chair pub and Killiney Avenue, opposite white stones.

Map No: 5

Entry no: 122

Simmonstown House

2 Sydenham Rd
Ballsbridge, Dublin 4
Co. Dublin

Tel: 01 6607260
Fax: 01 6607341
E-mail: info@simmonstownhouse.com
Web: www.simmonstownhouse.com

Finola and James Curry

Few places in Dublin can be more civilised than Simmonstown. James and Finola are great hosts and this is a charming unspoilt Victorian house in a quiet private road not far from good restaurants and the buzz of the city centre. Although we arrived late, we received a warm reception in every sense; fragrant lilies, original paintings hanging in the hall and Finola, who was friendly, welcoming and went out of her way to look after us. The elegant drawing room, with its marble chimney piece, gilded mirror and sumptuous fabrics in deep blues and purples, invites you to relax and unwind with a drink. A previous inspector was treated to some gospel singing, courtesy of other guests — we cannot guarantee this will happen during your stay, but it was typical of the friendly atmosphere here. Immaculate bedrooms have restrained decor, comfortable beds, crisp linen, luxurious bathrobes and gleaming bathrooms; some overlook a courtyard garden. Leave plenty of time for the gorgeous breakfast in the dining room which adjoins the drawing room. The food was so beautifully arranged, it seemed a shame to eat it — only we did because it would have been a shame to leave it.

Rooms: 4: 2 twins, 1 family,
1 single/double, all with en suite shower.
Price: IR£60—IR£70 p.p. Sing. supp.
IR£10.
Breakfast: Included — full Irish.
Meals: Available in Dublin.
Closed: Christmas & New Year.

How to get there: Central Dublin. Ask for directions when booking.

Waterloo House

8-10 Waterloo Rd
Ballsbridge, Dublin 4
Co. Dublin

Tel: 01 6601888
Fax: 01 6671955
E-mail: waterloohouse@eircom.ie
Web: www.waterloohouse.ie

Evelyn Corcoran

Waterloo is two large 1830s Georgian houses with twin doors like close-knit eyes that welcome you in. Evelyn's background is in hotels and elements of Waterloo are like a hotel but the welcome is sincere and friendly which is such a relief in a big city like Dublin. Helpful staff go out of their way to make sure guests are not treated as bednights. The houses have been knocked into one with high ceilings and big windows and are in a peaceful street close to the city centre. Everything here is clean, tidy and in perfect working order. Immaculate bedrooms have thick carpets, repro furniture and good-sized bathrooms. Reception doubles as a comfortable sitting area, or you can relax in the wicker-seated conservatory. Good breakfasts, in the plushly carpeted dining room set you up for a day of sight-seeing. *Parking for 8 cars in front of house.*

Rooms: 17: 5 twins & 12 doubles, 9 with en suite bathroom, 8 with en suite shower.
Price: IR£45 p.p. Sing. supp. IR£20.
Breakfast: Included — full Irish.
Meals: Available in Dublin.
Closed: Christmas week.

How to get there: From Merrion Row, near St Stephen's Green, to Baggott St that leads to Upper Baggott St. First right after bridge into Waterloo Road. House on left. 15 minutes walk from city centre.

Map No: 5

Entry no: 124

Number 31
31 Leeson Close
Dublin 2
Co. Dublin

Tel: 01 6765011
Fax: 01 6762929

Noel and Deidre Comer

Few places in Dublin compare to Number 31. This old coach house in a discreet mews near St Stephen's Green has loads of style and doesn't take itself too seriously. Noel's friendly professionalism keeps the atmosphere fun and upbeat — he knows the personal touch in an anonymous city makes all the difference. Stay in the coach house with its funky 1960s design, sunken black leather banquettes and modern art, or take a room in the more demure setting of a Georgian townhouse overlooking Fitzwilliam Place and reached by a connecting garden — you can come and go from either side. As someone once said, this place has a split personality to suit all tastes. The townhouse contains some huge rooms with original cornicing and plasterwork that Deirdre has transformed with a designer's eye. My favourite room was a cosy den in the coach house with a secluded patio. Attention to detail and a genuine enjoyment of what they do make the Comers wonderful hosts. *Children over 10 welcome. Secure parking.*

Rooms: 20 doubles & twins/triples,
17 with en suite bath, 3 with en suite shower.
Price: IR£55—IR£75 p.p.
Breakfast: Included — full Irish.
Meals: Available in Dublin.
Closed: Christmas week.

How to get there: From St. Stephen's Green, past Shelbourne Hotel, up Merrion Row, right along Pembroke St to end, then left into Leeson St. Leeson Close is first left. Entrance on right through arched wooden gate in high wall.

Entry no: 125

Map No: 5

Harvey's Guest House
11 Upper Gardiner Street
Dublin 1
Co. Dublin

Tel: 01 874 8384
Fax: 01 8745510
E-mail: harveysguesthse@iol.ie
Web: www.harveysguesthouse.com

Eilish Flood

Eilish is a special lady who runs this Georgian townhouse with true compassion and genuine warmth, unusual for a place right in the city. Comfortable, quirky rooms are on several floors that spread across two houses. Rooms on the ground floor at the rear are enclosed by a small backyard with an apple tree; upstairs rooms have the feel of a garret and rear rooms city rooftop views. French sleigh beds, generous bathrooms, lovely Victorian lights and her son's flair for DIY give them all character — there is a real family feel here and Eilish's older sister helps out with breakfasts (the Flood family were famous wine merchants in the 1880s). Harvey's is in an unfashionable part of Dublin, north of the River Liffey, but it is from here that James Joyce drew much of his inspiration for *Ulysses*. The Georgian architecture in this area is inspiring and nearby Mountjoy Square is considered one of the finest examples of its type. Not much further is the Writer's Museum, an art gallery and two theatres, while the river is a 15-minute walk along O'Connell Street. This is a good cure for the spent and saturated.

Rooms: 15: 6 doubles, 4 family, 3 twins, 2 singles, all with en suite bathroom.
Price: IR£25—IR£45 p.p. Sing. supp. IR£10.
Breakfast: Included — full menu.
Meals: Available in Dublin.
Closed: Never.

How to get there: From O'Connell St, right in Sean McDermott St, then second left into Gardiner St past Mountjoy Sq. House signed on left.

Aberdeen Lodge

53-55 Park Avenue
Ballsbridge, Dublin 4
Co. Dublin

Tel: 01 2838155
Fax: 01 2837877
E-mail: aberdeen@iol.ie
Web: www.halpinsprivatehotels.com

Pat Halpin

Pat fought hard to set up a small hotel amid the Regency mansions and embassies of leafy Ballsbridge. He won over local residents by promising to protect their peace and quiet. Today, he fulfils the same promise to guests. Aberdeen Lodge is a refuge from the hullabaloo of Dublin city yet the metro is close enough to catapult you back into the thick of things within minutes. Pat is a friendly professional with a quiet deferential manner. Nothing is too much trouble. When I asked for some information on obscure ferry crossings on the far side of Ireland, he must have made a dozen calls. This modest Victorian villa has been cleverly converted into a variety of contemporary rooms with all mod cons. Candy-striped curtains remind you of the seaside — Dublin's seafront is only 200 yards away — and Biedermeier-style furniture adds a touch of luxury. Rooms at the rear look onto a cricket pitch, an unusual sight in a country devoted to Gaelic football. Everything seems to run effortlessly, including room service that delivered a hearty snack at the shortest notice. Breakfast to piped classical music was revitalising. Ideal for those wanting the best of both worlds in this fair city.

Rooms: 17: 2 small suites, 2 family, 2 triples, 11 doubles/twins, all with en suite bathroom.
Price: IR£45—IR£55 p.p. Suites IR£65—IR£75 p.p. Sing. supp. IR£30.
Breakfast: Included — full menu.
Meals: Room service snacks from IR£2.50.
Closed: Never.

How to get there: From Merrion Square, Northumberland Rd to Merrion Road, then left into Ailesbury Rd, signed to Sydney Parade Dart Station, then first left into Park Avenue. House 500m on left.

Ashbrook House

River Road, Ashtown
Castleknock, Dublin 15
Co. Dublin

Tel: 01 8385660
Fax: 01 8385660
Web: www.sawdays.co.uk

Stan and Eve Mitchell

You would never guess you were in Dublin — I visited Ashbrook on a beautiful sunny day and felt I was back in the country. Fragrant roses climb the curved front façade of this 200-year-old Georgian manor with its white balustraded first-floor balcony. Old, white, shuttered windows, bay window seats with original glass and French doors look onto an immaculate lawn and grass tennis court, surrounded by trees. The canal passes by at the end of the garden, though not visibly, and Phoenix Park is close, too. The bedroom in the curved section was my favourite with its rounded door and windows and narrow balcony. All the rooms are pretty, done in pale pinks and creams and all are very different. There are good views all round the house. Eve runs the B&B side of things and does so with natural friendliness.

Rooms: 4 doubles/twins, all with en suite shower. Extra bathroom available.
Price: IR£30—IR£35 p.p. Sing. supp. IR£10.
Breakfast: Included — full Irish.
Meals: Available in Dublin.
Closed: Christmas & New Year.

How to get there: From Dublin airport, M50 south to N3 turn-off signed Blanchardstown. Left at first r'bout, over second r'bout, then left at Halfway House pub. Over rail crossing, first left, second entrance on left.

Map No: 5

Entry no: 128

Belcamp Hutchinson

Malahide Rd
Balgriffin, Dublin 17
Co. Dublin

Tel: 01 8460843
Fax: 01 8485703
E-mail: belcamphutchinson@eircom.net

Doreen Gleeson and Karl Waldburg

Dublin has been extending its girth right up to Belcamp Hutchinson's gravel front and lawns since 1786 when Francis Hely-Hutchinson originally built it, but it is probably still quicker to reach the city centre today than it was then — it takes about 20 minutes by car to reach St Stephen's Green. The house lies off a busy road that leads to the lovely village of Malahide but, once inside Belcamp's high walls surrounded by four acres of garden full of birds and flowers, you instantly forget the traffic. The Gleesons are renovating the old walled garden, growing a tunnel of roses and a hedge-maze. Good-natured old dogs will usher you into this beautiful Georgian home which feels like a small country house hotel. Doreen is tireless in her efforts to make sure guests are well looked after, collecting and dropping them off from the airport and getting up at all hours to make sure they catch their early flight home. Bedrooms are immaculately tidy with wooden floors, big comfortable zip-and-link beds, strong colours and modern furnishings. Escape the city to peace and quiet. *Dublin Airport is 10 minutes by car.*

Rooms: 8: 5 doubles, 3 doubles/twins, all with en suite bathroom.
Price: IR£44 p.p. No sing. supp.
Breakfast: Included — full Irish.
Meals: Available in Dublin.
Closed: Christmas & New Year.

How to get there: From Dublin, Malahide Road out of centre for about 4 miles. House signed on left. Entrance second left.

Redbankhouse and Restaurant

6 & 7 Church St, Skerries
Fingal
Co. Dublin

Tel: 01 8491005
Fax: 01 8491598
E-mail: redbank@eircom.net
Web: www.redbank.ie

Terry and Margaret McCoy

Terry epitomises all that is good about Ireland, a true original, dedicated to his own style. I am indebted to him because he hauled me out of a hole dug by a car hire firm which left me stranded at Dublin airport. Thanks to his contacts and resolute good humour, I was on the road by the morning. This refusal to be defeated helps explain his track record as an award-winning seafood chef, a former president of the Irish Restaurants Association and even a well-known face on Ireland's TV cooking show, *Pot Luck*. In his spare time, he sails dinghies and champions the cause of Skerries fishing village. The restaurant is the mainstay of this old bank house. Terry sources his ingredients locally — fresh fish from Skerries harbour, Dublin Bay prawns and more unusually, razorfish, whose long empty shells you see on beaches. Take your time over the menu with an apéritif and look out for the wine cellar in the old safe with its original vault door. Guests stay either in the old bank house next to the restaurant or in a nearby lodge. Rooms are hotel standard with all mod cons. Ideal to see Dublin by train, or to eat one last good meal before leaving Ireland. *Dublin Airport 20 minutes by car.*

Rooms: 12: Bank house: 6 doubles & 1 twin, 3 with en suite shower, 4 with en suite bath. Lodge: 3 doubles, 2 twins, all with en suite shower; 1 extra bedroom.
Price: IR£27—IR£37 p.p. Sing. supp. IR£10.
Breakfast: Included — full Irish.
Meals: Dinner in the restaurant IR£28—IR£30, start at 7pm, set menus. Sunday lunch IR£17.75, à la carte.
Closed: Christmas Eve, Christmas Day & Boxing Day.

How to get there: From Dublin, N1 to Blake's Cross, right signed Skerries & follow for 10 km under bridge, first left, continue down. Church St on the right opposite Londis shop.

Map No: 5

Entry no: 130

Munster

*"How beautiful it is to do nothing,
and then rest afterwards."*
Spanish proverb

Old Parochial House

Cooraclare
Kilrush
Co. Clare

Tel: 065 9059059
Fax: 065 9059059
E-mail: oldparochialhouse@eircom.net
Web: www.oldparochialhouse.com

Alyson and Sean O'Neill

Alyson and Sean bought this 1872 ecclesiastical house in 1986 and have done literally everything themselves — the plumbing, the carpentry, the masonry, wiring, painting, curtain-making; you name it, they have turned their hand to it. The house is painted in rich, deep colours; grey/blue downstairs, blue, burgundy and green upstairs. Big bedrooms have post beds, wooden floors and views. The place has a busy, family feel and a sense of being among friends, however short your stay. Families can wander off to meet the quiet riding pony, the goats and the free range hens in the front field. For those wanting more independence, stables have been converted into peaceful self-catering apartments with stone floors, wood beams, open plan living rooms with turf fires and more edible views over rolling countryside. This is a great place to unwind. Start the day with freshly-squeezed orange juice and bacon rashers voted the best around by the whole family at the start of each season. Explore prehistoric ringforts, relax on a nearby beach, or simply sit and contemplate the bog wood collection. Come nightfall nearby pubs serve good seafood and Irish music most nights.

Rooms: 4: 2 doubles, 1 double/twin, all with en suite shower; 1 double/twin with private shower.
Price: IR£20—IR£30 p.p. Sing. supp. IR£10.
Breakfast: Included — full Irish.
Meals: Light meals available. Village pub 5 mins walk. More within easy reach by car.
Closed: November—March.

How to get there: From Enis, N68 for 18 miles, then right to Cooraclare, following signs. In village, turn right at petrol station onto R483. House third on left.

Map no: 3

Entry no: 131

Berry Lodge
Annagh
Milltown Malbay
Co. Clare

Tel: 065 7087022
Fax: 065 7087011
E-mail: rita.meade@esatclear.ie
Web: www.sawdays.co.uk

Rita Meade

As I drove towards Berry Lodge in the teeth of a gale that threatened to overturn the car, I began to dream about fireplaces, hot food and friendly faces. This cosy cocoon-by-the-sea fitted the bill exactly. Rita is a warm, cheerful character and the voice of seasoning in County Clare, presenting a popular cooking show on local radio. You get to try what she tantalises her listeners with; salmon and crab roulade that looked almost too good to eat, home-made mango sorbet, a monkfish main course, a groaning pudding menu; excellence was piled on excellence. Afterwards, haul yourself upstairs to pretty bedrooms with spacious window-seats, firm orthopaedic beds, warm colours, patchwork quilts, pretty tied back curtains, wooden floors, armchairs, original fireplaces and if the weather is feeling generous, views of the sea. Rita wants guests to like it here. Breakfast completely absorbed the taste buds and practically warranted the bill on its own. As I left, local schoolkids were arriving for a cookery lesson — County Clare's answer to Ballymaloe is very much in demand.

Rooms: 5: 2 doubles, 3 triples, all with en suite shower.
Price: IR£22—IR£25 p.p. Sing. supp. IR£10.
Breakfast: Included — full Irish.
Meals: Restaurant dinners, 4 courses, IR£24, 7-10 pm, book 24 hours in advance.
Closed: 2 January—14 February.

How to get there: From Ennis, N85 to Inagh. Left in Inagh onto R460 signed Miltown Malbay. In village take N67 Killimer car ferry road, past Bellbridge Hotel, over the bridge, then second left. House first on right.

Entry no: 132   Map no: 3

Drumcreehy House

Ballyvaughan
Co. Clare

Tel: 065 7077377
Fax: 065 7077379
E-mail: b&b@drumcreehyhouse.com
Web: www.drumcreehyhouse.com

Bernadette and Armin Moloney-Grefkes

Nothing was going to stop Bernadette and Armin realising their dream of running a B&B in Ireland. They were working in Germany — in tourism and running a bistro, respectively — when they decided to take the plunge and look for somewhere to live on the north Clare coast. Bernadette used to come to this area, overlooking Galway Bay and the beautiful, alien wilderness of The Burren, when she was a child and Armin fell for its charms after they got married. Their intention had been to find an old house, but when nothing came up they built a new one in an old style. Drumcreehy is a triumph over complacent modern house-building. The lemon-coloured façade and white gabled dormer windows blend well into the surroundings and newly-planted whitethorn and fuchsia hedges will provide a colourful border. Inside, wooden floors, old walnut furniture and an open fire create a lovely atmosphere, while separate breakfast and dining rooms cleverly draw in the sun rays at the right times of the day. Bedrooms named after local wild flowers are spic and span with a mixture of old and new pine furniture and the buffet-style breakfast was exceptional. Great value. *Children over five welcome.*

Rooms: 10: 5 twins/doubles, 5 doubles, all with en suite shower.
Price: IR£25—IR£30.90 p.p. Sing. supp. IR£12.
Breakfast: Included — full menu.
Meals: Dinner IR£17. Book by noon the same day.
Closed: November—February. Off season by arrangement.

How to get there: From Ennis, R476 to Corofin. Through village, then right on R480 to Ballyvaughan. Right in village at Hylands Hotel. House 1 mile on right past blue cottage.

Map no: 3

Entry no: 133

Fergus View
Kilnaboy
Corofin
Co. Clare

Tel: 065 6837606
Fax: 065 6837192
E-mail: deckell@indigo.ie
Web: www.sawdays.co.uk

Mary and Declan Kelleher

This lovely family home lies close to The Burren, a unique lunar landscape of weathered limestone, prehistoric dolmens and rare flowers. Just a short walk in this beautiful wilderness is said to calm the most troubled mind. Declan, a college principal, is well read on the subject and will provide lots of useful information. But first I suggest you sample Mary's cooking; a combination of freshly baked soda bread, Irish cheese and home-made mint jelly was as simple as it was exquisite. Everything is done well here. The Kellehers work hard at making guests feel welcome in this former teacher's residence built to attract teachers to rural areas in the 1900s. A devotion to the Irish language and music is also evident, with original readers on phonetics displayed in the living room. The bedrooms are compact but comfortable with orthopaedic beds and snug, wooden windows to keep out the cold. The garden stretches down to the River Fergus which is hidden by a welter of colourful plants in the summer, while the ruins of an Elizabethan fortress and medieval churchyard beyond are worth exploring. Genuine Irish hospitality. *Self-catering cottage next door, sleeps 5, not suitable for children, IR£290—IR£465 .*

Rooms: 6: 1 large family, 3 doubles,
1 double/twin, all with en suite shower;
1 double, sharing bathroom.
Price: IR£24 p.p. Sing. supp. IR£8—
IR£12.
Breakfast: Included — full menu.
Meals: Dinner, 3 courses, IR£17.
Wine from IR£12—IR£15.
Closed: Mid-October—March.

How to get there: From Shannon, N18
through Ennis to r'bout signed Ennistymon. 2 miles on, right to Corofin. Follow R476 to Corofin, on to Kilnaboy. House on left after ruined church.

Entry no: 134   Map No 3

Clifden House

Corofin
Co. Clare

Tel: 065 6837692
Fax: 065 6837692
E-mail: clifdenhousecountyclare@eircom.net
Web: www.clifdenhousecountyclare.com

Jim and Bernadette Robson

The lakeside grounds at Clifden House are a romantic adventure for adults and a paradise for children; overgrown outbuildings, a treehouse, pathways, meadow, lakeshore — let serendipity be your guide. Jim and Bernadette have been painstakingly restoring this wonderful 1750s house since 1975. And as Jim says, it is quite clear what owns whom after that long. This is a labour of love and they make no apology for the property's more ramshackle features such as the mottled façade or the cracked mirrors in antique frames. It is all part of the experience. But what they have finished is lovely. Bedrooms have high ceilings and two have great views over Lake Inchiquin. The lake runs up to a meadow at the back of the house, yet it is hard to believe it even exists from the front. Beyond the lake rise the limestone hills of the Burren, their slopes dotted with the odd cottage. The garden is a jungle of ferns and trees and there is a river which runs through a disused mill site; a wander through Clifden's 15 acres is a romantic adventure. Come for interesting conversation, great food and the chance to do what you feel like.

Rooms: 4: 3 doubles, all with en suite bathroom; 1 twin with en suite shower.
Price: IR£35—IR£38 p.p. No sing. supp.
Breakfast: Included — full Irish.
Meals: Dinner IR£25. Book by noon the same day.
Closed: November—mid-March except for groups of 6 to 8.

How to get there: From Ennis, N85 Ennistymon Rd for 2 miles, then right on R476 to Corofin. Through village to shrine, turn left, then second right. House signed up drive.

Map no: 3   Entry no: 135

Riverrun Cottages

Riverrun House
Terryglass
Co. Tipperary

Tel: 067 22125
Fax: 067 22187
E-mail: riverrun@iol.ie
Web: www.riverrun.ie

Lucy and Tom Sanders

Tom and Lucy really have put down roots in the tiny, lake village of Terryglass. They started by turning a derelict church into a shop, a home and a pottery studio for Tom to work in. Then they built Riverrun just by the old stone bridge in 1992 with salvaged slates and local materials. It is a sensitive design inside and out that doesn't look or feel out of place with its surroundings. They started doing B&B but changed over to self-catering in 1999. Two apartments are in the main house and three cottages are in a terrace next door with pretty gabled doorways and rounded corners to soften the edges. Rooms are bright, simply painted rooms with coir matting and woodburning stoves; all look onto the lovingly tended garden reached through stable doors at the rear. Fully equipped kitchens have all you need. This quiet village has resident ducks cared for by a local man and two pubs that serve good food and good ale. At either you may well find yourself settling in for a long session so don't be alarmed if the clock ticks past closing time and the Gardaí show up. Just in case village life proves too hectic, you can always play a game of tennis, go for a bike ride or escape onto the lake in a 19ft fishing boat.

Rooms: 5 cottages, all with 2 bedrooms and 2 bathrooms, each sleeps 4.
Price: IR£205—IR£395 p.w. depending on season.
Breakfast: You cook, you choose.
Meals: Available locally or bring a cookbook.
Closed: Never.

How to get there: From Nenagh, N52 for 12 miles to Borrisokane. Left in village signed Ballinderry 5 miles. Right at x-roads with village stores, signed Terryglass 2 miles. Cottages in village centre near bridge.

Kylenoe House

Balinderry
Nenagh
Co. Tipperary

Tel: 067 22015
Fax: 067 22275

Virginia Moeran

Virginia puts you at such ease that when I visited on a hot August day, I completely forgot I was in a hurry. Out came a cheeseboard and a bottle of wine and we sat in the living room, nattering about horses, the merits of going to university and whatever else came to mind. It was the way you imagine spending a lazy Sunday afternoon without ever managing to. Kylenoe is a cosy, purpose-built home of a family that is "seriously into horses", you, too, can take one out with, or without, tuition. Virginia is a professional horse-breeder with a daughter at university and a teenage son living at home; you immediately feel part of the family. The bedrooms, when I finally got round to seeing them, were comfortable. The house has its own spring, too. The house is in a beautiful spot and the Moerans own a pier on nearby Lough Derg where you can swim or take out a boat; nearby is Terryglass, a pretty village with a harbour and craft shop. Virginia's other great strength is cooking and I knew that she had received many accolades. That she never mentioned it while I was there probably tells you more about her than we could.

Rooms: 3: 2 doubles, both with en suite bathroom; 1 double with private bathroom.
Price: IR£30—IR£35 p.p. Sing. supp. IR£5—IR£10.
Breakfast: Included — full Irish.
Meals: Dinner, 4 courses, IR£25.
Closed: Christmas.

How to get there: From Nenagh, N52 Borrisokane Rd for about 2 miles, then left on R493 to Ballinderry. Through village, then left at x-roads by village stores. Entrance on right after about 1.5 miles. House up drive.

Map no: 4

Entry no: 137

Annagh Lodge Country House

Coolbawn
Nenagh
Co. Tipperary

Tel: 067 24225
Fax: 067 24225
E-mail: annaghlg@hotmail.com
Web: www.annaghlodge.com

Rachel and Andrew Sterling

Andrew's parents courted at Shannon airport because there wasn't anywhere better to eat. Food since then has come a long way. Rachel's mother was part of the foodie revolution, making mustard that now sells worldwide, while Rachel has worked with Prue Leith. Dinner will never disappoint here as fresh local produce is used with cosmopolitan flair. I could go on, but Annagh is much more besides. A Georgian shooting lodge, it lies on 150 acres of lake, pasture and woodland near the shores of Lough Derg. You enter this warm, family home by the side of the old main entrance which was blocked off, according to tradition, after it was used to carry out a previous owner who died. Bedrooms are comfortable and include a four-poster, while the grounds are superb with horse-riding for children and nature trails. Plans are underway for a rare breeds farm and an obstacle course. The Sterlings have a young family and want visiting families to feel at home here, too. This is a lively, sociable house with a great sense of fun. *Self-catering in Victorian gate lodge, sleeps 2-4, IR£180—IR£250 p.w..*

Rooms: 5: 2 doubles, 1 family, all with en suite shower; 1 family with private bathroom; 1 twin sharing bathroom.
Price: IR£24 p.p. Sing. occ. IR£36.
Breakfast: Included — full menu.
Meals: Dinner, 3 courses, IR£23.
Closed: Never.

How to get there: From Nenagh, N52 towards Borrisokane for 1 mile, then left on R493 Lough Derg Drive, signed to house, for 8 miles. Entrance on left.

Ashley Park House

Nenagh
Co. Tipperary

Tel: 067 38223
Fax: 067 38013
E-mail: margaret@ashleypark.com
Web: www.ashleypark.com

The Mounsey Family

There is a tangible feel of the past at Ashley Park with its near-museum quality and its blissful detachment from the hustle and bustle. The peaty sweet smell of turf fires burned over many winters suffuses quiet rooms of dark, polished wooden floors and deeply carved furniture from the 1600s. The conservatory room at one end of this 1770 house is in a lighter style with exquisite Chinese art on the walls. Bathrooms are elegantly Victorian with chequered floors and the original metal and enamel intact. Bedrooms are big, the beds deeply carved. Take tea on the colonial veranda while you ponder the ruins of the island castle on their lake or stroll through the partially-restored walled garden with its new gazebo overlooking the orchard. Margaret's father Sean is an ever present force, feeding the wild ducks at first light. When I visited, this active 78-year-old was enjoying the pleasure of driving a brand new car. Children will love the secure cobbled, farmyard with its peacocks, guinea fowl, duck, hens and dovecote. You can fish on the lake or walk in the surrounding nature reserve where ancient woodland is home to the red squirrel.

Rooms: 6: 1 family, 3 doubles, all with en suite bathroom; 2 twins sharing bathroom.
Price: IR£25—IR£30 p.p. Sing. supp. IR£5.
Breakfast: Included — full Irish.
Meals: Dinner from IR£23.
Closed: Never.

How to get there: From Nenagh, N52 towards Borrisokane for 3.5 miles. Entrance on left after big lake.

Ballycormac House

Aglish
Borrisokane
Co. Tipperary

Tel: 067 21129
Fax: 067 21200
E-mail: ballyc@indigo.ie

John and Cherylynn Lang

"After six years of visiting Ireland with increasing frequency, and inevitably going home with yet another horse, we decided it would be cheaper to live here." Everything about the Langs and this quaint converted dairy house say they did the right thing. The building is a warren of tiny passages, low doorways and narrow staircases — everybody feels tall here. Enchanting cottage-style bedrooms have big, solid beds and bathrooms screened off with saloon doors. You will be warm, comfortable and well fed, as one enthusiastic guest assured me several times, describing it as the "best place to stay on earth". Cherylynn makes full use of home-grown organic fruit and vegetables, performing culinary backflips, twists and triple somersaults in their big, modern kitchen, while John provides liquid refreshment with copious enthusiasm. Meals are served round a big table in a snug dining room that feels part Gothic, part baronial. They are an effusive couple and well suited to the Irish *cráic* as well as the Irish love of horses. John doesn't take no for an answer, cajoling even the most reluctant guests onto one of their 21 horses, including a previous editor who found to his amazement that he quite enjoyed it.

Rooms: 5: 1 family, 2 doubles, 1 twin/double, 1 twin, all with en suite bathroom; 1 single with private bathroom.
Price: IR£25—IR£35 p.p. No sing. supp.
Breakfast: Included — full Irish.
Meals: Dinner, 4 courses, £22. Packed lunch for horse-riders by arrangement.
Closed: Never.

How to get there: From Nenagh, N52 towards Portumna, then right signed to house 0.25 miles after Borrisokane, down long straight road. Left at T-junc, then right in Aglish, signed to house.

Map no: 4

Inch House

Thurles
Co. Tipperary

Tel: 0504 51348/51261
Fax: 0504 51754
E-mail: inchhse@iol.ie
Web: www.tipp.ie/inch-house.htm

The Egan Family

Inch House emerges stately from behind its stand of beeches, a promise of comfort in an arable plain. The Egans moved here in 1985 and have tirelessly renovated this elegant Georgian house to create a spacious temple of ease and good taste — country living in the grand style. Most recently restored is the chapel where you may find a family relation saying mass. The Egans work well as a couple, Nora being the neat and practical nurse and John the farmer bursting with grand plans. The rest of the family lend tireless support. It is a job well done from the fine relief of the serpent ceiling-roses to the 44-foot pitch pine floorboards in the William Morris-papered blue, white and gilt drawing room. Ascend the wide, bifurcated, oak staircase and past the rich stained glass of the Ryan family with its motto, "Death rather than Dishonour". Mysteriously, the Ryans survived where fellow Catholics were dispossessed by Cromwell's penal law. Today, this is a place happily free of intrigue where you can recline on the finest linen in a Prince Albert bed or soak in a wood-panelled bathroom before an exquisite breakfast or dinner served on silver in the public restaurant.

Rooms: 5: 3 doubles, 2 twins, 4 with en suite bathroom; 1 double with en suite shower.
Price: IR£35 p.p. Sing. supp. IR£5.
Breakfast: Included — full Irish.
Meals: Dinner IR£27. Restaurant open 7pm-9.30pm, Tuesday to Saturday.
Closed: Christmas.

How to get there: From Dublin, N7 to Port Laoise. N8 Cork Rd & N75 to Thurles, through town square, then R498 Nenagh Rd for 4 miles. Stone entrance just past "The Ragg" x-roads.

Map no: 7

Entry no: 141

Mobarnane House

Fethard
Co. Tipperary

Tel: 052 31962
Fax: 052 31962
E-mail: info@mobarnanehouse.com
Web: www.mobarnanehouse.com

Richard and Sandra Craik-White

Lovers of Jane Austen would do well to pack a copy of *Emma* when they visit Mobarnane. It may be rural Tipperary, but the setting feels rural English — you can almost imagine Miss Woodhouse walking beside Mr Knightly around the lake or through the wild meadows that surround this historic house. The rear was originally a farmhouse, built in 1740 on the site of an old tower house, then a Georgian half with Doric columns and a classic fanlight was added on the front in 1820, two years after Austen's death. Inside, Richard and Sandra have created a graceful place to stay that befits the period. The elegant drawing room looks over fields to mature woodland, bedrooms are large and immaculately finished, with wooden shutters, deep carpets and original watercolours by Sandra's great-grandfather, and the formal dining room is decorated with beautiful friezes. Richard is a retired deputy public school head, who grew up nearby before moving to England to teach geology, and Sandra is a former nurse. Richard is passionate about cooking, something he says he inherited from his mother, while Sandra, who also grew up nearby, is the friendly, smiling welcome on arrival. You can't help but warm to this lovely house.

Rooms: 4: 2 twins, 2 doubles, all with en suite bathroom.
Price: IR£55—IR£65 p.p. Sing. supp. IR£10. 20% discount for 3 nights or more. House for rent to groups of 6-8.
Breakfast: Included — full menu.
Meals: Dinner IR£27.50. Supper by arrangement.
Closed: Never.

How to get there: From Cashel, Clonmel Rd for 0.5 miles, then left at graveyard onto R692, signed Fethard. After 7.5 miles, left signed Ballinure and Thurles. Entrance 1.5 miles on left.

Dualla House

Cashel
Co. Tipperary

Tel: 062 61487
Fax: 062 61487
E-mail: duallahse@eircom.net
Web: www.tipp.ie/dualla-house.htm

Mairéad Power

"Go placidly amid the noise and haste and remember what peace there may be in silence." So begins the poem, *Desiderata*, which hangs on the wall of this early 19th-century Georgian farmhouse. Mairéad learnt it off by heart because "it makes you think about the things that matter". The farm is an ordered lesson in sheep husbandry visited by other farmers. Pens with different breeds, including Cheviot and Suffolk, are laid out logically for lambing and shearing and are instructive fun for children. Mairéad started running this excellent B&B after her four children had grown up. One son still helps run the farm with husband Martin. It is an easy, clean and safe place to walk around and there is plenty to see. Well-proportioned rooms are furnished in a traditional farmhouse style, with some antiques, original polished floorboards in the breakfast room, fresh flowers and paintings brought back from Korea by her sister, who is a nun. Big, comfortable bedrooms have orthopaedic mattresses, clean, modern bathrooms and views over fields of sheep. Ideal for those who want to see the Rock of Cashel and stay in the countryside.

Rooms: 4: 2 family, 1 twin, 1 double, all with en suite bathroom.
Price: IR£20—IR£25 p.p. Sing. supp. IR£5—IR£10.
Breakfast: Included — full Irish.
Meals: Available in Cashel.
Closed: December—February.

How to get there: In Cashel, turn right at top of main street past church on left, then left signed Dualla for 3 miles. Entrance on left as road dips.

Map no: 7

Entry no: **143**

Ballyowen House
Dualla
Cashel
Co. Tipperary

Tel: 062 61265
E-mail: info@ballyowenhouse.com
Web: www.ballyowenhouse.com

The McCan Family

The accumulation of six generations of the McCan family fill the rooms at Ballyowen like layers of a crumbly cake. Historic memorabilia, paintings and bits and bobs collected since the family first arrived in 1864 are scattered about in a way that is refreshingly free of affectation. You are very much in a family home despite the monumental Georgian grandeur. The house was built in 1750 by the Pennefather family, Cromwellian settlers whose motto, 'Live and let live', is inscribed on the front of the building. The Venetian windows are similar to Cashel Palace, while decorative plasterwork in the drawing room is comparable to Glin Castle. The staircase climbs three floors to a domed skylight, while bedrooms of varying styles have beautiful parkland views. The B&B is run by Colm McCan and his wife Aoife, pronounced 'Eefeh', a young enthusiastic couple who are slowly introducing their own style to the house. Colm has an encyclopedic knowledge of family portraits hanging in the dining room while Aoife has a natural talent for cooking, using organic food produced on the 300-acre estate. Walk round a lake or through an old oak wood to the top of a small hill with beautiful views. A fabulous setting.

Rooms: 3: 1 double, 1 family, both with en suite bathroom; 1 twin with en suite shower.
Price: IR£27—IR£40 p.p. Sing. supp. IR£7.
Breakfast: Included — full menu.
Meals: Dinner from IR£15.
Closed: December—January.

How to get there: From Cashel, N8 north to Dublin for 4 miles, then right, signed Dualla. Entrance 1 mile on right.

Lismacue House

Bansha
Co. Tipperary

Tel: 062 54106
Fax: 062 54126
E-mail: lismac@indigo.ie
Web: www.lismacue.com

Katherine and Jim Nicholson

Horses figure prominently at Lismacue with 60 horses stabled in the yard. The night I visited, Kate was sitting up with a foaling mare. After the crab cake starter and locally-reared T-bone, we went to watch the new-born filly take its first tentative steps on the road to possible stardom before returning to a piquant cheeseboard and a glass of claret. Kate's family built Lismacue 200 years ago, having acquired the estate 100 years earlier, in full view of Galtymore mountain. It can be climbed or simply admired — you choose. There is also fishing in their river or riding in the Glen of Aherlow. The house is voluminous with high ornate ceilings, furniture sparingly arranged, block-printed wallpaper and luxurious carpets. The cosy clutter of the drawing room with its tapestry, fireplace and comfy chairs was a favourite place to slump, while vast, airy bedrooms with big, shuttered windows have beds that seem to float on pale wool carpets; one room has a four-poster. Nothing is contrived in this elegant, aristocratic and graceful home. A pleasure from the moment you drive up the beautiful lime tree avenue planted in 1760.

Rooms: 3 doubles, all with en suite bathroom; 2 doubles sharing bathroom.
Price: IR£48—IR£65 p.p. Sing. supp. IR£11.
Breakfast: Included — full Irish.
Meals: Dinner IR£26-IR£30. Packed lunches on request.
Closed: Christmas & New Year.

How to get there: From Cahir, N24 towards Tipperary for 12 miles. Entrance on right at bridge just before signpost for Bansha village. House at end of tree-lined avenue.

Map no: 7   **Entry no: 145**

Bansha House
Bansha
Tipperary
Co. Tipperary

Tel: 062 54194
Fax: 062 54215
E-mail: banshahouse@circom.net
Web: www.tipp.ie/banshahs.htm

John and Mary Marnane

Mary likes to invite guests in to the kitchen of this handsome early Georgian farmhouse. You will want to linger and chat away, soaking up the cosy atmosphere. The conversation will inevitably turn to horses which are sacred at Bansha and second only to guests. Mares, foals and racehorses are always visible somewhere on the 100-acre estate. Life feels settled here; the walls cloaked with red creeper, the gently swaying trees, horses lazily munching grass — it is worth packing some watercolours and a sketchbook. A row of Norman Rockwell prints leads upstairs to pastel bedrooms with thick walls and small but comfortable showers. The couple of rooms that do not have en suite bathrooms are possibly the nicest, which is so often the case. An informal drawing room is warmed by a log fire, while wholesome breakfasts are eaten at one table together. Nearby, there is superb walking in the Galtees and the Glen of Aherlow. Gay Byrne stayed here and loved it. *Self-catering cottage, sleeps 5, rates on request.*

Rooms: 8: 4 doubles, all with en suite showfer; 1 twin with en suite shower; 1 family, 1 triple, sharing bathroom & shower; 1 single with en suite shower.
Price: IR£24—IR£27 p.p. Sing. supp. IR£5.
Breakfast: Included — full Irish.
Meals: Dinner IR£16.50 at 7pm, by arrangement.
Closed: Christmas week.

How to get there: From Limerick, N24 south towards Tipperary. 5 miles past Tipperary, entrance to Bansha signed, turning on left. First big entrance on right opposite stand of evergreens.

Entry no: 146

Map no: 7

Ash Hill Stud

Ash Hill
Kilmallock
Co. Limerick

Tel: 063 98035
Fax: 063 98752
E-mail: ashhill@iol.ie
Web: www.ashhill.com

Belinda and Simon Johnson

Ash Hill is typical of many lovely old Irish houses. It was allowed to fall into disrepair before the present owners began lovingly restoring it. This 18th-century house sits at the end of a long drive and forms one side of an impressive stable yard where Simon keeps his horses. Originally the ancestral pile of Gulf War US general Colin Powell, the Johnsons are today breathing new life into the old bricks. Rooms are enormous with eye-catching details — original ceilings, an arched window in the children's room, free-standing antique bath tubs, wood panelling and ornate plasterwork. In winter, hunker down in the snug by a roaring fire. The house oozes style and Simon and Belinda have the friendly enthusiasm to fulfil its obvious potential. You will be well looked after here. *Self-catering apartment in converted stable wing, sleeps 4, IR£200—IR£300 p.w.*

Rooms: 4: 1 double, 1 double/triple, 1 triple, all with en suite bath. 1 twin, sharing bathroom.
Price: IR£30 p.p. Sing supp. IR£10 depending on season.
Breakfast: Included — full Irish.
Meals: Dinner IR£20—IR£30 by arrangement.
Closed: Christmas & New Year.

How to get there: From Limerick, take south ring road at Tipperary r'bout. At next r'bout take R512 to Kilmallock for 20 miles. Right in town centre onto R515. First gates on right after 0.5 miles.

Map no: 7

Entry no: 147

Flemingstown House

Kilmallock
Co. Limerick

Tel: 063 98093
Fax: 063 98546
E-mail: flemingstown@keltec.ie
Web: www.ils.ie/flemingstown/

Imelda Sheedy-King

Imelda is one of those people you can rely on in a crisis; she possesses a calm efficiency that inspires confidence. Not that running a B&B stretches her to such limits very often, but on my visit to this traditional Irish farmhouse near the historic town of Killmallock, a major farm drama couldn't dent her friendly willingness to show me around. This is a well-run B&B in a house that's been in the family for generations. Clean, comfortable guest rooms have king-size beds, pretty embroidered bedspreads, roomy showers and baths and views over fields and a lush orchard. There are lots of peaceful walks around the farm with more in the surrounding Golden Vale. What really sets this place apart is Imelda's fabulous cooking; she studied in Cork and caters for large functions in an industrial-sized kitchen. You eat round one big dining table in a pretty conservatory that sparkles with Waterford crystal — the stained glass windows were designed by the late Bill Malone, a specialist in church stained glass. You're in safe hands here.

Rooms: 5: 1 family, 4 doubles, all with en suite shower. Private bathroom also available.
Price: IR£25 p.p. Sing. Supp. IR£7.50.
Breakfast: Included — full menu.
Meals: Dinner IR£20. Packed lunch by arrangement.
Closed: November—February.

How to get there: From Limerick, R512 to Kilmallock. Through town towards Fermoy, house 2 miles on left set back from road.

Ballyteigue House

Rockhill
Bruree
Co. Limerick

Tel: 063 90575
Fax: 063 90575
E-mail: ballyteigue@eircom.net
Web: homepage.eircom.net/~ballyteigue

Richard and Margaret Johnson

Ballyteigue really has everything: beautiful furniture in big beautiful rooms, log fires, a gorgeous garden and views over the unspoilt Golden Vale where dairy herds convert emerald green pastures into 'liquid gold', the local expression for milk. In the distance, the smooth humps of the Ballyhoura Mountains provide a towering backdrop to this delightful setting. Margaret and Richard are unpretentious hosts. They enjoy meeting guests and suggesting local places to visit, such as the 13th-century abbey at Kilmallock or the prehistory of Lough Gur. Margaret has raised a large family in sometimes difficult circumstances and her resulting conviction that things do work out in the end is an inspiration. One day she promises to write a salacious account of the Anglo-Irish in Limerick, a tradition in keeping with the history of this fine Georgian farmhouse as novelist Dorothy Conyers once lived here. Comfortable bedrooms lead off a wide landing, home to a stuffed fox — it was saved from a hunt and given to Richard, a retired vet who looks after a few horses and some cattle on the farm. Breakfast is a home-made affair; the gooseberry jam is worth a visit in itself.

Rooms: 5: 3 doubles, 1 twin, all en suite; 1 single, sharing bathroom.
Price: IR£25—IR£26 p.p. Sing. supp. IR£6.
Breakfast: Included — full Irish.
Meals: Dinner IR£20 on request. Packed lunch on request.
Closed: Mid-December—mid-February unless by prior arrangement.

How to get there: From Croom, N20 south for 7 miles, then first right after O'Rourke's Cross junction, signed Rockhill Church. Up minor road for 1 mile, past church, then right up lane. House is signed.

Map no: 7

Entry no: **149**

The Mustard Seed at Echo Lodge

Ballingarry
Co. Limerick

Tel: 069 68508
Fax: 069 68511
E-mail: mustard@indigo.ie

Daniel Mullane

Named after a passage from the Bible, this impressive Victorian mansion, perched on the side of a dell above the village of Ballingarry, is a busy monument to indulgence and comfort. Every care has been taken: handmade Connemara carpets, the finest textiles, the best beds, power showers, pine floors, even a sloped ceiling suite. And sparkling amid this shrine to colour and good taste is the cheerful energy of Dan Mullane. Whether pouring fresh fruit juices at breakfast, planning the two old ladies' day out to Adare, welcoming the ambassador back from his bike ride, plucking greens from the garden, supervising his renowned restaurant, or fixing a nightcap for guests, his life is a vortex in which you become quickly cocooned. Dan takes a month off every year to go backpacking, and gathers maps, hangings, silk prints, new recipes and other worldly paraphernalia to delight the senses. The food and atmosphere in the dining room is spectacular, but in case your palate becomes a little jaded, there are six easy solutions — each one a local bar.

Rooms: 10: 1 family, 6 doubles, 3 twins, all with en suite bathroom.
Price: IR£65—IR£100 p.p. Sing. supp. IR£15-IR£30.
Breakfast: Included — full Irish.
Meals: Dinner IR£34.
Closed: Christmas & February.

How to get there: From Limerick, N21 through Adare. Left just after village, signed Ballingarry. Follow signs to house, taking right at village x-roads.

Glin Castle

Glin
Co. Limerick

Tel: 068 34173
Fax: 068 34364
E-mail: knight@iol.ie
Web: www.glincastle.com

Desmond and Olda FitzGerald

It has been called the most comfortable castle in the world. It is grand but intimate and has a cosy elegance and an unbroken link with the past. This has been the seat of the Knight of Glin for more than 700 years and is currently home to the 29th Knight, who inherited the castle in 1949 at the age of 12. He moved here in 1975 and has been studiously filling the house with lovely things. There is probably no finer collection of 18th- and 19th-century Irish furniture in Ireland. The house was built on the banks of the widest part of the River Shannon by John Bateman FitzGerald in the 1780s; the castellations were added in the 1820s, while the ornate woodwork was carved by local carpenters. A portrait of Fitzgerald hangs in the hall with its Corinthian columns and magnificent neo-classical plasterwork ceiling depicting the family crest. At the far end of the hall, a 'flying' staircase leads upstairs to exquisite bedrooms. Staff are extremely friendly and beautiful food is meticulously sourced and carefully prepared. Treat yourself to one of Ireland's rarest treasures.

Rooms: 15: 3 deluxe, 8 superior,
4 standard, all with en suite bathroom.
Price per room: IR£190—IR£300 p.p.
Breakfast: Included — full menu.
Meals: Dinner, 4 courses, IR£33.
Closed: November—March. Off-season by
prior arrangement.

How to get there: From Limerick, N69
west for 32 miles to Glin, then left up main
street and right at top of square. Entrance
straight ahead. Tabert car ferry 4 miles.

Ballyhowly Castle
Ballyhowly,

Tel: 000 00000
E-mail: no_chance@ballyhowly.eek
Web: www.no-itsgone.com

Oh for the open skies of Limerick! Indeed, was this not the place that inspired the epic verse: "There once was a castle in Limerick/Whose roof was no more than a gimmerick/ In summer or fall/ There was now't there at all/ Let's say it was just there to mimmerick." ? Be that as it may, this place is special in other ways, too: note the fenestration, the charming projection to one side and the great tower, leaning seductively against the other side. 'It is history itself that has left its mark.' Here Finnigan had his first wake, and Oliver Cromwell invented his famous metal helmet, the better to protect himself and his men from falling debris and the rain. It worked, but his holiday was a failure – or so the Irish say. Don't be fooled by the scale of the place; it is relaxed and easy-going and demands little of you other than a tent and portaloo. Come to be charmed by the past, alarmed by the present and terrified by the future – for there is a certain unpredictability about an old building that no longer quite knows whom it serves.

Rooms: Many and various 'spaces' - share with a friend or defend one for yourself.
Price: XXVII of the ancient land's finest coinage.
Breakfast: In the turrets or under parts of arches.
Meals: Stone and mud can be mixed down, seasoned with a little seawater andmake a delightful, mineral-rich 'stew', as local residents call it.
Closed: Keep you eyes peeled for a rain of arrows and rotten fruit. This is a sign that Ballyhowly is closed.

How to get there: Ask the locals or just trust your instincts...

Fitzgerald's Farmhouse & Riding Centre

Mount Marian
Abbeyfeale Hill, Abbeyfeale
Co. Limerick

Tel: 068 31217
Fax: 068 31558
E-mail: fitzfarmhouse@eircom.net

Kathleen and Tim Fitzgerald

Your kids are going to love this place. Kathleen and Tim, a gentle giant, have really found themselves running this riding centre, animal sanctuary and B&B. Lots of baby goats, kittens, ducks, rabbits, chickens and lambs inhabit a magical petland which children can safely explore. An obliging nanny-goat helped nurture grandchild Leon after it was found he was allergic to cow's milk. Tim has also designed a nature trail and Kathleen and Leon showed me round. It goes up past a pretty stream with secure fencing to a gazebo with lovely views and ends with a surprising exhibition of antique farm machinery. There is also a touch of the Wild West at the children's summer riding camps with campfire singalongs and a bunkhouse for children over 10 years to stay in. Mum and dad will prefer the pastel-coloured rooms inside the house; nothing fancy, just comfortable. Breakfast and dinner are served on blue gingham in a pink, pine-floored dining room but you are always welcome in the kitchen. There is lots for you to do here as well. Why not try a horse trek or a gallop on a beach, or else go touring knowing your children are in safe hands. Fitzgerald's is a rare, welcoming and affordable place to take your kids.

Rooms: 6: 2 doubles, 3 twins, 1 family, all with en suite bathroom.
Price: IR£20 p.p. Sing. supp. IR£6.
Breakfast: Included — full Irish/Continental.
Meals: Dinner IR£12.
Closed: Never.

How to get there: From Limerick, N21 towards Tralee for 40 miles into Abbeyfeale. Left in square, between O'Rourke's Bar and the Cellar Bar. House 1 mile up hill, signed on left.

Allo's Townhouse
41 Church Street
Listowel
Co. Kerry

Tel: 068 22880
Fax: 068 22803
E-mail: allosbar&bistro@microsoft.com

**Armel Whyte and
Helen Mullane**

"Outside of a dog, a book is Man's best friend. And inside of a dog, it's too dark too read." Groucho Marx would have got on famously in Listowel, home to Ireland's premier literary event, the Writer's Week. More bizarrely, it was once home to the world's first monorail. Every year, this pretty market town on the banks of the River Feale invites Irish and international authors to hang out for a week and talk about their books in the town's pubs, restaurants and excellent theatre. By far the best place to stay is Allo's Townhouse just off the main square and opposite the home of the late writer, Brian McMahon. Three stylish rooms have ornate mirrors, wiggly designer lampshades, a four-poster bed, oil paintings and a cherub pedestal and in bathrooms of green Connemara marble, there are lovely claw-footed baths. The traditional bar serves good bistro food on wooden tables in a lively atmosphere and a more upmarket restaurant next door does fresh fish and game that foodie guides rave about. There is also an amazing collection of Irish whiskeys behind the bar; one vintage malt costs IR£40 a shot. Armel and Helen are both chefs with a talent for spoiling even the most temperate souls.

Rooms: 3: 2 doubles with en suite bathroom; 1 twin with en suite shower.
Price: IR£35—IR£45 p.p. Sing. supp. IR£15.
Breakfast: Included — full menu.
Meals: Dinner, 2 courses, IR£25. Lunch from IR£6. Bar and restaurant closed for food on Sundays.
Closed: Christmas Day, New Year's Day & Good Friday.

How to get there: From Limerick, N69 to Tarbert, then onto Listowel. House on left with two bay trees outside.

Entry no: 154   Map no: 6

Castlemorris House

Ballymullen
Tralee
Co. Kerry

Tel: 066 7180060
Fax: 066 7128007
Web: www.sawdays.co.uk

Mary and Paddy Barry

Satisfied visitors keep writing to tell us that Mary and Paddy are doing a great job at Castlemorris. This imposing Georgian house stands on high ground on the edge of town with views over the Slieve Mish mountains in one direction and the rooftops of Tralee in the other. The drawing and dining rooms have thick carpets, real fires in winter and bay windows with views over a lovely garden. A broad staircase leads to large bedrooms of exquisite simplicity with huge beds — some with wrought-iron bedsteads and draped bedheads — and the odd sofa; the rooms up in the eaves are wonderful. An excellent base to head off in all directions (the Dingle Peninsula and the jewels of County Clare, perhaps) knowing that a warm welcome awaits your return.

Rooms: 6: 1 double, 1 double/twin, both with en suite bathroom; 3 doubles/twins, 1 double, all with en suite shower; 1 extra bathroom.
Price: IR£30—IR£35 p.p. Sing. supp. IR£10.
Breakfast: Included — full Irish.
Meals: Dinner, 3 courses, IR£20.
Closed: Never.

How to get there: From Limerick, N21 to Tralee, then left at first r'bout as you approach town, signed Dingle, and right at T-junc after 0.5 miles. House immediately on right.

Map no: 6

Entry no: 155

Coolclogher House

Mill Road
Coolclogher, Killarney
Co. Kerry

Tel: 064 35996
Fax: 064 30993

Mary Harnett

Coolclogher is a handsome early-Victorian house designed by Pugin in the Italianate style and set in a walled 60-acre estate near the tourist magnet of Killarney. Surrounded by mature gardens and parkland, the house has wonderful views of mountains and lakes. Mary and husband Maurice restored every room before opening their doors to guests in 1999 — they've paid equal attention to the gardens, too. Large, elegant bedrooms have lovely garden views and big, bright bathrooms. Relax in stylish and comfortable sitting rooms or the conservatory with its beautiful specimen camellia tree planted 170 years ago. Mary's direct and colourful outlook on life is infectious. She is good fun to be around, has huge energy and is extremely hospitable. The 22,000 acres of Killarney National Park and the lakes of Killarney are within walking distance. Rare peace and luxury in the heart of Ireland's busiest region. *Self-catering apartment in main house, sleeps 4, IR£560 p.w.*

Rooms: 4 doubles, all with en suite bathroom.
Price: IR£40—IR£65 p.p. No sing. supp.
Breakfast: Included — full Irish.
Meals: Available locally.
Closed: November—February.

How to get there: From Killarney, N71 Muckross Rd to Kenmare for 1 mile, then left at Gleneagle Hotel. Entrance 0.25 miles on right.

Entry no: 156

Map no: 6

Killarney Royal
College Street
Killarney
Co. Kerry

Tel: 064 31853
Fax: 064 34001
E-mail: royalhot@iol.ie
Web: www.killarneyroyal.ie

Joe and Margaret Scally

The Killarney Royal is an example of how a small hotel can be run in an atmosphere of friendly splendour. No self-righteous snobbery here. Rooms have real class yet dedicated staff give guests the sort of personal attention you would expect from a much smaller place. Neither compromises the other. Margaret and Joe are justly proud that the majority of the people who work here have been with the hotel for more than eight years. It has fostered a great team spirit. The pair were nurses before Margaret inherited the Royal. She comes from a family with a long pedigree of running hotels in Killarney and it would have been easy to sit back and tap the voracious demand in this busy tourist destination. Instead, she travelled Europe looking for new ideas to rejuvenate the hotel. The results are wonderful. In some cases, stunning. Luxurious rooms are all different, doffing their cap to the restrained elegance of French and Italian styles; many of the curtains were made by an old school friend. Margaret's tour de force is the split level dining room, the centrepiece being a chandelier hanging from a beautiful circular moulded ceiling. The Royal is a cut above the rest.

Rooms: 29: 5 suites, 10 twins,
14 double/twins, all with en suite
bathroom.
Price: IR£45—IR£75 p.p. Sing. supp.
IR£45.
Breakfast: Included — full menu.
Meals: Dinner, 4 courses, IR£25.
Closed: Christmas week.

How to get there: In Killarney town
centre. Ask hotel for directions.

Map no: 6

Entry no: 157

Fuchsia House

Muckross Road
Killarney
Co. Kerry

Tel: 064 33743
Fax: 064 36588
E-mail: fuchsiahouse@eircom.net
Web: www.fuchsiahouse.com

Mary and Tommy Treacy

Killarney has been given a hard time of late — an overfed child with a pretty face, claim the critics. True, the town is growing at a startling rate, but so is much of Ireland. Just to dismiss it as too touristy seemed churlish; it backs onto a beautiful national park and lies close to some of Ireland's most dramatic scenery. Yet I had my own misgivings as I hit the B&B strip along Muckross Road. It all looked so predictable and formulaic. Until, that is, I drew up outside Fuchsia House, a modern house built in 1992 in a Victorian style. I cannot think of anywhere else in the book that has swept away my preconceptions so swiftly. Once inside, the tawdry world of industrial B&B melts away. You have entered a home very much at peace with itself. Mary, a former French teacher, and husband Tommy, a local primary school teacher, are Francophiles and it has rubbed off on their home. Gorgeous bedrooms have a subtle elegance and the kitchen with its green Aga is a delight. But they make this joyful place. Mary is chatty and quick-witted and Tommy is a mellow fellow with a sage-like reverence for gardening. An unexpected pleasure.

Rooms: 10: 8 triples, 2 doubles, all with en suite bathroom.
Price: IR£30—IR£42 p.p.
Breakfast: Included — full Irish.
Meals: Available in Killarney.
Closed: Mid-November—February.

How to get there: From Killarney centre, N71 to Kenmare for 0.5 miles. House on right.

Beaufort House

Beaufort
Nr Killarney
Co. Kerry
Ireland

Tel: 064 44764
Fax: 064 44764
E-mail: info@beaufortireland.com
Web: www.beaufortireland.com

Donald and Rachel Cameron

Walking around the plush interior of Beaufort House reminded me of the story of the guests who once arranged to be Lord and Lady of the manor for the night. A delicious meal was prepared, the owners went off to play bridge, leaving the couple to play the part. Unfortunately, two over-exuberant dogs kept them confined to the kitchen all night. Rest assured, that won't happen here as the whole of this beautiful house is let to guests without interruption, though Donald and Rachel are never too far away if help is needed. He is an antiques expert and she restores old buildings. A wide staircase leads to large bedrooms with graceful antiques and lovely big bathrooms. The grand dining room has ancestral portraits on the walls and an ancient polished floor, so think feasts and fine wine rather than beans on toast. Historically, most of the house dates to 1640, though the façade and gardens arrived in the Georgian period. There are beautiful views over the secluded 42-acre estate, with two miles of private salmon fishing, towards the Gap of Dunloe in the distance. The courtyard cottages are equally nice and good for families and fishing parties. A perfect place to live out that Irish country house fantasy.

Rooms: Main house: 4 twins/doubles, all with en suite bathroom, sleeps 8. Courtyard cottages: 1 with 4 bedrooms, sleeps 8; 1 with 3 bedrooms, sleeps 6; 2 with 2 bedrooms, both sleep 4; all with en suite bathroom.

Price: Main house from IR£3,000 p.w.; Courtyard cottages IR£500—IR£900 p.w. depending on season.
Breakfast: You cook, you choose.
Meals: Available locally.
Closed: October—Easter.

How to get there: From Killarney, N72 Ring of Kerry Rd west to Killorglin for 5 miles, then left over stone bridge. Entrance immediately left after bridge.

Map no: 6   **Entry no: 159**

Carrig House

Caragh Lake
Killorglin
Co. Kerry

Tel: 066 9769100
Fax: 066 9769166

Frank and Mary Slattery

After 20 years of searching, Frank knew Carrig was the place he had been looking for. Reached by a long wooded drive, this mid-19th-century country house looks out onto the timeless beauty of Caragh Lake. It is a beautiful spot and Frank and Mary run things with good-natured professionalism. He is full of likeable charm and disarming patter, while she looks after you with sincere warmth and a big smile. Dinner here is a great occasion. You ponder the menu with an aperitif next to a fire in the snug drawing room, then are led into the intimate atmosphere of the bay-windowed dining room that overlooks the lake. The food is excellent. A wild mushroom starter followed by Barbary duck and a poached pear dessert were memorable. Comfortable bedrooms mix old and modern. The junior suite with lake views and the double with wisteria creeping round the windows both had a lovely old-fashioned grace befitting a house of this period. The garden has nearly 1,000 different plant species. There are walks through woods with secluded seating areas and a path down to the lake and a small jetty. Fishing, golf and hill walking can be arranged. *Children over 10 welcome.*

Rooms: 6: 3 doubles, 3 twins, all with en suite bathroom.
Price: IR£50—IR£70 p.p. Sing. supp. IR£20.
Breakfast: Included — full menu.
Meals: Dinner, 4 courses, IR£30.
Closed: January—March.

How to get there: From Killorglin, N70 towards Glenbeigh for 3 miles, then left signed Caragh Lake for 1.5 miles. Turn right at village shop, entrance on left.

Caragh Lodge

Caragh Lake
Killorglin
Co. Kerry

Tel: 066 9769115
Fax: 066 9769316
E-mail: caraghl@iol.ie
Web: www.caraghlodge.com

Mary and Graham Gaunt

Caragh has one of the most beautiful gardens in Ireland, a legacy of the Reverend Kennedy, who built this Victorian fishing lodge 100 years ago and planted many of the trees and shrubs. Azaleas, camellias, rhododendrons and magnolias bring colour and scent, while tree ferns and various types of bamboo have an almost semi-tropical influence on shadier parts of the garden. It's a lovely place to stroll before dinner with views across the lawn over Caragh Lough and the Ring of Kerry. Meals here are renowned. Mary personally supervises everything, whether it be the deliciously light shortbread served with tea in the elegant drawing room or the Kerry lamb cooked with fresh herbs from the garden; a chef at one of Ireland's best houses told me she did the "best duck in Ireland". The dining room is reminiscent of a gentleman's club with fine furniture and silverware and immaculate linen, all bathed in the glow of an open fire. There are two rooms in the main house, while the rest are in an annexe next door with either terraces or balconies. Rooms are hotel standard. Take a sauna, play tennis or simply revel in contentment. *Children over 10 years welcome.*

Rooms: 15: Main house: 2 double/twins, both with en suite bathroom. Annexe: 1 suite, 11 double/twins, 1 single, all with en suite bathroom.
Price: IR£62.50-IR£110 p.p. Single IR£85.
Breakfast: Included — full menu.
Meals: Dinner, 4 courses, IR£33.
Packed lunch by arrangement.
Closed: Mid-October—mid-April.

How to get there: From Killorglin, N70 towards Glenbeigh for 3.5 miles. Left at blue sign for Caragh Lodge, left again at T-junc. House on right.

Map no: 6

Entry no: 161

The Old Anchor

Main Street
Annascaul
Co. Kerry

Tel: 066 9157382
Fax: 066 9157382
E-mail: dropanchor@eircom.net
Web: www.dingle-peninsula.ie/annascaul

Marie Kennedy

The most unlikely things are likely to happen at the Old Anchor. Where other places have a view, a lovely garden or gorgeous antiques, here you meet the village. Within a few hours of arriving, the resident magician had shown me a few tricks, the keeper of folk tales had sung a hilarious song about lost love, and a woman from Alabama had cooked us real southern fried chicken just the way her mom taught her. So it was entirely plausible that the duffed up leather ration bag hanging on the wall in the dining room once belonged to Antarctic explorer Ernest Shackleton — Tom Crean, a member of his expedition, was born in Annascaul. The fun often continues next door in Dan Foley's, the 'most photographed pub' in Ireland. Marie is a quiet, considerate constant amid this social maelstrom. She runs painting courses with established artists from a studio behind the guesthouse. Inspiration is guaranteed with the beautiful Dingle Peninsula on the doorstep; long sandy beaches, pebble coves and mountain ranges dotted with prehistory are close enough to walk to. Comfortable bedrooms and a hearty breakfast set you up for a day's exploration. This is the Ireland I hoped to discover.

Rooms: 10 double/twins, all with en suite shower.
Price: IR£22 p.p. Sing. supp. IR£5.
Breakfast: Included — full Irish.
Meals: Dinner, 3 courses, IR£18. Packed lunch IR£4.
Closed: Never.

How to get there: From Killarney, N72 to Castlemaine, left on R561 towards Dingle, then right on N86 towards Tralee.
Annascaul 0.5 miles. House in middle of village, on right.

The Old Farmhouse

Minard West   **Tel:** 066 9157346
Lispole   **E-mail:** grundbrk@indigo.ie
Co. Kerry   **Web:** www.sawdays.co.uk

Jill Sanderson

A friendly lurcher will welcome you enthusiastically to The Old Farmhouse, bounding out of a mature English country garden. The combination is unusual for deepest rural Ireland but then Jill moved here in 1989 after an interesting and varied life at home and abroad. A keen sailor, she skippered a handsome 11-ton teak sloop for 16 years before taking the helm of a bookshop on the east coast of England. Now she has settled for a 130-year-old stone house, transforming three acres into a hillside oasis of hardy flowering perennials and shrubs. This is a blissfully television-free house, ideal for the discerning walker and nature lover. The furniture is a mixture of family things and lovingly-restored Irish pieces. There are books and pictures all over the place and a photo album of her exploits on the high seas. Rooms are simple but inviting and each has breathtaking views of Dingle Bay. Sit out on a sunny day with a cup of tea and a slice of banana bread or hole up in the sitting room and lose yourself in a book by the turf fire. Just gently ebb and flow.

Rooms: In separate wing: 2 twins, sharing shower room.
Price: IR£22.50 p.p.
Breakfast: Included — full Irish.
Meals: Farmhouse supper IR£10, by arrangement.
Closed: Never.

How to get there: From Tralee, N86 to Dingle via Camp and Annascaul. 4 miles on, left at Sullivan's Bar in Lispole. Take uphill road to Minard Castle. First right at top. Continue for 1km. Single-storey pink house with whitish garden walls and black iron gates on right.

Map no: 6   **Entry no: 163**

Greenmount House

Gortonora
Dingle
Co. Kerry

Tel: 066 9151414
Fax: 066 9151974
E-mail: mary@greenmounthouse.com
Web: www.greenmounthouse.com

Mary and John Curran

Although Greenmount is not the most beautiful house in the world to look at, it has been cleverly designed on the inside by a young local architect; it was his end of year project and he passed with flying colours. The result is very large, split-level suite-style bedrooms with simple wallpaper, thick carpets, a sitting area and doors that lead out onto a balcony — the standard rooms have the same facilities but are naturally smaller. The two parts of the house are connected by a long conservatory dining room lit beautifully by natural light. The house is on a hill overlooking Dingle Bay with its famous resident, Fungi the dolphin and you come to the Dingle for fabulous walking across dramatic cliff, hill and sea scenery studded with prehistory. Do, though, bear in mind that in the middle of summer it gets very crowded. Mary is wonderfully friendly and likes to ensure every guest feels they can relax and unwind here, even after 20 years in the business. I was knocked out by the deliciously moist Citrus Cake.

Rooms: 12: 7 suites, all with en suite bathroom; 6 doubles, all with en suite shower.
Price: IR£25—IR£50 p.p. Sing. supp. IR£10.
Breakfast: Included — full Irish.
Meals: Available in Dingle.
Closed: Christmas.

How to get there: N86 into Dingle, right at r'bout, right at next junction, up hill, house on left.

Entry no: 164

Map no: 6

Captain's House
The Mall
Dingle
Co. Kerry

Tel: 066 9151531
Fax: 066 9151079
E-mail: captigh@eircom.net
Web: homepage.eircom.net/~captigh

Mary and Jim Milhench

Sometimes the rain wallops the Dingle Peninsula so hard the distinction between land and sea blurs and you wish you had packed a life-jacket. Then the torrents lift as suddenly as they arrived and a magic light cuts through the storm clouds gilding the landscape with droplets of silver. I arrived in these conditions at the Captain's House. The sun burst though the slate-grey sky, illuminating Jim and Mary's small but beautifully-formed garden on a finger of land by a stream. Cross a footbridge and walk up to the conservatory dining room where Mary beckons you in with a big smile to a downstairs full of cosy snugs, with antiques, comfy chairs and the sweet aroma of turf fires. Inviting bedrooms feel like ship's cabins; compact, comfortable, with antique dressers and good beds. Jim used to be a captain in the Merchant Navy and this warren-like 1840 house is full of nautical memorabilia. These days he sails a Galway Hooker, and yes, he has seen Funge the dolphin. Breakfast is varied, the grilled Dingle kipper is particularly good. The weather won't trouble you here.
Luxury self-catering bungalow with sea views, sleeps 8, IR£850—IR£1,050 p.w.

Rooms: 9: 1 suite, 1 double, both with en suite bathroom; 4 doubles, 1 twin, 2 singles, all with en suite shower.
Price: IR£25—IR£30 p.p. Sing. supp. IR£5.
Breakfast: Included — full menu.
Meals: Available in Dingle.
Closed: Mid-November—mid-March.

How to get there: N86 to Dingle, then right at r'bout signed Connor Pass and town centre. House 200m on left with footbridge over stream.

Map no: 6

Gorman's Clifftop House

Glaise Bheag
Ballydavid, Dingle Peninsula,
Co. Kerry

Tel: 066 9155162
Fax: 066 9155162
E-mail: gormans@eircom.net
Web: www.gormans-clifftophouse.com

Sile and Vincent Gorman

Here is a rare opportunity to hear Gaelic spoken as this is a *gaeltacht* region where people speak it as their first language. The house is a warm refuge set just back from cliffs at the south-western edge of Ireland, overlooking a bay and the magical sight of the Three Sisters peninsula beyond. Sile — Gaelic for Sheila — is friendly, down-to-earth and full of life, just the person to welcome you in on a howling winter evening. All the rooms in this recently modernised house have big, comfy beds, stripped-pine cupboards and dressers and are decorated in warm, attractive colours. The small, friendly restaurant has gorgeous views over the Atlantic and serves wonderful food from Vincent's Ballymaloe-inspired repertoire — the Dingle Bay prawns are excellent. Afterwards, sit and chat in front of an open fire. By day, hire a bike for the Slea Head Drive, explore the interior with its many ancient archaeological sites or just let the sea captivate your imagination. The Gormans are a naturally hospitable family, the youngest being a little boy from Guatemala who loves meeting guests.

Rooms: 9: 2 double/triples,
3 twin/doubles, 2 doubles, 2 twins,
all with en suite bathroom.
Price: IR£30—IR40 p.p. Sing. supp.
IR£6—IR12.
Breakfast: Included — full Irish/buffet.
Meals: Set menus from IR£25 or à la carte.
Closed: Mid-January—February.

How to get there: From Dingle, R559
with harbour on left to r'bout. Go straight

across, signed An Fheothanach. After 4 miles, keep left at fork, house a further
4 miles beside round house.

Glanleam House

Glanleam
Valentia Island
Co. Kerry

Tel: 066 9476176
Fax: 066 9476108

Meta Kreissig

Glanleam is a botanical paradise. Sheltered by a collar of tall forested hills overlooking a wide bay, the estate's 192 acres contain some of Ireland's most spectacular gardens. Between the house and the sea is a restored tropical forest of ferns, myrtle, bamboo and trees normally associated with Madagascar or Mauritius, including the only surviving camphor tree in the UK or Ireland. If Meta has time, she may take you for a walk and explain how she restored the gardens from an overgrown jungle. The house itself is 1820s and was the Knight of Kerry's residence. Today, modern vies with antique for supremacy inside; a huge dripping 42-light candelabra with a long brass stalk dominates the hall, then there is the enormous Bonsack bathroom with its gold swan-shaped taps and the purple velveteen sofa covers in the drawing room. Large bedrooms have spectacular views over the bay and a solitary lighthouse. Both Meta and daughter Jessica are accomplished cooks with meals served in the grand dining room. Outside, rare Soay sheep and Connemara ponies dot this beautiful island landscape.

Rooms: 7: 4 twin/doubles, 2 doubles, 1 suite, all with en suite bathroom.
Price: IR£35—IR£85 p.p. Sing. supp. IR£30, at owner's discretion.
Breakfast: Included — full Irish/Continental.
Meals: Dinner IR£25. Lunch IR£8.
Closed: November—mid-March.

How to get there: From Killarney, N72 to Killorglin, then N70 Ring of Kerry Rd to Cahersiveen. Follow signs to Renard Point, then car ferry to Knights Town on Valentia Island. House signed in village. Or: 3 miles after Cahersiveen, right on R565 to Portmagee and island.

Map no: 6

Entry no: 167

Iskeroon

Bunavalla
Caherdaniel
Co. Kerry

Tel: 066 9475119
Fax: 066 9475488
E-mail: info@iskeroon.com
Web: www.iskeroon.com

Geraldine and David Hare

David and Geraldine are an easy-going young couple who have renovated a wonderfully remote one-storey house right by the sea on the Ring of Kerry. All the rooms are decorated in bold colours and are full of space and light. The layout is unusual with bedrooms on one side of a corridor and bathrooms and loos on the other. Iskeroon blossoms in the summer. Follow a windy path through a restored semi-tropical garden with tree-ferns down to a private jetty where you can swim in the crystal clear sea. The water is shallow and safe. David also uses the jetty for fishing and lobster-potting. If he has time (normally he's a TV producer) he'll take guests fishing with him. Geraldine is a painter who draws inspiration from views across Derrynane Bay that change chameleon-like according to the weather. Iskeroon has excellent breakfast, the warmest welcome and lots to do in a tranquil setting. What else could you want? *Children over 12 welcome. Self-catering apartment opening in 2002, sleeps 4.*

Rooms: 3: 2 doubles, 1 twin, all with private bathroom (dressing gowns provided).
Price: IR£38 p.p. Sing. supp. IR£10.
Breakfast: Included — full Irish.
Meals: Available locally.
Closed: October—April.

How to get there: Between Caherdaniel and Waterville. At Scarriff Inn take road down hill to the bottom signed Bunavalla Pier, bearing left at each hairpin. At pier, left through gate marked 'private', over beach to very end. House is pink.

Entry no: 168

Map no: 6

Derreensillagh

Castlecove
Co. Kerry

Tel: 064 45347
Fax: 064 45588
Web: www.sawdays.co.uk

Tim and Bronwen Youard

Everyone must circumnavigate the Ring of Kerry at least once in their lives and Derreensillagh makes an ideal base camp. It is right on the Ring itself built on a hillside. Below the house is a colony of up to 80 seals to visit. Above, the views become more spectacular the higher you climb. Right at the top is a small plateau garden wilderness where you can sit in summer. After that you are into pure countryside. Tim and Bronwen are very entertaining, very caring, running the B&B as well as a salmon-smoking business. They have modified this sweet, old, beamed farmhouse to make it completely wheelchair-friendly, with ramps outside and surreptitious design inside. No ugly chrome bars. The whitewashed bedrooms are charming with wooden ceilings, seagrass matting, hot towel rails and every conceivable little extra. Horsehair mattresses are handmade, sheets are pure cotton, pillow cases antique and embroidered. There are radios, chocolates, notepaper, hairdryer, tea, coffee, fresh milk, jar of sweeties... You really do get pampered here.

Rooms: 2/3: 1 double with en suite bath; 1 two-room family suite sleeping 4/5 with en suite shower.
Price: IR£25 p.p. Sing. supp. IR£5.
Breakfast: Included — full Irish.
Meals: Available in Sneem and Caherdaniel.
Closed: Never.

How to get there: From Kenmare, N70 to Sneem. Continue on N70, signed Waterville. 6 miles on, pass "Community Alert" sign. House on next right-hand bend, 1 mile before Castlecove.

Map no: 6

Entry no: 169

Tahilla Cove Country House

Tahilla
Co. Kerry

Tel: 064 45204
Fax: 064 45104
E-mail: tahillacove@eircom.net
Web: www.tahillacove.com

James, Deirdre and Dolly Waterhouse

James's father, Charles Waterhouse, built Tahilla shortly after retiring from the armed forces following the British withdrawal from India in 1947. Perhaps this part of 'Ireland's Riviera', with its lush semi-tropical vegetation and balmy micro-climate, reminded him in some way of the Raj. Or perhaps it was the local girl he married that convinced him to settle here. This quaint guesthouse tumbles down into a beautiful, secluded cove in Kenmare Bay, surrounded by 14 acres of landscaped gardens and mature woodland. Today, James runs the place with his wife Deirdre, a local doctor, and his mother Dolly, a great character who will happily relate the whole history of this unique place. Old-fashioned bedrooms have modern comforts and most have sea views and a private balcony or terrace. Walk through oak groves to idyllic viewpoints where seals can be seen basking on rocks, swim off the private pier or mess about in a small rowing boat, before returning for afternoon tea on the sun terrace. Dinner is a relaxed affair — more house party than stuffy restaurant. The family are warm, friendly hosts upholding a fine tradition established more than half a century ago.

Rooms: 9: 5 double/twins, 3 twins, all with en suite bathroom; 1 double/twin with en suite shower.
Price: IR£38—IR£43 p.p. Sing. supp. IR£20. Special rates available.
Breakfast: Included — full Irish.
Meals: Dinner IR£18, except Tuesdays. Bar lunch and packed lunch also available.
Closed: Mid-October—March.

How to get there: From Kenmare, N70 towards Sneem for 11 miles. House left down drive, signed.

Rockcrest

Killarney Road
Kenmare
Co. Kerry

Tel: 064 41016/41132
Fax: 064 42135

Grainne O'Connell

Killarney's popularity is Kenmare's gain. This handsome town seems to escape much of the coachload tourism that descends on its bigger neighbour further west. This is helped because the only way to get there from Killarney is by a twisting road through some of the most craggy, desolate scenery in Ireland. Be warned: the journey takes much longer than you think. I started to wonder whether I had taken a wrong turn as thick mist wrapped the car like a blanket. Don't lose heart — it is a wonderful relief to finally see the warm orange glow of the settlement ahead of you. This is one of the first buildings that comes into view, perched above the road on the right and was the first bungalow ever to be built in Kenmare. But this 1955 house, available for self-catering, is no ordinary bungalow inside. A large hallway leads to rooms with wooden floors, rugs, oak furniture, big beds and an open fire. The kitchen has everything you need to fend for yourself and patio doors lead onto a paved sun terrace. It feels comfortable without being cluttered and is a two-minute walk from the town centre with its busy restaurants and colourful pubs. This matches the best B&B, only you cook breakfast when you want and how you want.

Rooms: 3 bedrooms, all with en suite bathroom, sleeps 6.
Price: IR£300—IR£750 p.w. depending on season.
Breakfast: You cook, you choose.
Meals: Available locally.
Closed: Never.

How to get there: In Kenmare, N71 Killarney Road from town centre for 0.5 miles, then left up lane. Entrance immediately left.

Map no: 6

Entry no: 171

Shelburne Lodge

Cork Rd
Kenmare
Co. Kerry

Tel: 064 41013
Fax: 064 42135

Maura and Tom O'Connell-Foley

In Kenmare, folk say Maura has the Midas touch. By that they mean she excels at everything she does, whether it be her renowned restaurants or the wonderful Shelburne Lodge which has her colourful personality stamped all over it. Lovely yellow bedrooms with huge mirrors, beautiful limed antique furniture, modern art and thick rugs on wooden floors show a great eye for elegant but unstuffy interior design. This 1740s house is country-style elegant and extremely welcoming. A secluded coach house overlooking the garden and grass tennis court has recently been converted with the same flair. Arrive to a warm welcome, settle on a sofa by a large log fire with a cup of tea that appears to arrive by magic and just soak up the relaxed atmosphere. The whole family is easy going and friendly and Tom's encyclopedic knowledge of the Kenmare region will inspire you to explore. Walks up steep country lanes lead to sweeping views of the River Kenmare and the surrounding hills. In the evening, try out Maura's restaurant where simple, delicious food and a great atmosphere are guaranteed. Outstanding.

Rooms: 9: Main house: 3 king-size doubles, 2 queen-size doubles, 2 twins,
all with en suite bathroom. Coach house:
1 double, 1 family, both with en suite shower.
Price: IR£35—IR£50 p.p. Sing. supp. IR£15.
Breakfast: Included — full Irish.
Meals: Available in Kenmare.
Closed: December—February

How to get there: From Killarney, N71 to Kenmare. Follow signs to Kilgarvan on the Cork Rd. House 0.5 miles on left.

Entry no: 172

Map no: 6

Sallyport House

Glengarriff Road
Kenmare
Co. Kerry

Tel: 064 42066
Fax: 064 42067
E-mail: arthurs@sallyporthouse.com
Web: www.sallyporthouse.com

The Arthur Family

You can thank an enterprising grandfather who exported railway sleepers to England for the lovely antiques here. Rather than use more conventional ballast for the return boat journey, he brought back beautiful furniture. The Arthurs are justifiably proud of his collection and put it to full use in every room. This extraordinary man also bought the local workhouse, knocked it down and used the stone to build Sallyport in 1932 — you can see the worn stepping stone in the hallway. Bedrooms lead off a central landing and have silk bedspreads, thick carpets, full baths, lots of light, mod cons and views over the orchard to Muxnaw Mountain and the Caha Mountains. Walk from the house through the park or stroll along the River Kenmare in the evening. Breakfast is wonderful, with smoked salmon on the menu. When I visited, staff remained friendly despite being at the beck and call of visiting foreign bigwigs. Kenmare is a pretty town with lots of life and is a good base to explore the rings of Kerry and Beara.

Rooms: 5: 1 twin/double, 3 doubles, 1 family, all with en suite bath.
Price: IR£35—IR£50 p.p.
Breakfast: Included — full menu.
Meals: Available in Kenmare.
Closed: November—March.

How to get there: From Killarney, N71 to Kenmare. Follow Bantry signs through town. House on left before suspension bridge.

Map no: 6

Entry no: 173

Ceann Mara

Kenmare
Co. Kerry

Tel: 064 41220
Fax: 064 41220

Thérèse Hayes

It is typical of Thérèse's innate modesty that she didn't put her house forward for consideration because she thought it was too modern. That may be the case but few houses have such a magnificent setting and few people are as likeable. Her garden, which she describes as "a favourite child", extends from the back of the house down to the shoreline of Kenmare Bay with the Caha Mountains behind. The sunsets alone are reason enough to stay here. Thérèse, a geography and English teacher at the local secondary school during term-time, takes great care of her guests, providing memorable breakfasts — kedgeree, local cheeses, stewed fruits and home-made scones, as well as the usual Irish fry. Bedrooms are small and sweet; the best has a beautiful view of the bay through large purpose-built windows. There are no TVs here. Her philosophy is to encourage rather than force guests to listen to music or read a book in the comfortable sitting room. Idea for bird-watchers and wonderful value.

Rooms: 4: 1 twin with en suite shower; 1 double with en suite bath; 2 doubles with en suite shower.
Price: IR£18 p.p. Sing. supp. IR£7.
Breakfast: Included — full Irish.
Meals: Dinner IR£15, by arrangement. Good restaurants in Kenmare.
Closed: End September—May.

How to get there: From Kenmare, follow Cork Rd, signed Kilgarvan. 1 mile from Post Office, just past ruined church, house signed right, down 100yd drive.

Entry no: 174

Map no: 6

Rock Cottage

Barnatonicane
Nr Schull
Co. Cork

Tel: 028 35538
Fax: 028 35538
E-mail: rockcottage@eircom.net
Web: www.mizen.net/rockcottage

Barbara Klötzer

Barbara is a no-nonsense woman with a great sense of humour and polymathic talents. Speaking in a weird and wonderful mix of German and Cork accents, she explained how she fought tooth and nail to restore a property she fell in love with and bought before even having it surveyed. As its name implies, this south-facing 1826 Georgian hunting lodge is built on a huge slab of rock; hence the split levels on the ground floor. Its slate-clad front and white sash windows look irresistible as you come up the drive and guests often extend their stay as excellent cooking and enticing bedrooms cast their spell. Rooms are done in simple bright colours with wood floors, pine beds, wicker chairs and views over lightly-wooded paddocks that contain Fruitabix-addicted sheep and a horse and a donkey who are great pals. Behind the house, a path through gorse bushes leads up a small hill where you can sit and gaze at the spectacular view over Dunmanus Bay to Sheep's Head. A successful shoe designer and accomplished chef, Barbara is now excelling at B&B in a region where she spent many a happy holiday as a child. *Self-catering cottage, sleeps 2-3, IR£200—IR£370 p.w.*

Rooms: 3: 2 family, both with en suite shower; 1 double with private bathroom.
Price: IR£25—IR£30 p.p. Sing. supp. IR£10.
Breakfast: Included — full menu.
Meals: Dinner, 3 courses, from IR£25. Supper on request.
Closed: Never.

How to get there: From Cork, N71 west. Just before Bantry, left on R591, signed Durrus. In Durrus, left on Goleen Rd for 8 miles. Entrance on right past small cemetery.

Map no: 6

Entry no: 175

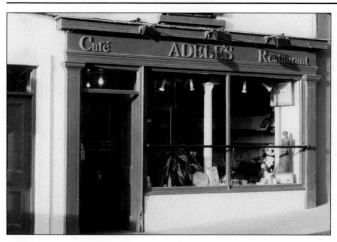

Adèle's

Main Street
Schull
Co. Cork

Tel: 028 28459
Fax: 028 28865
E-mail: adele@adelesrestaurant.com
Web: www.adelesrestaurant.com

Adèle and Simon Connor

Adèle's is a perfect combination of café, restaurant and B&B with a charm all of its own. The smell of good cooking is the first thing that greets you as you walk in off Schull's pretty main street. Bread, pastries, cakes and savoury snacks are baked on the premises with no additives and are tailored towards vegetarians and vegans. Pitch pine tables, candles, friendly staff — it is a lovely, unfussy place to sit back with a newspaper and watch the world go by. Adèle and her son Simon are both skillful bakers and she runs things with relaxed good humour. Up the little staircase are three small rooms with dark wooden floors, sweet little windows and window boxes. One room has a view of Clear and Sherkin Islands off nearby Baltimore. One shower and the 'first bath to be fitted in Schull' services all. Be careful not to follow the example of one guest who was soaking in the bath between the ground floor café and the first floor restaurant as the café filled up and had to run the gauntlet, dressed in just a towel, back to his room. Schull is a cosmopolitan place full of walkers, anglers and sailing enthusiasts. It is also the unlikely home of Ireland's only planetarium.

Rooms: 3: 1 twin, 2 doubles, all sharing shower & bathroom.
Price: IR£20 p.p. No sing. supp.
Breakfast: Included — Continental.
Meals: Dinner IR£15—IR£25. Lunch IR£5—IR£10.
Closed: November—Easter. (Open Christmas & New Year).

How to get there: From Cork, N71 to Ballydehob, then R592 to Schull. Building right side of Main Street in village.

Grove House

Colla Road
Schull
Co. Cork

Tel: 028 28067
Fax: 028 28069
E-mail: billyoshea@yahoo.com
Web: www.cork-guide.ie/schull/grove/welcome.html

Billy and Mary O'Shea

A sense of history drifts through Grove House like an unseen guest. Opening first as a hotel in the early 1900s, it became a popular haunt for many a distinguished guest. Bernard Shaw stayed here, as did Irish painter Jack Yeats. With its big airy rooms and commanding views over Schull harbour, it is easy to see what attracted them. Billy and Mary have done wonders with this remarkable house, mixing strong colours, antiques, modern paintings and handmade rugs on polished wooden floors to great effect. Uncluttered bedrooms are full of eccentric detail such as panelled headboards salvaged from a bank and an original Victorian loo with a square wooden seat. Schull has changed little in the past century. The narrow main street remains unspoilt with great traditional pubs. You could almost bottle their smoky, timeworn atmosphere and take it home as a souvenir. Billy is great company, cheery, helpful, the typical Irishman known to all in the village as I discovered when he took me on a whirlwind tour of his favourite haunts, while Mary is a helpful, friendly host who makes a truly superb breakfast that more than counteracts the night before. The Gubbeen bacon was probably the best I have tried in Ireland. You will have a lot of fun here.

Rooms: 5: 3 doubles, 1 twin, all with en suite shower; 1 double with en suite bathroom.
Price: IR£30—IR£40 p.p. Sing. supp. IR£10.
Breakfast: Included — full Irish or Continental.
Meals: Available in Schull.
Closed: Never.

How to get there: From Cork, N71 to Ballydehob, then R592 to Schull. At top of of main street, left opposite AIB bank. House 500m on right.

Map no: 6

Entry no: 177

Baltimore Bay

Baltimore
Co. Cork
La Jolie Brise

Tel: 028 20600 Chez Youen
Tel: 028 20136
Fax: 028 20495
E-mail: baltimorebay@youenjacob.com
Web: www.youenjacob.com

Youen Jacob

Two Youen Jacobs make this family business tick. Youen elder sailed from Brittany to Ireland with a cargo of furniture 30 years ago and never returned. He never even made it to his planned destination. Instead, he married a schoolteacher from nearby Sherkin Island and opened a seafood restaurant. This corpulent character is every bit the grizzled seafarer with wispy, white beard and a gruff but warm personality. Youen Junior is equally passionate about the sea and has sailed for Ireland at Olympic level; he will arrange sailing lessons. There are two restaurants now: the more upmarket Chez Youen; and La Jolie Brise, named after a sailing boat that won the Fastnet race two years running, where laid-back staff serve "the cheapest oysters in Ireland" and breakfast whenever you want; Youen treats the place as his office — I was given an impromptu lesson in the art of chewing rather than swallowing oysters whole. The guesthouse is above the bustling cafe. Rooms are adequate; five have harbour views; the rear ones look over a small garden. Baltimore, has everything you want from an old Irish fishing village — views, seafood, boats and folk music. *One double has full disabled facilities.*

Rooms: 8: 4 doubles, 4 triples, all en suite.
Price: IR£32.50 p.p.
Breakfast: Included — full Irish. Eaten in La Jolie Brise.
Meals: IR£10 in La Jolie Brise; IR£18— IR£35 at Chez Youen.
Closed: Never.

How to get there: From Cork, N71 to Skibbereen, then road signed Baltimore. La Jolie Breeze is light blue building in corner of small square on waterfront.

Blair's Cove House

Durrus
Co.Cork

Tel: 027 61127
Fax: 027 61487
E-mail: blairscove@eircom.net

Phillipe and Sabine De Mey

Phillipe and Sabine, from Belgium and Germany respectively, have devised a great system whereby breakfast comes to you rather than you go to it. Wake up to a beautiful spread ordered the night before and relax in front of a view of the bay. You can even try champagne and oysters. Blair's Cove is a late 18th-century Georgian house with a courtyard of cobbled paths, flowers and a lily pond. Stone outbuildings have been beautifully converted by local craftsmen into guest suites and a magnificent restaurant with a high-beamed ceiling. Each suite is self-contained with kitchen, sitting area and dining area. They are all different with wooden floors, terracotta tiles, coir matting, antique furniture, Victorian bedsteads and modern art on the walls. This is sophisticated comfort. In season, gorgeous seafood platters are laid out in the restaurant and meat is cooked on a woodburning grill. The atmosphere is wonderful. On summer evenings, you can dine in the conservatory overlooking the courtyard. The De Meys are good at detail and know how to spoil you. *Two self catering cottages: one on the estate, sleeps 8, IR£410—IR£800 p.w. and one at Dunmanus Pier further along coast, sleeps 4, IR£240—IR£500 p.w.*

Rooms: 3 courtyard apartments, 1 with 1 double, 1 twin, both en suite, sleeps 4; 2 with 1 double with en suite bathroom, both sleep 2.
Price: IR£55—IR£75 p.p. Sing. supp. IR£15.
Breakfast: Included — full menu.
Meals: Dinner, 3 courses, IR£31. Restaurant closed Nov-Mid-March and on Sundays and Mondays except in July & Aug.
Closed: Never.

How to get there: From Cork, N71 west. Just before Bantry, left on R591, signed Durrus. In Durrus, left on Goleen Rd for 1.5 miles. Entrance on right before sharp right bend. Take care when turning in or out.

Map no: 6

Entry no: 179

Bantry House

Bantry
Co. Cork
Ireland

Tel: 027 50047
Fax: 027 50795
E-mail: bantryhouse@iol.ie
Web: www.cork-guide.ie/bnry_hse.htm

Egerton Shelswell-White

This is one of the most beautiful houses in Ireland. The original Queen Anne house was added to in 1820, then again in the 1830s by the then Viscount Berehaven, who travelled extensively in Europe buying the priceless furniture and furnishings that fill the house today. There are three sections to the house: a guest wing with luxurious bedrooms furnished for comfort rather than authenticity; a family wing; and the stately reception rooms of the main house that were first opened to the public in 1945. The style of the huge drawing room, dining room, library and halls doff the cap to Versailles, where many of the wonderful antiques originate. In the evening, sit in front of an open fire in the incredible library with a pre-dinner drink. Bedrooms either have views of the vertiginous Italian terraced gardens, or to the front, across lawns, past cannons and a stone balustrade, over Bantry Bay to the heather-red Caha Mountains. The view from the top of the recently-restored garden is peerless, as the whole house joins the picture. Egerton, who inherited the house in 1978, is immensely friendly, plays the trombone and organises annual chamber music concerts in the house. A rare treat.

Rooms: 8: 2 twins, 4 doubles, 1 suite, all with en suite bathroom; 1 family with private bathroom.
Price: IR£75—IR£85 p.p. Sing. supp. IR£10. Child sharing parents' bedroom IR£20, occupying own room IR£35.
Breakfast: Included — full Irish.
Meals: Dinner, 3 courses, IR£25, by arrangement. Lunch in the tearoom from IR£3.

Closed: November—February. Last week in June.

How to get there: From Cork, N71 to Bantry. Big entrance on right just before village.

Entry no: 180   Map no: 6

Butlerstown House
Butlerstown, Timoleague
Bandon
Co. Cork

Tel: 023 40137
Fax: 023 40137
E-mail: mail@butlerstownhouse.com
Web: www.butlerstownhouse.com

Elisabeth Jones and Roger Owen

Lis and Roger are a relaxed, friendly Welsh couple who laugh a lot and make their guests feel instantly at home. The proportions of this fine Georgian house are perfect — the elegant staircase, the large airy rooms, the incredible cornice work and tall windows with views across fields to the sea. Four-poster beds and a 14ft mahogany dining table match the architectural splendour, while log fires, candlelit dinners, loads of hot water and a mammoth but homely kitchen make this a warm, informal country house. Breakfasts are a gourmet affair. As well as the full Irish spread, laverbread, cockles, wild Ummera smoked salmon, smoked haddock and Castletownshend kippers are worth a special mention. This house is a treat and one of our favourites in this part of Ireland. *Children over 12 years welcome. House available for self-catering (up to 10 people) from June to September.*

Rooms: 4: 2 doubles & 2 twins, 1 with en suite shower, 2 with en suite bath, 1 with private shower.
Price: £35—IR£55 p.p., depending on season and length of stay. No sing. supp.
Breakfast: Included — full menu.
Meals: Available locally.
Closed: Never.

How to get there: From Cork, N71 to Bandon, then R602 to Timoleague, then Barryroe, then Butlerstown. House signed to right as you approach village.

Map no: 7

Entry no: 181

Sea Court

Butlerstown
Timoleague, Bandon
Co. Cork

Tel: 023 40151/40218 or
US: 001 513 9613537
E-mail: seacourt_inn@yahoo.com

David Elder and Monica Bohlen

Every year, David and Monica cross the Atlantic to spend 10 glorious weeks in their
second home which they throw open to B&B guests, too. David, a law professor in
Kentucky, fell in love with this fine 1760 country house on a visit in 1983; Monica
took a little more persuading as it was little more than a dilapidated pile. Today, their
devotion to Georgiana has brought this graceful house back to life. It is a
magnificent example of the unpretentious style of Irish Georgian where space, light
and minimal detail were considered sacred. A sloped gravel drive brings you to the
front of the house and you step from the car by three terraced lawns, linked by
elegant stone steps. The view stretches down the hill through exotic trees and two
acres of restored orchard towards the sea at Seven Heads point; perhaps it is the sea
air that makes people sleep so well here — David says everyone does. Or maybe it is
the head-clearing simplicity of the huge, sparsely furnished bedrooms. Ask to see the
curious free-standing Edwardian bath and shower contraption in one bathroom
which looks like a museum piece and is yours to try out. An authentic pleasure.

Rooms: 6: 1 family, 2 doubles, 2 twins,
all with en suite bath; 1 double with private
bath.
Price: IR£25 p.p. No sing. supp.
Breakfast: Included — full Irish.
Meals: Dinner IR£22.50 for groups of
four or more. Book by noon the same day.
Closed: September—May for B&B. Self-
catering available all year.

How to get there: From Cork, N71 to
Bandon, R603 to Timoleague, cross causeway, then left signed Courtmacsherry,
past abbey on right. Ignore bridge signed Courtmacsherry & go straight on,
signed Butlerstown. Just before village, right on sharp left bend. Entrance on left
through white pillars.

Entry no: 182

Map no: 7

Kilbrittain Castle

Kilbrittain
Co. Cork

Tel: 023 49601
Fax: 023 49702
E-mail: timcob@iol.ie
Web: www.sawdays.co.uk

The Cahill-O'Brien Family

This is a rare opportunity to stay in Ireland's oldest inhabited castle. Irish chieftains, Norman invaders, Cromwellian troops and Anglo-Norman planters have all sought Kilbrittain's protection since its construction in 1035. Now the Cahill-O'Brien family maintain it as a B&B with enthusiastic affection. Sweep down and up the magnificent concave drive, past the Irish setters at the gate to the forbidding stone façade with its external double staircase; Today, you enter on the ground floor through a huge oak door into the guard room, then under a 'murder hole' and up a spiral staircase to a beautiful stone-floored gallery. From the guests' dining room, with its open fire and old leaded windows, look over a wooded valley to Courtmacsherry Bay or sit in the lounge next door with its magnificent fireplace and dream. Dark wood beams and thick doors lead to modern bedrooms and 1970s bathrooms. Fishing, tennis, scuba-diving, sailboarding, and sailing are available nearby, as is the unique Old Head links golf course. *No children under three.*

Rooms: 5: 3 family, 1 double, all with bath/shower; 1 double with shower.
Price: IR£45 p.p. Sing. supp. IR£10. Children under 12 sharing parents' bedroom, 50% discount.
Breakfast: Included — full Irish.
Meals: Available locally.
Closed: October—April.

How to get there: From Cork, N71 to Bandon, then R603 to Kilbrittain for 6 miles. In village, left at hairdressers, then first right. Entrance 200m on right.

Map no: 7

Entry no: 183

Leighmoneymore

Dunderrow
Kinsale
Co. Cork

Tel: 021 4775312
Fax: 021 4775692
E-mail: leighmoneymore@eircom.net
Web: www.sawdays.co.uk

Dominique O'Sullivan-Vervaet

Dominique is naturally friendly in six languages — Dutch, English, French, Italian, Spanish and German. Born in Belgium, she moved to Ireland to raise a family and now runs an informal B&B down a tiny lane just inland from the hustle and bustle of Kinsale. The farmhouse was built as a dowry in 1912 on land that extends to a secluded sea inlet banked by forrested hills. Sit on a jetty at the shore's edge and pass the time in blissful isolation. The bedrooms — in the old part of the house and in a new annexe that is in keeping with the original — have polished wooden floors, big brass beds, large bathrooms and distant views over rolling countryside. The family suite has interlinking twin and double rooms and a bathroom with a beautiful claw-footed bath. Downstairs, the sitting room in the older part of the house is full of plants and comfortable sofas. Delicious breakfasts with tempting dishes such as mangoes in lime juice are served around a big table in the bay-windowed dining room or in the new conservatory. Children will love the peacocks.

Rooms: 5: 1 family suite, 3 doubles, 1 twin/double, all with en suite bath.
Price: IR£28 p.p. Sing. supp. IR£10.
Breakfast: Included — full Irish/buffet.
Meals: Available in Kinsale.
Closed: November—mid-March.

How to get there: From Cork, N71 to Inishannon, then R605 towards Kinsale, past Innishannon House Hotel, for about 3.5 miles. House signed on right down lane.

The Gallery
The Glen
Kinsale
Co. Cork

Tel: 021 4774558
E-mail: carole@gallerybnb.com
Web: www.gallerybnb.com

Carole and Tom O'Hare

You cannot miss The Gallery's eye-catching yellow front as you near the centre of Kinsale. Tom claims they were the first to do it, but like all good ideas, he chuckles, "everyone copied them". This is a one-off sort of place, friendly, small and personal. Tom is a jazz musician and music teacher, and breakfast is not complete without some mellow tunes playing in the background. He sometimes plays the vibraphone or piano in the evening; satisfied guests say it does wonders for the digestion. Carole is an accomplished painter; all the pictures on the walls in this informal house are hers. The bedrooms are compact with seagrass matting, white walls and wooden beds, and the tiled en suite showers are bigger than expected. The rear of the house looks onto the old lighthouse, left over from the days when the road was a waterway. Quite a lot of Kinsale has been reclaimed from the old wharves and docks. Tom will fill you in about this historic town, and the annual arts festival in September which he helps run. Amid all the talk of money that threatens to spoil Kinsale's unique character, it is good to still find the Bohemian spirit that first drew so many people here.

Rooms: 5: 1 family, 4 doubles, all with en suite shower.
Price: IR£22.50—IR£32.50 p.p. Sing. supp. up to IR£10.
Breakfast: Included — full Irish.
Meals: Available locally.
Closed: Christmas.

How to get there: From Cork into Kinsale, straight on at Post Office, right at White House Hotel, 50yds on left.

The Old Rectory
Rampart Lane
Kinsale
Co. Cork

Tel: 021 4772678
Fax: 021 4772678
E-mail: dpringle@gofree.indigo.ie

Martha and David Pringle

It is not certain whether the starchy looking clergy pictured in the old photographs at The Old Rectory would quite approve of the temple of fun that Martha and David have created. Today, it is more likely to be the aperitif to a good night out rather than to prepare withering performances from the pulpit. But I think even the most ardent zealot would find it hard not to warm to the easy-going nature of this happy sanctuary in the whirligig of Kinsale. Expect to be treated and entertained like old friends over a glass of wine in the mini-bar that looks onto the secluded walled garden of this attractive Georgian building. Martha and David moved down from Dublin a few years ago after selling a consultancy business. The bedrooms are opulent; one has a four-poster with a gorgeous Paisley gold bedspread, the rose room is gracefully feminine, while the blue room has the fanciest bathroom in Kinsale complete with jacuzzi bath and mini-steam room. Revel or relax here — the choice is yours.

Rooms: 3: 1 double with en suite bath; 2 doubles, both with private bathroom.
Price: IR£40—IR£60 p.p.
Breakfast: Included — full Irish/buffet.
Meals: Available in Kinsale.
Closed:

How to get there: From Cork, N71 to Kinsale. Keep left past Blue Haven Hotel, then right up hill, past church on left, then left into Blind Gate as main road veers sharp right. Rampart Lane first left. House first right.

Entry no: 186

Map no: 7

Macalla Cheoil

33 Cork Street   **Tel:** 021 4772907
Kinsale
Co. Cork
Please note: pictures of property were unavailable at time of going to press.

Pat and Bernadette Crowley

"There's sure no passion in the human soul, but finds its food in music," wrote the 18th-century dramatist George Lillo; sentiments shared by Pat and Bernadette, two accomplished musicians who have renovated this historic 1760 Georgian townhouse to teach Irish folk music. Macalla Cheoil means 'echo of music' in Gaelic; and you will hear just that drifting from a converted music studio on the first floor of their informal family home. Bernadette is a music teacher and plays the fiddle, while Pat is a pianist. Both play regularly at the Spaniard pub, the best local music venue. The Crowleys are continuing a teaching tradition in the house started by Tom Johnson, founder of the Irish Labour party. He set up a school here for underprivileged children in the 1880s after falling in love with a local teacher. The bedrooms on the upper floors are furnished in a modern style with bold, bright colours on the walls and polished wooden floors; the double has a superb view over Kinsale harbour. Downstairs, striking modern prints by Gertrude de Genhardt continue the musical theme, while the red wooden kitchen, designed by a shipwright, leads to a conservatory and garden with a decked sitting area. Ideal for laid-back music lovers.

Rooms: 3: 1 double, 1 family, 1 twin, all with en suite shower.
Price: IR£25—IR£28 p.p. Sing supp. IR£10.
Breakfast: Included — full menu.
Meals: Available in Kinsale.
Closed: Never.

How to get there: From Cork, N28 to Kinsale. Entering town, keep straight into Pearce St rather than main road round to left. Left at junction, then first right and right again up hill. House on right 100yds after Desmond Castle.

Map no: 7   **Entry no: 187**

Farran House

Farran
Cork
Co. Cork

Tel: 021 7331215
Fax: 021 7331450
E-mail: info@farranhouse.com
Web: www.farranhouse.com

Patricia Wiese and John Kehely

Patricia and John's restoration of this grand mid-18th-century country house in 12 acres west of Cork city is a model for all Georgian houses in Ireland. Rather than paper over the cracks, these two young photographers stripped back the house to a bare shell, removed the problem, then put it back together again. The work was time-consuming but now the house, built in the mid-1770s, looks amazing and is capable of withstanding another couple of hundred years. Rooms are sensitively done, with antiques, pine floors, amazing window shutters, kilims from Afghanistan and paintings by Patricia's grandmother. I liked the bathrooms because they more than match the large bedrooms. There is lots of room to relax in — play the Bechstein in the drawing room, play snooker on a full-size billiards table or simply sit on a patio overlooking the Lee Valley. Indulge yourself in luxurious surroundings or step out to explore the mature beech woodland — home to myriad wild animals and birds. *Self-catering in main house, sleeps 8, IR£2,100—IR£2,500 p.w. or converted coach house, sleeps 6, IR£394—IR£433 p.w.*

Rooms: 4: 2 doubles, 1 family, 1 twin, all with en suite bathroom.
Price: IR£49—IR£55 p.p. Sing. supp. IR£12.
Breakfast: Included — full menu.
Meals: Dinner, 3 courses, IR£25.
Closed: November—March. Large groups off season by arrangement.

How to get there: From Cork city, N22 to Killarney for 10 miles, then second right after Dan Sheahan's pub, up steep lane. First entrance on left.

D'Arcy's

7 Sidney Place
Wellington Rd
Cork
Co. Cork

Tel: 021 4504658/4504522
Fax: 021 4502791
E-mail: accommodation@darcysguesthouse.com
Web: www.darcysguesthouse.com

Clare D'Arcy

Not until you enter D'Arcy's do you realize what a large building this is. Built in 1810 for Murphys the brewery (Clare thinks), it has ceilings and rooms that seem immeasurable, becoming lower and smaller as the house rises. And it does! Clare jokes that she does not charge for the step aerobics; there are 92 steps in all from the cosy breakfast area in the basement to the top floor bedrooms. D'Arcy's stands on the north bank of the River Lee close to the hubbub of Cork city. Inside, vivid yellows, mauves, pinks and reds grab the eye, as do the abstract paintings by one of Clare's daughters. The big bedrooms have outstanding views over the city; the higher you are the better the view. The rooms themselves do the job and are surprisingly peaceful for somewhere so close to the buzz of Ireland's southern capital. Breakfast is freshly squeezed, freshly ground and freshly baked with hot porridge and cream and home-made preserves. Clare brims with genuine good humour, always ready to crack a joke to put you at ease, while the rest of the family in the house happily mucks in. A friendly introduction to Cork.

Rooms: 6: 2 doubles, both with en suite shower; 4 doubles, sharing 2 showers, 1 bath & 2 toilets.
Price: IR£25—IR£30 p.p. Sing. supp. IR£5.
Breakfast: Included — full Irish.
Meals: Available locally.
Closed: Christmas.

How to get there: In Cork City centre. Ask for directions when booking.

Map no: 7

Entry no: 189

Allcorn's Country Home

Shournagh Rd
Blarney
Co. Cork

Tel: 021 4385577
Fax: 021 4382828
E-mail: allcorns_blarney@hotmail.com
Web: www.allcorns.com

Helen Allcorn

On a crisp, frosty morning, Helen Allcorn's wooden house reminded me of those Christmas card houses where snow-edged windows emit a welcoming, orange glow. It even smells cosy. Helen built the house herself 13 years ago, enchanted by the position in a wooded valley by the River Shournagh. It is modern and extremely comfortable, with the river an ever-present gurgle in the background. Guests will enjoy Helen's simple philosophy of doing-as-you-would-be-done-by. She loves animals and people in equal measure, and her pets are often strays in need of a good home; guests' pets are also welcome by arrangement. Downstairs, there are polished wooden floors, country baskets, rugs, flowers, pine furniture, and woodburning stoves; it is the sort of place where you just want to pad around all day in thick socks. It was a credit to the house's insulation that it was so warm inside on such a bitter morning. The bedrooms upstairs are equally pretty, with Egyptian cotton bed linen and plenty of space to shower. Breakfast is also a treat which should not be hurried.

Rooms: 4: 3 doubles with en suite shower;
1 single with private bath/shower.
Price: IR£21—IR£23 p.p.
Breakfast: Included — full Irish.
Meals: Available locally.
Closed: November—March.

How to get there: From Blarney, R617 Killarney Rd
for 1 mile, then right at major turn by River
Shournagh, signed to house. Entrance second on left.

Entry no: 190   Map no: 7

Maranatha Country House

Tower
Blarney
Co. Cork

Tel: 021 4385102
Fax: 021 4382978
E-mail: info@maranathacountryhouse.com
Web: www.maranathacountryhouse.com

Olwen and Douglas Venn

Olwen has created an extraordinary place to stay on a hill surrounded by monkey-puzzle trees and rhododendrons. This incurable romantic loves daring, sensual designs. In each bedroom, she has created a different fantasy centred round large, ornate four-poster or king-size beds. One resembles a flower garden, another a cool forest, while the magnificent regal suite is sumptuously decorated in claret damask drapes, deep burgundies, pinks and real lilacs; it even has its own whirlpool. In one room alone, more than 400 yards of material have been used. Olwen is enormously enthusiastic about the house and shows great daring in her designs; incredibly, she professes to have no previous experience of interior design — a born natural. Eating here is an experience, too, with wonderful breakfasts served in a beautiful flower-filled conservatory. The house is secluded by mature woodland in which they have designed special walks. Douglas and Olwen are very personable and know how to treat their guests well. A great place with a big heart.

Rooms: 6: 4 family/doubles and 2 doubles, all with ensuite bathroom.
Price: IR£21—IR£50 p.p. Sing. supp. IR£6—IR£15.
Breakfast: Included — full Irish.
Meals: Available locally.
Closed: November—March.

How to get there: From Cork, N20 then R617 through Blarney. Right up hill, 1.5 miles on, signed to house just after Tower village sign.

Map no: 7   **Entry no: 191**

Glenview House
Midleton
Co. Cork

Tel: 021 4631680
Fax: 021 4634680
E-mail: glenviewhouse@esatclear.ie
Web: www.dragnet-systems.ie/dira/glenview

Ken and Beth Sherrard

Ken and Beth's enthusiasm is palpable; they are proud of their home and of the guests who have become good friends, many of whom will go nowhere else in Ireland. In front of the 1780 Georgian house, the view is exhilarating. Lawns dive into a wedge of pines to an unseen, gurgling river that urges you to explore. Across the water, the valley rises in a huge sweep of larches and forested land. Quiet seclusion is yours among birds, horses, sheep, and all so close to the pretty market town of Midleton. The large bedrooms have spectacular views. Tall, sash windows, big, comfortable beds, long mirrors, and antiques — no expense has been spared. And one room has a wonderful turn-of-the-century Heath-Robinson-like brass shower. This is a friendly house with bags to do — fishing on the river, riding nearby, lawn tennis, or simply ambling in acres of woodland. *Two self-catering coach house cottages, one with full disabled facilities, sleep 2-6, IR£320—IR£620 p.w. Guide dogs welcome.*

Rooms: 4: 1 twin, 3 doubles, all with en suite bathroom.
Price: IR£40—IR£50 p.p. Discretionary sing. supp.
Breakfast: Included — full Irish.
Meals: Dinner IR£25. Book by noon on day of arrival.
Closed: Never.

How to get there: Drive into Midleton. Do not take bypass. At large r'bout, L35 to Fermoy. 2.5 miles on, left signed Leamlara in forestry area, then immediately right. Follow sign to Glenview; first entrance on left at top of hill.

Rathcoursey House

Ballinacurra
Midleton
Co. Cork

Tel: 021 4613418
Fax: 021 4613393
E-mail: beth@rathcoursey.com
Web: www.rathcoursey.com

Beth Hallinan

We all dream of discovering the perfect place in the perfect setting but wonder whether it really exists; well, Rathcoursey comes close. Owner Beth Hallinan is an accomplished chef who needed a change from running a busy restaurant in London, so when this derelict 1773 farmhouse on 35 acres came on the market, she snapped it up and and waved goodbye to the metropolitan lifestyle. That was in early 1999. Since then, she has renovated the house, exquisitely, and transformed the grounds, planting 3,000 trees and an orchard in the shape of a comet. She has even cleared a path through woodland to the local pub. A long avenue gently rises, up and up, until it opens into a clearing and a house the colour of dried apricots comes into view, sitting on the brow of a hill overlooking an unspoilt sea inlet of Cork Harbour. Luxurious rooms look as if they have evolved over many years in assured hands; the 'baptismal font' bathroom alone is incredible. Beth has a rare talent and it is to her credit that any praise offered is shrugged off with a graceful smile. A very special place — even ambassadors have pleaded to stay here.

Rooms: 5: 5 doubles, 2 with en suite shower, 3 with en suite bathroom. Extra bathroom with bath/shower.
Price: IR£55 p.p. House available to groups for longer periods.
Breakfast: Included — full menu
Meals: Dinner, by arrangement, IR£25.
Closed: Never.

How to get there: From Cork, N25 to Midleton. At r'bout, Whitegate road for 3 miles, then right to East Ferry. 2 miles on, look out for black arrows, and follow signs up narrow lane to house.

Map no: 7

Entry no: 193

Old Parochial House

Castlemartyr
Midleton
Co. Cork

Tel: 021 4667454
Fax: 021 4667429
E-mail: oldparochialhouse@eircom.net
Web: www.oldparochialhouse.com

Kathy and Paul Sheehy

Once home to the local priest, once a bawdy casino, Old Parochial House has always been a focal point for the local community since it was built in 1784, so there was sigh of relief in Castlemartyr when it was bought by folk with local connections. Kathy and Paul gamely undertook the huge task of renovating a house that had been neglected for 100 years to stunning effect. Mindful of preserving its character rather than its notorious past, they have created an informal atmosphere of relaxed elegance with maximum comfort. Downstairs, the drawing room has womb-like sofas and armchairs to flop in, floor-to-ceiling windows, a lovely fireplace, wood floors, cornicing that Paul restored painstakingly with a toothpick, and sound-proofed and cold-tight sash windows. In warm weather, you can sit in the conservatory among the tomato plants and grape vines. Upstairs, there is a four-poster in one room, a big brass bed in another, thick carpets, sparkling bathrooms and plenty of space. Kathy and Paul are a young, enthusiastic couple who take a lot of pride in what they do. Enjoy the results.

Rooms: 3: 2 doubles with en suite bath; 1 twin/double with en suite shower.
Price: IR£35—IR£40 p.p. No sing. supp.
Breakfast: Included — full Irish.
Meals: Available locally.
Closed: Christmas & New Year.

How to get there: From Cork, N25 to Waterford, bypassing Midleton. Next village Castlemartyr. Cross bridge, then immediately right signed Shanagarry, then keep immediately left. House first on left.

Entry no: 194

Map no: 7

Spanish Point Restaurant

Ballycotton
Co. Cork

Tel: 021 4646177
Fax: 021 4646179
E-mail: spanishp@indigo.ie

John and Mary Tattan

What strikes you most about Mary is she makes time for you; in my case, she was happy to natter away while she sliced two fresh salmon into steaks for the menu that night. She used to run the kitchen herself, cooking what John landed in his deep sea trawler, but now she has hired a French chef with ambitions to win a Michelin rosette. Their seafood restaurant perches on small cliffs looking over Ballycotton Bay. Below, a small, rocky cove is accessible via a steep path. From the large conservatory section of the restaurant, you can watch the clouds rolling in off the slate-grey Atlantic, casting their shadow over Lighthouse Island just off shore. To the right is the harbour where John moors his trawler. He is a seine-net fisherman by trade, meaning the fish are landed on the boat alive which improves their quality. Upstairs, the rooms are identical with low double beds and pink carpets; two of them have sea views. Ballycotton is a sweet little fishing village that has changed little over the years. This is a place for foodies who want to eat the freshest seafood in unpretentious surroundings and to mull on the larger issues of life while gazing out to sea. *There are plans to add more rooms with sea views.*

Rooms: 5: 3 doubles, 2 family, all with en suite shower.
Price: IR£25—IR£35 p.p. Sing. supp. IR£10.
Breakfast: Included — full Irish.
Meals: Dinner IR£30. Lunch IR£15. Packed lunch from IR£7.
Closed: January—mid-February.

How to get there: From Cork, N25 towards Youghal. Right in Midleton to Ballycotton. Entering village, restaurant signed on left.

Map no: 7

Entry no: 195

Glenally House

Youghal
Co. Cork

Tel: 024 91623
Fax: 024 91623
E-mail: enquiries@glenally.com
Web: www.glenally.com

Fred and Herta Rigney

Fred and Herta couldn't quite shrug off the settled metropolitan lifestyle they left behind in London when they took the brave step of decamping to southern Ireland to restore a classic Georgian building. Modern contrasts with original in this 1826 house on the outskirts of Youghal, pronounced 'yawl'. Sleek Italian furniture sits next to antique thrones, central heating next to wooden shutters and polenta is as likely to be served as soda bread. Both are design junkies and incurable foodies. The rooms are full of surprises, like the 19th-century Spanish wrought iron canopied bed that defies description except to say that it probably started life as a flying machine. I could go on, but you discover the rest. Fred and Herta are a contrast, too. He is a Dubliner, avuncular, tall, with a well-trimmed white beard, while Herta is naturally industrious and visually creative, decorating the rooms with fresh flowers from the garden. Both love gardening the seven acres of wild and cultivated land. Eating and drinking brings the most pleasure. Arriving late, I found them sitting outside in candlelight. "Would you like some cheese and a glass of wine?" Fred asked and the evening began from there.

Rooms: 4: 3 doubles, all with en suite shower;
1 twin with private bathroom.
Price: IR£25—IR£40 p.p. Sing. supp. IR£10.
Breakfast: Included — full menu.
Meals: Dinner, 4 courses, IR£24.
Closed: Christmas, New Year & January.

How to get there: From Youghal, N25 Waterford Rd out of town. Over r'bout, past Esso garage, then first left into small lane. After 75m, turn right into cul-de-sac. House at bottom.

Entry no: 196

Map no: 7

Conna House
Conna   **Tel:** 058 59419
Co. Cork

Michael and Maura Verling

There are no regulations here. The emphasis is on a relaxed homely atmosphere where no part of the house is blocked off to guests. "Except our bedroom," says Maura, smiling. Four good-sized rooms have large single beds that convert into doubles, high pink bedsteads, workmanlike en suite showers and views over green hills and some unlikely palms in the garden. Blue patterned carpets lead downstairs to the sitting room and into the dining room through a large arch. Here, Maura serves home-made meals that had one group of Italians applauding at the end. "I love feeding people," she says. This is fishing and horse country. Riding, hunting and point-to-pointing are all available locally, while the house is within casting distance of the River Bride for trout fishing and salmon fishing can be arranged on the River Blackwater. Maura has an infectious humour and many a happy time is spent nattering in the cosy kitchen. *Self-catering mews cottage, sleeps 4, IR£250 p.w.*

Rooms: 4 twin/doubles, all with en suite shower.
Price: £25 p.p. Sing. supp. £5.
Breakfast: Included — full Irish.
Meals: Dinner IR£25, B.Y.O wine. Packed lunch for fishermen IR£5.
Closed: October—Easter.

How to get there: From Cork, N8 Dublin Rd. Before village of Rathcormack, right signed Conna, follow straight for 8 miles. House signed on right before village.

Map no: 7   **Entry no: 197**

Ballyvolane House

Castlelyons
Co. Cork

Tel: 025 36349
Fax: 025 36781
E-mail: ballyvol@iol.ie
Web: www.ballyvolanehouse.ie

Jeremy and Merrie Green

Tell anyone in southern Ireland that you are staying at Ballyvolane and you will get a nod of approval, as this is one of most stylish old houses in Ireland — gracefully furnished, luxuriously comfortable, set in one of Ireland's most idyllic private estates and, above all, run by a delightful couple. Jeremy and Merrie are masters at looking after guests with Jeremy's charming Anglo-Irish aplomb complementing the boisterous exuberance of Merrie. The house built in 1728, then remodelled 120 years later in the Italianate style is surrounded by woodland, restored trout lakes, formal terraced gardens and a croquet lawn. The pillared hall with its fine, high ceilings features a Bluthner baby grand piano which guests are welcome to play, while in the grand dining room, Egyptian lucifers stand attendant while guests dine around a magnificent table sparkling with the best silverware — expect a feast. Bedrooms lie off a long narrow corridor and are all different with huge beds, antique furniture, thick carpets, tall windows, and comfortable armchairs; one of the bathrooms has an amazing early 19th-century bath. The Greens justly deserve their reputation. *Private salmon fishing on 13km of the River Blackwater.*

Rooms: 6: 2 doubles, 3 twins, all en suite bathroom; 1 double with en suite shower.
Price: IR£40—IR£50 p.p. Sing. supp. IR£15.
Breakfast: Included — full Irish.
Meals: Dinner IR£26. Packed lunch for fishermen IR£6.
Closed: Christmas.

How to get there: From Cork, N8 towards Fermoy for about 15 miles, then right onto R628 Tallow Rd before Rathcormac. Follow signs to house from Tallow turn-off.

Castlehyde Hotel

Fermoy
Co. Cork

Tel: 025 31865
Fax: 025 31485
E-mail: cashyde@iol.ie
Web: www.castlehydehotel.com

Helen and Erik Speekenbrink

By happy coincidence, John Barry's moody theme tune to the *Ipcress File* was playing in the car as I drove slowly through a stone archway into the magnificent courtyard at Castlehyde. The music matched the atmospheric surroundings. I was starring in my own 1960s spy movie. Down one side runs a wonderful flagstoned veranda, with rooms leading off, supported by 200-year-old pitchpine columns salvaged from a wharf at nearby Cork city — imagine sitting content in all weathers with a book or a glass of wine. Dutch couple Erik and Helen have done a wonderful job converting this ruined 17th-century dower house into a small hotel run with friendly professionalism. It took two years to find the right materials and the right furniture but it has paid off — Lloyd Loom chairs, Italian marble, silk curtains, tapestry pillows, all combine beautifully in simple, elegant rooms done in country house, cottage and French styles. Buffet breakfasts and superb evening meals are served in a dining room that looks onto landscaped gardens and mature woodland. You are in the heart of the Blackwater Valley, a Mecca for fishermen, walkers and dreamers. *Outdoor heated pool open all year. Five self-catering cottages also available, IR£325—IR£750 p.w..*

Rooms: 14: 10 courtyard rooms, 4 woodland rooms, twins/doubles, all with en suite bathroom.
Price: IR£52.50—IR£75 p.p. Sing. supp. IR£25.
Breakfast: Included — full menu/buffet.
Meals: Dinner IR£22.50.
Closed: Never.

How to get there: From Fermoy, N72 to Mallow for 2 miles. Entrance on left, signed.

Map no: 7

Entry no: 199

Glanworth Mill

Glanworth
Fermoy
Co. Cork

Tel: 025 38555
Fax: 025 38560
E-mail: glanworth@iol.ie
Web: www.iol.ie/glanworth

Lynne Glasscoe and Emelyn Heaps

There is not enough room here to mention all the good things about Glanworth. It is an absolute gem on all counts. Its position is the first thing that strikes you; built into a cliff-face with an imposing Norman Castle perched like a hat above, and next to a 15th-century, narrow, stone-arched bridge, that crosses the River Funcheon. Inside, the river turns the huge mill-wheels behind a glass wall in the tea rooms, which is an unusually soothing experience. The setting is stupendous and film crews regularly turn up to capture its magic. All this has not gone to the heads of Lynne and Emelyn, however, who are two of the most relaxed people you could hope to meet. Their calm spirit seems to have rubbed off on the young staff, who cheerfully keep the restaurant and tearooms ticking over. Downstairs is a library with a stone fireplace and beamed mantlepiece where a few tunes are tinkled on a piano on Sundays. The writer-themed rooms are enchanting, and the pièce de résistance has to be the Seamus Murphy room where the back wall is an exposed, white-painted rock-face. All is bright and beautiful here and full of country style.

Rooms: 10: 7 doubles and 3 twins/doubles, all with en suite bath.
Price: IR£50 p.p. Sing. supp. IR£10.
Breakfast: Included — full Irish.
Meals: Dinner (6 nights/wk) in Fleece 'n' Loom, à la carte. Average main course IR£14.50. Closed Sunday night. Mill Tea Rooms for casual dining.
Closed: 24 December—4 January & Good Friday.

How to get there: From Dublin, N8 south. Between Mitchelstown and Fermoy, right signed Glanworth. Continue for 5 miles, over old bridge. House under castle on right by the river.

Creagh House

Main Street
Doneraile
Co. Cork

Tel: 022 24433
Fax: 022 24715
E-mail: creaghhouse@eircom.net
Web: www.creaghhouse.ie

Michael O'Sullivan and Laura O'Mahony

Michael and Laura began with the intention of buying a small holiday cottage and ended up acquiring a life's work. By any architectural standards, this 1837 Georgian townhouse is a monster. Nothing prepares you for the sheer scale and beauty of the rooms as you approach the austere weathered limestone front. It was built like a fortress by the Creagh family after they were targeted during the Doneraile Conspiracy of 1829. "You can't change a bulb here without scaffolding," Michael jokes. Both he and Laura are environmental consultants with a great sense of fun. They want you to relax here rather than pay homage. The two distinguished reception rooms with high decorated ceilings of beautifully restored plasterwork are the largest from this period outside Dublin and were the setting for many a society ball in the late 1800s; hard to imagine the dining room was briefly an amusement arcade. The bedrooms, particularly those at the front, have an unfussy grandeur that invokes the true spirit of Irish Georgian. Out back they plan to restore the garden using accurate descriptions from two novels written by Canon Sheehan, who lived next door and wrote in the garden. An astonishing place to stay.

Rooms: 3: 1 double, 2 twins, all with en suite bath/shower.
Price: IR£55—IR£60 p.p. Sing. supp. IR£10—IR£12.
Breakfast: Included — full menu.
Meals: Supper IR£10. Give 24 hours notice. Available locally.
Closed: Christmas.

How to get there: From Cork, N20 Limerick Rd through Mallow to New Twopothouse, then right to Doneraile. House on left at bottom of long main street before bridge.

Map no: 7

Entry no: 201

Assolas Country House

Kanturk
Co. Cork

Tel: 029 50015
Fax: 029 50795
E-mail: assolas@eircom.net
Web: www.assolas.com

Joe and Hazel Bourke

Catholic monks lived at Assolas until Elizabeth I ordered them out in the 16th century. Today, that monastic dedication to self-sufficiency has been revived under the careful supervision of Joe and Hazel, the latest in a long line of Bourkes to live here. They grow a dizzying variety of organic fruit and vegetables for the table in a large walled garden; old Irish apple varieties fill puddings and compots, tangy crab apples create delicious mint jelly, peppery nasturtiums make distinctive bread, while the resident bees with so much blossom on their doorstep produce the most fragrant honey. Few kitchen gardens in Ireland are managed this well and similar standards apply to the rest of this family-run affair; the service is exemplary and the rooms are impeccable. The house is a rare example of an Irish Queen Anne manor house built in 1740 with rounded ends; some of the larger bedrooms have beautiful curved walls. The quiet courtyard rooms are behind the house, while the grounds — manicured lawns, wild meadow, mature trees and the River Owenbeg, a Blackwater tributary that was beautifully landscaped into the garden in the 1700s — provide the ideal stroll before dinner. This is a treat in a secret part of Ireland.

Rooms: 9: House: 6 doubles, all with en suite bath/shower; Courtyard: 3 doubles, all with en suite bathroom.
Price: IR£55—IR£83 p.p. Sing. supp. IR£10—IR£15.
Breakfast: Included — full menu.
Meals: Dinner IR£32.
Closed: November—February. Groups all year by arrangement.

How to get there: From Mallow, N72 west towards Killarney for 8 miles, then right towards Kanturk. House signed on right after 1 mile. Follow signs to house.

Entry no: 202   Map no: 7

Glenlohane

Kanturk
Co. Cork

Tel: 029 50014
Fax: 029 51100
E-mail: info@glenlohane.com
Web: www.glenlohane.com

Desmond and Melanie Sharp Bolster

Glenlohane was built by Desmond's ancestor in 1741 and has remained in the family ever since. The Sharp and Bolster clans are spread thickly over the north Cork region, having rooted here several centuries ago. Desmond returned to the fold after a stint in the US where he met Melanie, an American heavily under the influence of Ireland. They are great characters, full of anecdotes and humour. This working estate has 300 acres of sheep fields, horse paddocks and parkland. Nearby Mount Hilary beckons the walker. You can fish on the renowned River Blackwater with some advance notice and ride just about anywhere. Foxhunting is available in the winter. Desmond keeps pet hens who provide eggs for breakfast, while Melanie is the custodian of several stray dogs who love strangers. Relax in informal rooms full of antiques and family memorabilia; the stuffed birds of paradise in the hallway are beautiful. Large bedrooms are clean, fresh, with lots of windows and proper bathrooms. Great fun and sophisticated comfort. *Children over 12 welcome. Groups can reserve the whole house.*

Rooms: 4: 1 double, 2 twins, all with en suite bath and shower; 1 twin with en suite shower.
Price: IR£55—IR£65 p.p. Sing. supp. IR£10. Book in advance.
Breakfast: Included — full Irish.
Meals: Dinner IR£25, except on Sundays.
Closed: Never.

How to get there: From Kanturk, take R576 towards Mallow. Bear left on R580 towards Buttevant. First right towards Ballyclough, first entrance on left after 2.5 km, signed 'Glenlohane Bird Sanctuary'.

Map no: 7   **Entry no: 203**

Buggy's Glencairn Inn
Glencairn
Co. Waterford

Tel: 058 56232
Fax: 058 56232
E-mail: buggysglencairninn@eircom.net
Web: www.buggys.net

Ken and Cathleen Buggy

Ken and Cathleen steadfastly refuse to blow their own trumpet, so I must let others do it for them. Buggy's has "a wealth of uniqueness", wrote one fan, while another said he would have been furious if he had bought our book and not found it mentioned; all this before I had even seen the place. Buggy's Glencairn Inn is a small pub, a small restaurant and a small B&B — small but perfectly formed. Dump your stuff on a wonderful double bed, soak in a hot bath, then slip downstairs for a pint of Guinness by a log fire in a snug, wooden pub. Dinner is in the even cosier restaurant next door with stone floors, country artefacts and red and white check tablecloths. Food is utterly delicious. After coffee, amble back to the bar for a few nightcaps and a chat with Ken if he is around. His wry observations are hilarious; he might even guess the car you drive. Both he and Cathleen are great company and have many entertaining tales to retell from years in the hotel trade both in Ireland and abroad. If you were driving through the dark wondering where the hell to pass the night and you stumbled upon Buggy's, you would know some of your sins had been forgiven.

Rooms: 4: 3 doubles, 1 twin, all with en suite bathroom.
Price: From IR£32 p.p. Sing. supp. IR£10.
Breakfast: Included — full Irish.
Meals: Dinner IR£18—IR£22.
Closed: Christmas Day & Good Friday.

How to get there: From Lismore, N72 Tallow Rd for 0.75 miles, then right at Horneybrooks car showroom signed Glencairn. House is 2 miles on right in village, opposite T-junc.

Entry no: 204

Map no: 7

Hanora's Cottage

Nire Valley
Ballymacarbry
Co. Waterford

Tel: 052 36134
Fax: 052 36540
E-mail: hanorascottage@eircom.net
Web: www.hanorascottage.com

Seamus and Mary Wall

Once in a while, we all hanker to escape from it all, to go somewhere where no-one can find us, where we will be pampered and provided for. This is just such a place. Seamus and Mary have created a refuge of luxury set deep in the heart of the beautiful Nire valley next to a crystal clear brook. A short distance on, the road literally stops and nature takes over, rising into the Comeragh Mountains and the towering peak of Knockaunapeebra. The Walls first moved here in 1967, opening a tea shop in the original cottage built for Seamus's great grandparents. Today, it is hard to imagine such humble beginnings. Rooms are sumptuous and sensual with jacuzzi and double jacuzzi baths. They have thought of everything. Hanora's breakfast provides the idea start to your day in the mountains — exotic bread baked each morning by Seamus, porridge, scones, cheeses, smoked salmon, fresh fruit... not to mention the scrambled eggs, sweet bacon and coffee. Then after the exertions of the day, you can sample the talented cooking of son Eoin and wife Judith, who both trained at Ballymaloe. A blissful retreat from the white noise of modern life. *Restaurant open to non-residents by reservation.*

Rooms: 10: 6 doubles, 4 twins, all with en suite bathroom.
Price: IR£45—IR£65 p.p. Sing. supp. IR£10.
Breakfast: Included — full Irish.
Meals: Dinner IR£30 except Sundays. Free packed lunch for walkers.
Closed: Christmas.

How to get there: From Clonmel, cross bridge and follow R671 Dungarven Rd to Ballymacarbry. House signed left over small bridge by Melody's Lounge. House 3.5 miles up twisty road by Nire church.

Map no: 7

Entry no: 205

The Old Rectory

Stradbally   **Tel:** 051 293280
Kilmacthomas
Co. Waterford

Julian and Alison Burkitt

Arriving at this happy, settled house, it strikes you that maybe once there was a halcyon past where life's embrace was softer and kinder to the spirit and time drifted gently with the seasons. Imagine a comfy armchair by a log fire, gin and tonic in hand, a cat asleep on your lap and dogs curled up around your feet and you will begin to understand why guests find it so hard to leave the cosy environment that Julian and Alison have created here. They are a warm, intelligent couple who love to chat and will ensure you feel instantly at home. The rectory is built round a small courtyard and stands in a sylvan setting. Bedrooms have been left as they were originally intended, so no sign of cramped showers or noisy ventilator fans here. Old-fashioned carpets, rugs, and curtains mix well with bold blues, pinks and yellows on the walls. Beware, these comfortable bedrooms weaken your resolve to get up for breakfast. However, seductive smells wafting from the kitchen will generally do the trick. Stradbally is a lovely coastal village with a great cove for summer bathing, while drives along the coast to Annestown are outstanding. *Self-catering apartment overlooking courtyard, sleeps 4* .

Rooms: 2 doubles, both with bathroom next door.
Price: IR£30 p.p. Sing. supp. IR£8.
Breakfast: Included — full Irish.
Meals: Dinner IR£21 by arrangement. Light supper IR£15 on request.
Closed: Christmas.

How to get there: From N25 Cork to Waterford road, turn off at Griffins garage towards Stradbally for 5 miles. Entrance on right, in village centre after small green.

Entry no: 206   Map no: 7

Knockmahon Lodge

Bunmahon
Co. Waterford

Tel: 051 292249
Fax: 051 292422
E-mail: ktoebbe@aol.com
Web: www.knockmahonlodge.com

Karen Többe

Karen is a German with an Irish sense of humour. Praise this clean, uncluttered B&B for its smooth efficiency and she replies, laughing: "I have to — *I'm German*." She even has a dog called Fritz who I was assured understood German. The lovely garden is just as immaculate with seating overlooking Bunmahon beach and the rugged Copper Coast. The shoreline was named after the mines that operated here in the 19th century and this 200-year-old house was once home to the director of a mining company. Good-sized bedrooms are welcoming and unfussy with roomy bathrooms and sea views; two are in an annexe which would suit families. Karen is an incredibly obliging woman, who never likes to see people go hungry; she is tangibly happy in this corner of Ireland that, they say, gets less rain and more sun. Take a delicious packed lunch and explore the industrial archaeology left by the mining era or walk along the spectacular coast to nearby Bunmahon, once the lively centre of the copper industry. Above all, come to be inspired by the sea.

Rooms: 3 double/twins with en suite shower.
Price: IR£25—IR£35 p.p. Sing. supp. IR£10.
Breakfast: Included — full Irish.
Meals: Dinner IR£18. Lunch IR£12. Packed lunch IR£12.
Closed: December—January.

How to get there: From Waterford, N25 Dungarven Rd for 5 miles, then left at The Sweep pub on R681 for 10 miles through Kill to Bunmahon. In village, right then right.

Map no: 7

Entry no: 207

Annestown House

Annestown
Co. Waterford

Tel: 051 396160
Fax: 051 396474
E-mail: relax@annestown.com
Web: www.annestown.com

John and Pippa Galloway

With the views from Annestown, a shack would suffice. Instead, you have the added comforts of a gorgeous 1830s country house. From your clifftop eyrie, gaze across the Celtic Sea, then turn to look across fields to the Comeragh Mountains. The terraced lawns draw you to the cliff's edge where a small path winds down to a sandy bay that arcs round to the next headland. The house has been in John's family for years and is full of assorted memorabilia accumulated by previous generations. It feels old fashioned but you would not want it any other way. The library has a full-size billiards table and complete sets of 1820s editions of Voltaire and Scott, while the snug is full of technicolour rows of hardback novels and botanical reference books. All the bedrooms are large, with lovely views and modern bathrooms, and some have huge beds. John is a seriously nice chap, while Pippa crackles with energy. They thrive on good company and fondly remember the guests who volunteer to play the piano. You will love this place, whether it is playing tennis on the grass court in summer, or huddling round a warm fire in winter after a particularly long walk for a pint of Guinness — Annestown is said to be the only village in Ireland without a pub.

Rooms: 5: 4 doubles, all with en suite bathroom; 1 double with en suite shower.
Price: IR£33—IR£40 p.p. Sing. supp. IR£15
Breakfast: Included — full Irish.
Meals: Dinner IR£20—IR£23. House wines from IR£15.
Closed: December—February except for groups by arrangement.

How to get there: From Waterford, follow signs to Tramore. Through town centre, up steep hill. Continue past golf club until sharp bend signed to Annestown. Continue into Annestown, house signed on left.

Entry no: 208   Map no: 8

The Old Rectory Kilmeaden House

Kilmeaden   **Tel:** 051 384254
Co. Waterford   **E-mail:** kilmeadenhouse@eircom.net
                                    Web: www.kilmeaden.com

Jerry and Patricia Cronin

Kilmeaden is a rural idyll. The combination of sun, buzzing bees, fragrant blossom, manicured lawns and shady groves made me want to lie down on the grass and go to sleep. On hot days, doors are thrown open at both ends of the large hall and wrought-iron chairs laid out by the lawn at the back. Here you can sit looking over a magnificent garden with terraces of vegetables and beds of wonderful roses. Beyond this lovely garden, paddocks and trees provide quiet seclusion from the bustle of nearby Waterford city. A tight entrance through pillared gates leads up a gravel drive to this imposing, creeper-clad late Georgian rectory. As a local surgeon, Jerry is familiar with attention to detail, and with wife Patricia's flare for elegant interior design, they have meticulously restored the house, doing up all the rooms and opening up the long hall with an arched recess; it now houses a grand piano. The results are exceptional. Large bedrooms overlook the garden are immaculate with thick carpets, luxurious beds, and big, white bathrooms. No expense has been spared in this deeply peaceful setting. *Children over 12 welcome.*

Rooms: 5: 3 doubles, 2 twins, all with en suite bathroom.
Price: IR£60 p.p. Sing. supp. IR£20.
Breakfast: Included — full Irish.
Meals: Light evening meals available. Give 24 hours notice.
Closed: October—April.

How to get there: From Waterford, N25 towards Cork for 8 miles. Right signed Carrick-on-Suir. A tight turn through gates 300m on right leads to house.

Map no: 8   **Entry no: 209**

Sion Hill House and Gardens

Ferrybank
Waterford City
Co. Waterford

Tel: 051 851558
Fax: 051 851678
E-mail: sionhill@eircom.net

George and Antoinette Kavanagh

What a beautiful position overlooking Waterford City and the River Suir. It is easy to see why George and Antoinette, a gentle, modest couple, are passionate about their historic home and garden. Two lovely pavilions sit either side of the house, while sentry holes in the stone steps are reminders that big houses needed protection in the past. Inside, Sion Hill is full of interesting memorabilia — nothing arrived without a story — and good-sized bedrooms have lovely antiques, large beds and fine views of the wonderful garden and river. The Kavanaghs have restored the original five-acre garden laid out 250 years ago using plans discovered in Waterford Library. The result is a living encyclopedia of botany containing more than 1,000 species of rhododendron, azalea, rose, hydrangea and many other rare plants. Pathways lead to fragrant groves, a walled garden, a pond surrounded by ancient tree ferns, and an 11th-century Coptic monk lodged in an old garden wall — just how this Egyptian relic got here remains a mystery. With George as your guide, not even the world's smallest rhododendron will escape your attention but do allow yourself time — he has the infectious enthusiasm of an academic.

Rooms: 4: 2 family with en suite bath;
1 double, 1 family, both with en suite shower.
Price: IR£25—IR£35 p.p. Sing. supp. IR£10.
Breakfast: Included — full Irish.
Meals: Available in Waterford.
Closed: Christmas.

How to get there: From Waterford city centre, N25 over bridge towards Rosslare. Entrance on left, 100m after Jury's Hotel.

Brown's Townhouse

29 South Parade
Waterford
Co. Waterford

Tel: 051 870594
Fax: 051 871923
E-mail: info@brownstownhouse.com
Web: www.brownstownhouse.com

Leslie and Barbara Brown

Behind Leslie's deadpan telephone manner is a friendly, helpful and mischievously humorous man who makes people laugh. Running a B&B is the perfect vehicle for his wry and mildly subversive nature as is the internet; he is a self-taught expert, consulting surreal think-tanks in Hawaii to design websites in his spare time. A lot of thought has gone into this Victorian townhouse with charming results. Both he and Barbara, who is an accountant, are keen patrons of modern Irish art. The walls are full of their expanding collection of paintings, while window boxes provide more splashes of colour. Comfortable bedrooms with large beds have big, sash windows. There is a funky orange and blue family room at the top of the house, reached via a tiny staircase, while others are done in an older style; one has its own roof terrace garden. Brown's is on a quiet residential street with easy and safe parking and only a short walk from Waterford's lively city centre and the waterfront. Ideal for the Waterford Show held during the summer. In the morning, breakfast is served around a big dining table with pancakes, home-made jams and bread, fruit salad and a full fry-up. Great value.

Rooms: 6: 3 double/twins, 1 family, all with en suite shower; 1 twin with en suite bathroom; 1 suite with bath.
Price: IR£25—IR£35 p.p. Sing. supp. IR£5.
Breakfast: Included — full menu.
Meals: Available in Waterford.
Closed: Christmas & January.

How to get there: Arriving in Waterford from Dublin, cross bridge, left down the quay, follow road round to right. At second traffic lights after Tower Hotel turn left, over hump-backed bridge, past park. House on right.

Map no: 8

Entry no: 211

Foxmount Country House

Passage East Road
Waterford
Co. Waterford

Tel: 051 874308
Fax: 051 854906
E-mail: foxmount@iol.ie
Web: www.iol.ie/tipp/foxmount.htm

Margaret and David Kent

If there were awards for outstanding contributions made to B&B in Ireland, David and Margaret would get my vote. They have been putting up guests in the utmost comfort for more than 30 years. The guest book says it all. People come back time and time again to Foxmount, a peaceful, secluded 17th-century farmhouse set in 200 acres of farmland just three miles from the sea. Margaret is such a pleasant, confident woman, and justifiably proud of her home. No description would be complete without mentioning her wonderful cooking. She uses fresh beef and dairy products from the farm, as well as lamb, local wild salmon, free-range chickens, free-range eggs, unsprayed fruit, vegetables and fresh herbs. "I will not deviate from my butter-and-cream policy," she says emphatically and quite right, too, as the results are mouth-watering. Dinner is served at separate tables though a dinner-party atmosphere usually develops, then guests come together for coffee in front of the marble fireplace in the big drawing room. Bedrooms are lovely, with split levels, proper bathrooms and creeper-framed windows overlooking a valley on one side, the farmyard on the other. You will be happy here.

Rooms: 5: 5 double/twins, 4 with en suite bath and shower, 1 with en suite bathroom.
Price: IR£35 p.p. Sing. supp. IR£10.
Breakfast: Included — full Irish.
Meals: Dinner IR£20, B.Y.O. wine.
Closed: November—February.

How to get there: From Waterford, take Dunmore Rd for 3 miles, left towards Passage East and follow signs to Foxmount.

Gaultiere Lodge

Woodstown
Co. Waterford

Tel: 051 382549
Fax: 0903 22003
E-mail: castleffrench@eircom.net

John and Jill Thomas

Time and time again in Ireland you stumble on the Georgian legacy; hunting lodges, mansions, farmhouses, all faithfully executed in the Palladian style. And Gaultiere is no exception. What makes this 18th-century hunting lodge unique is its position. The back garden leads right onto a clean, sandy beach with views over the widest part of Waterford Harbour to County Wexford. Walk with the sand between your toes for more than a mile. Let the wind and surf inspire you. Built on a bank of rock, the house is effectively upside down, with the entrance on the same level as the bedrooms and the dining room and kitchen underneath. From the road, it appears to be surrounded by impregnable walls breached only by a stone-stepped entrance underneath the gnarled boughs of an evergreen holm oak that leads to a raised lawn and gardens. When I visited, the bedrooms were being decorated in a comfortable country house style, but I only had eyes for the huge window view. Jill and John are friendly horse folk who originally come from Cornwall. B&B is a new venture for them but they have everything going for them. *Children over 8 welcome.*

Rooms: 4: 2 doubles, 2 twins, all with en suite bathroom.
Price: IR£45—IR£55 p.p. Sing. supp. IR£20.
Breakfast: Included — full Irish.
Meals: Available in Dunmore East.
Closed: Never.

How to get there: From Waterford, R684 Dunmore East Rd for 6 miles, then left, signed Woodstown. Through village towards beach, right at T-junc. Lodge behind high wall 0.25 miles on left.

Map no: 8

Entry no: 213

Meanings of place names

Gaelic	Anglicised form	Meaning	Example
Achadh	Agha	Field	*Aghamore* - big field
Ard	Ard	Hill	*Ardmore* - big hill
Áth	Ath	Ford	*Athlone* - ford of Luan
Abhainn	Avon	River	*Avonbeg* - small river
Baile	Bally	Town	*Ballynamuck* - town of the pigs
Beann	Ben	Mountain	*Bengorm* - blue mountain
Bóthar	Boher	Road	*Bohereeen* - little road
Cathair	Caher	Fort	*Caherlough* - fort of the lake
Carrick	Carrick	Rock	*Carrickfergus* - rock of Fergus
Calseal	Cashel	Stone Fort	*Cashel Murnhan* - fort of Munster
Cloch	Clogh	Stone	*Clogheen* - little stone
Cluain	Clon	Meadow	*Clonmel* - meadow of honey
Creag	Creg	Stony	*Cregmoher* - stony field
Cruach	Croagh	rounded hill	*Croaghpatrick* - Patrick's hill
Doire	Derry	Oak grove	*Derrybeg* - little oak grove
Drium	Drom	Ridge	*Drumquinn* - Quinn's ridge
Dún	Dun	Fort	*Dundalk* - fort of Dealgan
Inis	Ennis	Island	*Enniskillen* - Island of Kethleen
Gleann	Glen	Valley	*Glenroe* - red valley
Gort	Gort	Garden	*Gortboy* - yellow garden
Ceann	Ken	Head	*Kinvara* - head of the sea
Cill	Kill	Church	*Kildare* - second church
Cnoc	Knock	Hill	*Knockanean* - hill of the birds
Coill	Kyle	Wood	*Kyleglass* - green wood
Lios	Lis	Fort	*Lismore* - big fort
Loch	Lough	Lake	*Loughrea* - grey lake
Mullach	Mullagh	Summit	*Mullaghmore* - big summit
Poll	Poul	Hole	*Poulaphuca* - hole of the demon
Rath	Rath	Fort	*Rathdrum* - the fort on the ridge

Meanings of place names

Sean	Shan	old	*Shandangan* - old stronghold
Sliabh	Slieve	mountain	*Slievenamon* - mountain of women
Teampall	Temple	church	*Templemore* - big church
Tír	Teer	district	*Teervarna* - district of the gap
Tobar	Tubber	well	*Toberaheeny* - Friday's well

One or two words differing in Ireland

Press	Cupboard
Gardaí	The police (general)
Garda	A policeman
Fir	Gents (toilets)
Mná	Ladies (toilets)
Bruscar	Rubbish
Bord Fáilte	The Irish Tourist board

Pronunciation

Most Irish place names are loose anglicisations of Gaelic words. This means that often the pronunciation is not what you'd expect... in fact hardly ever. Here are some to help you out.

Youghal	Yawl
Dunlaoghaire	Dun'leary
Tuam	Tchoom
Laois	Leash
Abbeyleix	Abbey'leex
Oughterard	Ookterard (as in look)
Nenagh	Neenah
Inistioge	Ini'steeg
Athy	Ath'eye (as in high)
Clones	Clonez (2 syllables)
(River) *Suir*	Shore

Louth, *Meath* and *Westmeath* are all pronounced as if they had an 'e' on the end, as in 'seethe'.

Guinness

What is it?

Guinness is a stout with a distinctive malty flavour and a creamy head. Contrary to Guinness folklore, the water used to make the brew comes from the Wicklow Mountains rather than the River Liffey that runs through Dublin. The Guinness brewery at St James's Gate in Dublin today spreads over 65 acres. It was started by Arthur Guinness in 1759 and he signed a 9,000-year lease at an annual rent of £45 a week. Guinness is now exported to 120 countries.

How is Guinness made?

Irish barley is malted, flaked and roasted, then ground together to form a grist. The grist is mixed with hot water and mashed into a porridge that is strained into a mash tun and left to stand for an hour to produce a dark, sweet wort. Hops are then added in 20-ton kettles and boiled at a high temperature for 90 minutes, then strained. The hopped wort is cooled and yeast added to ferment for 48 hours. The yeast is removed and the liquid is now stout. It is left for up to 10 days, then pumped into kegs.

Why is Guiness black?

Guinness is black because of the way the ingredients are prepared. The malted barley is roasted in a similar way to coffee beans, which is what gives Guinness the dark, ruby colouring.

Why does Guinness have a white head?

The creamy white head is created from the 'iniation' and 'surging' of bubbles of nitrogen and carbon dioxide as the beer is poured. The gas enters the keg and forces the beer out. It is actually the nitrogen which causes the tight, white creamy head.

Guinness cocktails

Black and Tan	Guinness mixed with a lighter coloured beer such as pale ale or lager.
Black Velvet	Guinness and champagne in equal proportions.
A Purple Meaney	Half Guinness, half bitter and a dash of blackcurrant cordial.
Golden Cream	Add 8-10 fluid ounces of bottled Guinness to a pint glass. Allow to settle, then add several scoops of vanila ice-cream. Wait one minute, then serve with a long ice-cream spoon.

Irish Folk Songs

A few verses from some traditional Irish folk songs to help you out if you are ever in an Irish pub (or any kind) of singalong.

Danny Boy
Oh, Danny Boy, the pipes... the pipes are calling,
From glen to glen and down the mountain side.
The summer's gone and all the leaves are falling,
Tis you, Tis you must go and I must bide.

But come ye back, when summer's in the meadow,
and all the valley's hushed and white with snow.
And I'll be here in sunshine or in shadow,
Oh, Danny Boy, Oh, Danny Boy, I love you so!

When Irish Eyes Are Smiling
When Irish eyes are smiling
Sure it's like a morning spring.
In the lilt of Irish laughter,
You can hear the angels sing.
When Irish hearts are happy,
All the world seems bright and gay.
And when Irish eyes are smiling,
Sure, they steal your heart away.

Chorus: When Irish eyes are smiling
         Sure it's like a morning spring.
         In the lilt of Irish laughter,
         You can hear the angels sing.
         When Irish hearts are happy,
         All the world seems bright and gay.
         And when Irish eyes are smiling,
         Sure, they steal your heart away.

Cockles and Mussels
In Dublin's Fair City, where the girls are so pretty,
'Twas there I first met MY sweet Molly Malone.
She drove a wheel-barrow thro' streets broad and narrow,
Crying "COCKLES AND MUSSELS, a-live, a-live-o!"

The Wild Rover
I've been a wild rover for many a year
And I spent all my money on whiskey and beer
And now I'm returning with gold in great store
And I never will play the wild rover no more

Chorus: And it's no nay never
         No nay never no more
         Will I play the wild rover
         No nay never no more

Saint Patrick - Naomh Pádraig

Saint Patrick's Day (March 17th), is an Irish holiday honoring Saint Patrick, the missionary credited with converting the Irish to Christianity.

Saint Patrick was not actually Irish. Historical sources report that he was born around 385 AD in Scotland (near Kilpatrick). His parents were Calpurnius and Conchessa, who were Romans living in Britain in charge of the colonies. His real name is believed to be Maewyn Succat (he took on Patrick, or Patricus, after he became a priest).

He was kidnapped at the age of 16 by pirates and sold into slavery in Ireland. During his 6-year captivity (he worked as a shepherd), he began to have religious visions, and found strength in his faith. He finally escaped (after voices in one of his visions told him where he could find a getaway ship) and went to France, where he became a priest (and later a bishop).

When he was about 45years old, Saint. Patrick travelled back to Ireland. He had a dream in which the people of Ireland were calling out to him "We beg you, holy one, to come and walk among us once more". Patrick began preaching the Gospel throughout Ireland. He and his disciples preached and converted thousands and began building churches all over the country. He used the shamrock, which resembles a three-leafed clover, as a metaphor to explain the concept of the Trinity (father, son, holy spirit).

Legend has it that Saint Patrick drove all the snakes out of Ireland - that they all went into the sea and drowned. The snake was a revered pagan symbol, and perhaps this was a figurative tale alluding to the fact that he drove paganism out of Ireland.

Patrick preached and converted all of Ireland for 40 years. He worked many miracles and wrote of his love for God in Confessions. After years of living in poverty, traveling and enduring much suffering he died on March 17, 461.

Green is associated with Saint Patrick's Day because it is the colour of spring, Ireland, and the shamrock.

An Irish blessing for St. Patrick's Day:

May your blessings outnumber the shamrocks that grow
And may trouble avoid you wherever you go.

Gaelic phrases for St. Patrick's Day

Lá Fhéile Pádraig - St. Patrick's Day
(LAW AY-luh PAW-rihg)

Beannachtaí na Féile Pádraig oraibh! - Happy St. Patrick's Day to You All!
(BAN-uhkh-tee nuh FAY-luh PAW-rihg O-rihv)

Quick reference indices

WHEELCHAIR

These owners have told us that they have facilities suitable for people in wheelchairs. It is essential that you confirm on the telephone what is available.

Co. Donegal
4 • 10

Co. Monaghan
13 • 14

Co. Londonderry
21

Co. Antrim
23

Co. Down
33

Co. Mayo
38

Co. Galway
44

Co. Sligo
64 • 68

Co. Meath
77

Co. Westmeath
86

Co. Offaly
93

Co. Kilkenny
107

Co. Wexford
112 • 113

Co. Wicklow
121

Co. Dublin
124

Co. Tipperary
139

Co. Limerick
150

Co. Kerry
169 • 170

Co. Cork
178 • 192 • 193 • 198

ACCESS

These houses have bedrooms or bathrooms that are accessible for people of limited mobility. Please phone beforehand to confirm details and special needs.

Co. Donegal
3 • 4 • 7 • 10

Co. Monaghan
13

Co. Londonderry
21

Co. Antrim
23 • 26

Co. Down
28 • 33

Co. Galway
40 • 43 • 48 • 50 • 51 • 52 • 54 • 56

Co. Sligo
64 • 68

Co. Louth
71 • 72

Co. Meath
76 • 77 • 79 • 81

Co. Westmeath
86

Co. Laois
96

Co. Carlow
98

Co. Kilkenny
100 • 103 • 106

Co. Wexford
110

Quick reference indices

Quick reference indices

PETS WELCOME

The owners of these houses are happy to discuss the idea of your bringing your prize pet on holiday.

A short history of the Company

Perhaps the best clue as to why these books have their own very particular style and 'bent' lies in Alastair's history.

After a law degree, a stint as a teacher in Voluntary Service Overseas led to a change in direction. He became a teacher (French and Spanish) and then a refugee worker, then spent several years in overseas development work before settling into environmental campaigning, and even green politics. Meanwhile, he was able to dabble - just once a year - in an old interest, taking clients on tours of special places all over Europe. This grew, eventually, into a travel company (it still exists as Alastair Sawday's Tours, operating, inter alia, walking and biking tours all over Europe).

Trying to take his clients to eat and sleep in places that were not owned by corporations and assorted bandits he found dozens of very special places in France - farms, châteaux etc - a list that grew into the first book, French Bed and Breakfast. It was a celebration of 'real' places to stay and the remarkable people who run them.

So, this publishing company is based on the success of that first and rather whimsical French book. It started as mild crusade, and there it stays. For we still celebrate the unusual, the beautiful, the highly individual. We have no rules for owners; they do things their own way. We are passionate about rejecting the ugly, the cold, the banal and the indifferent and we are still passionate about promoting the use of 'real' food. Alastair is a trustee of the Soil Association and keen to promote organic growing especially.

It is a source of huge pleasure to us that we seem to have pressed the right button: there are thousands and thousands of people who, clearly, share our views and take up our ideas. We are by no means alone in trumpeting the virtues of standing up to the monstrous uniformity of so much of our culture.

The greatest accolade we have had was in The Bookseller magazine, which described us as 'head and shoulders above the rest'. That meant a lot. But even more satisfying is that we are building a company in which people matter. We are delighted to hear of new friendships between those in the book and those using it and to know that there are many people - among them artists, farmers, champions of the countryside - who have been enabled to pursue their unusual lives thanks to the extra income the book brings them.

Of course we want the company to flourish, but this isn't just about money; it is about people, too.

Alastair Sawday
Special Places to Stay series

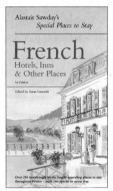

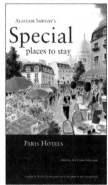

Tel: 01275 464891
Fax: 01275 464887
www.sawdays.co.uk

The Little Earth Book

The Little Earth Book

Alastair Sawday, the publisher of this (wonderful) guidebook, is also an environmentalist. For over 25 years he has campaigned, not only against the worst excesses of modern tourism and its hotels, but against environmental 'looniness' of other kinds. He has fought for systems and policies that might enable our beautiful planet - simply - to survive. He founded and ran Avon Friends of the Earth, has run for Parliament, and has led numerous local campaigns. He is now a trustee of the Soil Association, experience upon which he draws in this remarkable new book.

Researched and written by an eminent Bristol architect, James Bruges, *The Little Earth Book* is a clarion call to action, a mind-boggling collection of mini-essays on today's most important environmental concerns, from global warming and poisoned food to economic growth, Third World debt, genes and 'superbugs'. Undogmatic but sure-footed, the style is light, explaining complex issues with easy language, illustrations and cartoons. Ideas are developed chapter by chapter, yet each one stands alone. It is an easy browse.

The Little Earth Book provides hope, with new ideas and examples of people swimming against the current, of bold ideas that work in practice. It is a book as important as it is original. One has been sent to every M.P. Now you, too, can learn about the issues and join the most important debate of this century.

Oh - one last thing: *The Little Earth Book* is a damned good read! Note what Jonathon Porritt says about it:

"The Little Earth Book is different. And instructive. And even fun."

Did you know.....

- If everyone adopted the Western lifestyle we would need five earths to support us

- 60% of infections picked up in hospitals are now drug-resistant

- Environmental disasters have already created 80 MILLION refugees.

Order Form UK

All these books are available in major bookshops or you may order them direct. Post and packaging are FREE.

	Price	No. copies
Special Places to Stay: **Portugal**		
Edition 1	£8.95	
Special Places to Stay: **Spain**		
Edition 4	£11.95	
Special Places to Stay: **Ireland**		
Edition 3	£10.95	
Special Places to Stay: **Paris Hotels**		
Edition 3	£8.95	
Special Places to Stay: **Garden Bed & Breakfast**		
Edition 1	£10.95	
Special Places to Stay: **French Bed & Breakfast**		
Edition 6	£13.95	
Special Places to Stay: **British Hotels, Inns** and other places		
Edition 2	£10.95	
Special Places to Stay: **British Bed & Breakfast**		
Edition 5	£12.95	
Special Places to Stay: **French Hotels, Inns** and other places		
Edition 1	£11.95	
Special Places to Stay: **Italy** (from Rome to the Alps)		
Edition 1	£9.95	
The Little Earth Book	£4.99	

Please make cheques payable to: **Alastair Sawday Publishing**   **Total** [   ]

Please send cheques to: Alastair Sawday Publishing, The Home Farm, Barrow Gurney, Bristol BS48 3RW. **For credit card orders call 01275 464891 or order directly from our website www.sawdays.co.uk**

Name:

Address:

Postcode:

Tel: Fax:

If you do not wish to receive mail from other companies, please tick the box ❏   Ire 2

Order Form USA

All these books are available at your local bookstore, or you may order direct. Allow two to three weeks for delivery.

Special Places to Stay: British Hotels, Inns and other places Price No. copies

	Price	No. copies
Edition 2	$17.95	

Special Places to Stay: British Bed & Breakfast

Edition 5	$19.95	

Special Places to Stay: French Hotels, Inns and other places

Edition 1	$19.95	

Special Places to Stay: French Bed & Breakfast

Edition 6	$19.95	

Special Places to Stay: Garden Bed & Breakfast

Edition 1	$17.95	

Special Places to Stay in Ireland

Edition 3	$17.95	

Special Places to Stay in Spain & Portugal

Edition 3	$19.95	

Special Places to Stay: Italy (from Rome to the Alps)

Edition 1	$14.95	

Shipping in the continental USA: $3.95 for one book, $4.95 for two books, $5.95 for three or more books. Outside continental USA, call (800) 243-0495 for prices. For delivery to AK, CA, CO, CT, FL, GA, IL, IN, KS, MI, MN, MO, NE, NM, NC, OK, SC, TN, TX, VA, and WA, please add appropriate sales tax

Please make checks payable to: **The Globe Pequot Press**   **Total**

To order by phone with MasterCard or Visa: (800) 243-0495. 9 a.m. to 5 p.m. EST; by fax: (800) 820-2329, 24 hours; through our Website: www.globe-pequot.com; or by mail: The Globe Pequot Press, P.O. Box 480, Guilford, CT 06437.

Name: _____ Date: _____

Address: _____

Town: _____

State: _____ Zip code: _____

Ire 2 Tel: _____ Fax: _____

Report Form

Comments on existing entries and new discoveries.

If you have any comments on entries in this guide, please let us have them. If you have a favourite house, hotel, inn or other new discovery, please let us know about it.

Report on:

Entry no: _____ Edition: _____

New recommendation: _____

Name of property: _____

Address: _____

_____

_____ Postcode: _____

Tel: _____

Comments: _____

_____

_____

_____

_____

_____

_____

From: _____

Address: _____

_____

_____ Postcode: _____

Tel: _____

Please send the completed form to: **Alastair Sawday Publishing, The Home Farm Stables, Barrow Gurney, Bristol BS48 3RW**

Thank you.

Index by house name

Index by house name

Index by house name

Index by place name

Index by place name